The Object-Oriented Thought Process

Second Edition

Matt Weisfeld

DEVELOPER'S LIBRARY

Sams Publishing, 800 East 96th Street, Indianapolis, Indiana 46420

The Object-Oriented Thought Process, Second Edition

International Standard Book Number: 0-672-32611-6

Library of Congress Catalog Card Number: 2003113099

Printed in the United States of America

First Printing: December 2003

06   05   04   03   4   3   2   1

Trademarks

Warning and Disclaimer

Bulk Sales

Sams Publishing offers excellent discounts on this book when ordered in quantity for bulk purchases or special sales. For more information, please contact

U.S. Corporate and Government Sales
1-800-382-3419
corpsales@pearsontechgroup.com
For sales outside of the U.S., please contact

International Sales
1-317-428-3341
international@pearsontechgroup.com

Associate Publisher
Michael Stephens

Acquisitions Editor
Todd Green

Development Editor
Songlin Qiu

Managing Editor
Charlotte Clapp

Senior Project Editor
Matthew Purcell

Production Editor
Seth Kerney

Indexer
Erika Millen

Proofreader
Carla Lewis

Technical Editor
Bob Reselman

Reviewers
Handel A. Gibbings
Dennis Vargo

Publishing Coordinator
Cindy Teeters

Interior Designer
Gary Adair

Cover Designer
Alan Clements

Page Layout
Susan Geiselman

❖

To Dad & Sammy

❖

Contents at a Glance

Table of Contents

About the Author

Matt Weisfeld is an assistant professor at Cuyahoga Community College (Tri-C) in Cleveland, Ohio. Matt is a member of the information technology faculty, teaching programming languages such as C++, Java, and C# .NET. Prior to joining Tri-C, Matt spent 20 years in the information technology industry gaining experience in software development, project management, business development, corporate training, and part-time teaching. Matt holds an M.S. in computer science and an MBA in project management. Besides the first edition of *The Object-Oriented Thought Process*, Matt has published two other computer books, and more than a dozen articles in magazines and journals such as *Dr. Dobb's Journal*, *The C/C++ Users Journal*, *Software Development Magazine*, *Java Report*, and the international journal *Project Management*. Matt has presented at conferences throughout the United States and Canada.

Acknowledgments

As with the first edition, this book required the combined efforts of many people. I would like to take the time to acknowledge as many of these people as possible, for without them, this book would never have happened.

First and foremost, I would like to thank my wife Sharon for all her help. Not only did she provide support and encouragement throughout this lengthy process, but, as with the first edition, she edited every chapter of the initial draft.

I would also like to thank my mom and the rest of my family for their continued support.

I have really enjoyed working with the people at Sams on both editions of this book. Working with editors Todd Green, Seth Kerney, Matt Purcell, and Songlin Qiu has been a pleasure.

Thanks to Dennis Vargo, Handel Gibbings, and Bob Reselman for their help with the technical editing of the manuscript.

Finally, thanks to my daughters Stacy and Stephanie, and my cat Duffy for keeping me on my toes. Stacy produced many of the manuscript's initial figures.

We Want to Hear from You!

As the reader of this book, *you* are our most important critic and commentator. We value your opinion and want to know what we're doing right, what we could do better, what areas you'd like to see us publish in, and any other words of wisdom you're willing to pass our way.

As an associate publisher for Sams Publishing, I welcome your comments. You can email or write me directly to let me know what you did or didn't like about this book—as well as what we can do to make our books better.

Please note that I cannot help you with technical problems related to the topic of this book. We do have a User Services group, however, where I will forward specific technical questions related to the book.

When you write, please be sure to include this book's title and author as well as your name, email address, and phone number. I will carefully review your comments and share them with the author and editors who worked on the book.

Email: `feedback@samspublishing.com`

Mail: Michael Stephens
            Associate Publisher
            Sams Publishing
            800 East 96th Street
            Indianapolis, IN 46240 USA

For more information about this book or another Sams Publishing title, visit our Web site at `www.samspublishing.com`. Type the ISBN (excluding hyphens) or the title of a book in the Search field to find the page you're looking for.

Introduction

This Book's Scope

As the title suggests, this book is about the object-oriented (OO) thought process. Obviously, choosing the theme and title of the book are important decisions; however, these decisions were not all that simple. Numerous books deal with one level or another of object orientation. Several popular books deal with topics including OO analysis, OO design, OO programming, design patterns, OO databases, the Unified Modeling Language (UML), various OO programming languages, and many other topics related to OO programming.

However, while poring over all of these books, many people forget that each one of these topics are built on a single foundation: how you think in OO ways. It is unfortunate, but often software professionals dive into these books without taking the appropriate time and effort to *really* understand the concepts in them.

I contend that learning OO concepts is not accomplished by learning a specific development method or a set of tools. Doing things in an OO manner is, simply put, a way of thinking. This book is all about the OO thought process.

Separating the methods and tools from the OO thought process is not easy. Many people are introduced to OO concepts via one of these methods or tools. Many C programmers were first introduced to object orientation by migrating directly to C++—before they were even remotely exposed to OO concepts. Some software professionals were first introduced to object orientation by presentations that included object models using UML—again, before they were even exposed directly to OO concepts.

It is important to understand the significant difference between learning OO concepts and using the methods and tools that support the paradigm. In his article "What the UML Is—and Isn't," Craig Larman states

> Unfortunately, in the context of software engineering and the UML diagramming language, acquiring the skills to read and write UML notation seems to sometimes be equated with skill in object-oriented analysis and design. Of course, this is not so, and the latter is much more important than the former. Therefore, I recommend seeking education and educational materials in which intellectual skill in object-oriented analysis and design is paramount rather than UML notation or the use of a case tool.

Although learning a modeling language is an important step, it is much more important to learn OO skills first. Learning UML before OO concepts is similar to learning how to read an electrical diagram without first knowing anything about electricity.

The same problem occurs with programming languages. As stated earlier, many C programmers moved into the realm of object orientation by migrating to C++ before being directly exposed to OO concepts. Many times developers who claim to be C++ programmers are simply C programmers using C++ compilers.

This problem is even more of an issue now that object-oriented languages like Java, C# .NET, Visual Basic .NET, and so on have become so popular. There are many Visual Basic programmers who now must make the leap to Visual Basic .NET. Likewise, many C++ programmers, who might not be conforming to strict OO practices, are being asked to migrate to Java or C#, where they have no choice but to think in OO ways.

Early versions of Visual Basic are not OO. C is not OO, and C++ was *developed* to be backward compatible with C. Because of this, it is quite possible to use a C++ compiler writing only C syntax while forsaking all of C++'s OO features. Even worse, a programmer can use just enough OO features to make a program incomprehensible to OO and non-OO programmers alike.

Thus, it is of vital importance that while you're on the road to OO development, you first learn the fundamental OO concepts. Resist the temptation to jump directly into a programming language (such as C++, C# or Java) or a modeling language (such as UML), and take the time to learn the object-oriented thought process.

This book is a concepts book intended to introduce programmers to object-oriented technologies. One of these audiences is, of course, structured programmers making the leap to O-O. Thus, I have included some material that is, in fact, a bridge between structured and object-oriented technologies. Chapter 6 is a good example of this approach - I have included techniques that will be familiar to structured programmers. It is important to understand that Object-oriented and structured practices are not mutually exclusive. Structured techniques are used throughout O-O designs (just consider a for loop or if statement).

In my first class in Smalltalk in the late 1980s, the instructor told the class that the new OO paradigm was a totally new way of thinking. He went on to say that although all of us were most likely very good programmers, about 10%–20% of us would never really grasp the OO way of doing things. If this statement is indeed true, it is most likely because some people never really take the time to make the paradigm shift and learn the underlying OO concepts.

What's New in the Second Edition

As stated often in this introduction, my vision for the first edition was primarily a conceptual book. Although I still adhere to this goal for the second edition, I have included several application topics that fit well with object-oriented concepts. These applications include the following:

- Object modeling
- Object persistence

- XML
- Objects and the Internet
- The enterprise
- Design patterns

The chapters that cover these topics are still conceptual in nature; however, several of the chapters include Java code that shows how these concepts are implemented.

The Intended Audience

This book is a general introduction to fundamental OO concepts. The intended audience includes designers, developers, project managers, and anyone who wants to gain a general understanding of what object orientation is all about. Reading this book should provide a strong foundation for moving to other books covering more advanced OO topics.

Of these more advanced books, one of my favorites remains *Object-Oriented Design in Java* by Stephen Gilbert and Bill McCarty. I really like the approach of the book, and have used it as a textbook in classes I have taught on OO concepts. I cite *Object-Oriented Design in Java* often throughout this book, and I recommend that you graduate to it after you complete this one.

Other books that I have found very helpful include *Effective C++* by Scott Meyers, *Classical and Object-Oriented Software Engineering* by Stephen R. Schach, *Thinking in C++* by Bruce Eckel, *UML Distilled* by Martin Fowler, and *Java Design* by Peter Coad and Mark Mayfield.

While teaching intro-level Java to programmers at corporations and universities, it quickly became obvious to me that most of these programmers easily picked up the Java syntax. However, these same programmers struggled with the OO nature of the language.

This Book's Scope

It should be obvious by now that I am a firm believer in becoming comfortable with the object-oriented thought process before jumping into a programming language or modeling language. This book is filled with examples of Java code and UML diagrams; however, you do not need to know Java or UML to read it. After all I have said about learning the concepts first, why is there so much Java code and so many UML diagrams? First, they are both great for illustrating OO concepts. Second, both are vital to the OO process and should be addressed at an introductory level. The key is not to focus on Java or UML, but to use them as aids in the understanding of the underlying concepts.

The Java examples in the book illustrate concepts such as loops and functions. However, understanding the code itself is not a prerequisite for understanding the concepts; it might be helpful to have a book at hand that covers Java syntax.

I cannot state too strongly that this book does **not** teach Java or UML, both of which can command volumes unto themselves. It is my hope that this book will whet your appetite for other OO topics, such as OO analysis, object-oriented design, and OO programming.

This Book's Conventions

The following conventions are used in this book:

- Code lines, commands, statements, and any other code-related terms appear in a monospace typeface.
- Placeholders that stand for what you should actually type appear in *italic monospace*. Text that you should type appears in **bold monospace**.
- Throughout the book, there are special sidebar elements, such as:

Note

A note presents interesting information related to the discussion—a little more insight or a pointer to some new technique.

Tip

A tip offers advice or shows you an easier way of doing something.

Caution

A caution alerts you to a possible problem and gives you advice on how to avoid it.

Source Code Used in this Book

You can download all the source code and examples discussed within this book from http://www.samspublishing.com. Simply type this book's ISBN (0672326116) into the "search" window, press Enter, and you'll be taken to a page with links to the source code.

1

Introduction to Object-Oriented Concepts

ALTHOUGH IT MIGHT BE QUITE surprising, object-oriented (OO) software development has been around since the early 1960s. Although objects have become much more prevalent in today's software industry, many software shops have yet to venture into the OO arena. It is no secret that the software industry can be slow-moving at times. It is also true that, when working systems are in place, there has to be a compelling reason to replace them. This has hindered the propagation of OO systems. There are a lot of non-OO *legacy systems* (that is, older systems that are already in place) that seem to be working just fine—so why risk potential disaster by changing them? In most cases you should not change them, at least not simply for the sake of change. There is nothing inherently wrong with systems written in non–OO code. However, brand-new development definitely warrants the consideration of using OO technologies.

Although there has been a steady and significant growth in OO development in the past 10 years, an entirely new venue has helped catapult it further into the mainstream. The emergence of the Web has opened a brand-new arena, where much of the software development is new and mostly unencumbered by legacy concerns. Even when there are legacy concerns, there is a trend to wrap the legacy systems in object wrappers.

Object Wrappers

Object wrappers are object-oriented code that includes structured code inside. For example, you can take a structured module and *wrap* it inside an object to make it look like an object.

Objects are slowly but surely making their way into our professional information systems (IS) lives—and they cannot be ignored. With the success of Java and the introduction of Microsoft's .NET technologies, objects are becoming a major part of the IS equation. With the explosion of the Internet, now many years in the making, the electronic highway is really becoming an object-based highway. And as businesses gravitate toward the Web, they are gravitating toward objects, because the technologies used for the Web are mostly OO in nature.

This chapter is an overview of the fundamental OO concepts. The topics covered touch on most, if not all, of the topics covered in subsequent chapters, which explore the issues in much greater detail.

Procedural Versus OO Programming

Before we delve deeper into the advantages of OO development, let's consider a more fundamental question: What exactly is an object? This is both a complex and a simple question. It is complex because shifting gears to learn a totally new way of thinking is not an easy task. It is simple in the sense that most people already think in terms of objects.

For example, when you look at a person, you see the person as an object. And an object is defined by two terms: attributes and behaviors. A person has attributes, such as eye color, age, height, and so on. A person also has behaviors, such as walking, talking, breathing, and so on. In its basic definition, an *object* is an entity that contains *both* data and behavior. The word *both* is the key difference between the more traditional programming methodology, procedural programming, and OO programming. In procedural programming, code is placed into totally distinct functions or procedures. Ideally, as shown in Figure 1.1, these procedures then become "black boxes," where inputs go in and outputs come out. Data is placed into separate structures, and is manipulated by these functions or procedures.

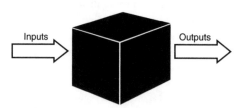

Figure 1.1 Black boxes.

Difference Between OO and Procedural

This is the key difference between OO and procedural programming. In OO design, the attributes and behavior are contained within a single object, whereas in procedural, or structured design, the attributes and behavior are normally separated.

Procedural programming has been the mainstay since the Bronze Age of computers—so why change? First, as illustrated in Figure 1.2, in procedural programming the data is separated from the procedures, and sometimes the data is global, so it is easy to modify data that is outside your scope. This means that access to data is uncontrolled and unpredictable (that is, several functions may have access to the global data). Second, because you have no control over who has access to the data, testing and debugging are much more difficult. Objects address these problems by combining data and behavior into a nice, complete package.

Figure 1.2   Using global data.

Proper Design

We can state that, when properly designed, there is no such thing as global data in an OO model. This fact provides a high amount of data integrity in OO systems.

Objects are much more than primitive data types, such as integers and strings. Although objects do contain entities such as integers and strings, which represent the attributes, they also contain methods, which represent the behaviors. In an object, you use the methods to operate on the data. Perhaps more importantly, you can control access to members of an object (both attributes and methods). This means that some members, such as data types and methods, can be hidden from other objects. For instance, an object called `Math` might contain two integers, called `myInt1` and `myInt2`. Most likely, the `Math` object also contains the necessary methods to set and retrieve the values of `myInt1` and `myInt2`. It might also contain a method called `Sum()` to add the two integers together.

Data Hiding

In OO terminology, data is referred to as attributes, and functions are referred to as methods. Restricting access to certain attributes and/or methods is called *data hiding*.

By combining the data and methods in the same entity, which in OO parlance is called *encapsulation*, we can control access to the data in the `Math` object. By defining these integers as off-limits, another logically unconnected function cannot manipulate the integers `myInt1` and `myInt2`—only the `Math` object can do that.

Sound Class Design Guidelines

Keep in mind that it is possible to create poorly designed classes that do not restrict access to class attributes. The bottom line is that you can design bad code just as efficiently with OO design as with any other programming methodology. Simply take care to adhere to sound class design guidelines (see Chapter 5, "Class Design Guidelines," for class design guidelines).

What happens when another object—for example, `myObject`—wants to gain access to the sum of `myInt1` and `myInt2`? It asks the `Math` object: `myObject` sends a message to the `Math` object. Figure 1.3 shows how the two objects communicate with each other via their methods. The message is really a call to the `Math` object's `Sum` method. The `Sum` method then returns the value to `myObject`. The beauty of this is that `myObject` does not need to know how the sum is calculated (although I'm sure it can guess). In this example, you can change how the `Math` object calculates the sum without making a change to `myObject` (as long as the means to retrieve the sum do not change). All you want is the sum—you *don't care* how it is calculated.

Calculating the sum is not the responsibility of `myObject`—it's the `Math` object's responsibility. As long as `myObject` has access to the `Math` object, it can send the appropriate message and then obtain the result. In general, objects should not manipulate the internal data of other objects (that is, `myObject` should not directly change the value of `myInt1` and `myInt2`). And, for reasons we will explore later, it is normally better to build small objects with specific tasks rather than build large objects that perform many.

myObject

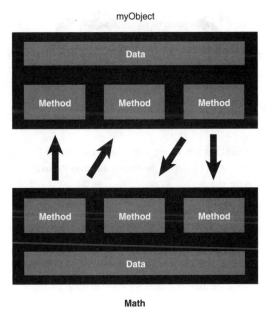

Math

Figure 1.3   Object-to-object communication.

Moving from Procedural to Object-Oriented Development

Now that we have a general understanding about some of the differences about procedural and object-oriented technologies, let's delve a bit deeper into both.

Procedural Programming

Procedural programming separates the data of the program from the operations that manipulate the data. For example, if you want to send information across a network, only the relevant data is sent (see Figure 1.4), with the expectation that the program at the other end of the network pipe knows what to do with it. In other words, some sort of handshaking agreement must be in place between the client and server to transmit the data. In this model, no code is actually sent over the wire.

OO Programming

The fundamental advantage of OO programming is that the data and the operations that manipulate the data (the code) are both encapsulated in the object. For example, when an object is transported across a network, the entire object, including the data and behavior, goes with it. In Figure 1.5, the Employee object is sent over the network.

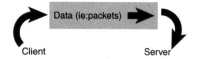

Figure 1.4   Data transmitted over a wire.

> **Proper Design**
>
> A good example of this concept is a Web object, such as a Java applet. The browser has no idea of what the
> Web object will do. When the object is loaded, the browser executes the code within the object and uses
> the data contained within the object.

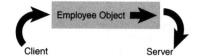

Figure 1.5   Objects transmitted over a wire.

What Exactly Is an Object?

Objects are the building blocks of an OO program. A program that uses OO technology is basically a collection of objects. To illustrate, let's consider that a corporate system contains objects that represent employees of that company. Each of these objects is made up of the data and behavior described in the following sections.

Object Data

The data stored within an object represents the state of the object. In OO programming terminology, this data is called *attributes*. In our example, as shown in Figure 1.6, employee attributes could be Social Security numbers, date of birth, gender, phone number, and so on. The attributes contain the information that differentiates between the various objects, in this case the employees. Attributes are covered in more detail later in this chapter in the discussion on classes.

Object Behaviors

The *behavior* of an object is what the object can do. In procedural languages the behavior is defined by procedures, functions, and subroutines. In OO programming terminology these behaviors are contained in *methods*, and you invoke a method by sending a message to it. In our employee example, consider that one of the behaviors required of an employee object is to set and return the values of the various attributes. Thus, each attribute would have corresponding methods, such as `setGender()` and `getGender()`. In this case, when another object needs this information, it can send a message to an employee object and ask it what its gender is.

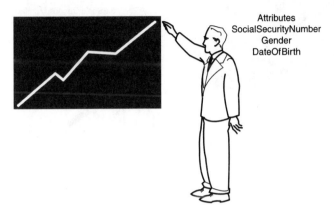

Attributes
SocialSecurityNumber
Gender
DateOfBirth

Figure 1.6   Employee attributes.

Getters and Setters

The concept of getters and setters supports the concept of data hiding. Because other objects should not directly manipulate data within another object, the getters and setters provide controlled access to an object's data. Getters and setters are sometimes called accessor methods and mutator methods, respectively.

Note that we are only showing the interface of the methods, and not the implementation. The following information is all the user needs to know to effectively use the methods:

- The name of the method
- The parameters passed to the method
- The return type of the method

To further illustrate behaviors, consider Figure 1.7.

In Figure 1.7, the `Payroll` object contains a method called `CalculatePay()` that calculates the pay for a specific employee. Among other information, the `Payroll` object must obtain the Social Security number of this employee. To get this information, the payroll object must send a message to the `Employee` object (in this case, the `getSocialSecurityNumber()` method). Basically, this means that the `Payroll` object calls the `getSocialSecurityNumber()` method of the `Employee` object. The employee object recognizes the message and returns the requested information.

To illustrate further, Figure 1.8 is a class diagram representing the `Employee`/`Payroll` system we have been talking about.

Employee Object

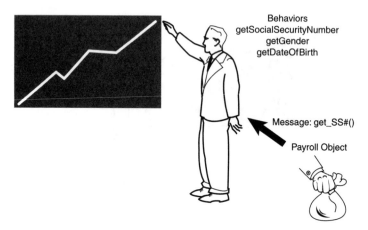

Figure 1.7   Employee behaviors.

Employee
–socialSecurityNumber:String –gender:boolean –dateOfBirth:Date
+getSocialSecurityNumber:String +getGender:boolean +getDateOfBirth:Date +setSocialSecurityNumber:void +setGender:void +setDateOfBirth:void

Payroll
–pay:double +calculatePay:double

Figure 1.8   Employee and payroll class diagrams.

UML Class Diagrams

Because this is the first class diagram we have seen, it is very basic and lacks some of the constructs (such as constructors) that a proper class should contain. Fear not—we will discuss class diagrams and constructors in more detail in Chapter 3, "Advanced Object-Oriented Concepts."

Each class diagram is broken up into two separate sections (besides the name itself). The first section contains the data (attributes), and the second section contains the behaviors (methods). In Figure 1.8, the `Employee` class diagram's attribute section contains `SocialSecurityNumber`, `Gender` and `DateofBirth`, while the method section contains the methods that operate on these attributes. You can use programming tools such as Rational Rose or TogetherJ to create and maintain class diagrams that correspond to real code.

Modeling Tools
Rational Rose and TogetherJ are visual modeling tools that provide a mechanism to create and manipulate class diagrams using the Unified Modeling Language (UML). UML is discussed throughout this book, and you can find a description of this notation in Chapter 10, "Object Modeling with UML."

We will get into the relationships between classes and objects later in this chapter, but for now you can think of a class as a template from which objects are made. When an object is created, we say that the objects are instantiated. Thus, if we create three employees, we are actually creating three totally distinct instances of an `Employee` class. Each object contains its own copy of the attributes and methods. For example, consider Figure 1.9. An employee object called `John` (John is its identity) has its own copy of all the attributes and methods defined in the `Employee` class. An employee object called `Mary` has its own copy of attributes and methods. They both have a separate copy of the `DateOfBirth` attribute and the `getDateOfBirth` method.

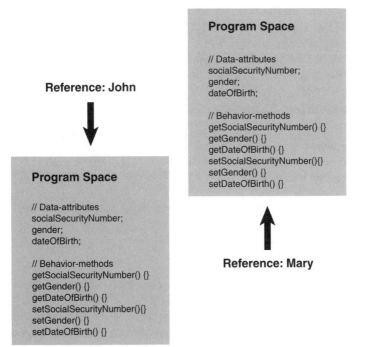

Figure 1.9   Program spaces.

An Implementation Issue

Be aware that there is not necessarily a physical copy of each method for each object. Rather, each object points to the same physical code. However, this is an implementation issue left up to the compiler/operating platform. From a conceptual level, you can think of objects as being wholly independent and having their own attributes and methods.

What Exactly Is a Class?

In short, a class is a blueprint for an object. When you instantiate an object, you use a class as the basis for how the object is built. In fact, trying to explain classes and objects is really a chicken-and-egg dilemma. It is difficult to describe a class without using the term *object*, and to describe an object without using the term *class*. For example, a specific bike is an object. However, someone had to have the blueprints (that is, the class) to build the bike. In OO software, unlike the chicken-and-egg dilemma, we do know what comes first—the class. An object cannot be instantiated without a class. Thus, many of the concepts in this section are similar to those presented earlier in the chapter, especially when we talk about attributes and methods.

To explain classes and methods, it's helpful to use an example from the relational database world. In a database table, the definition of the table itself (fields, description, and data types used) would be a class (metadata), and the objects would be the rows of the table (data).

This book focuses on the concepts of OO software, and not on a specific implementation (such as Java, C#, Visual Basic .NET or C++), but it is often helpful to use code examples to explain some concepts, so Java code fragments are used in this chapter to help explain some concepts when appropriate. The following sections describe some of the fundamental concepts of classes and how they interact.

Classes Are Object Templates

Classes can be thought of as the templates, or cookie cutters, for objects as seen in Figure 1.10. A class is used to create an object.

A class can be thought of as a sort of higher-level data type. For example, just as you create an integer or a float:

```
int x;
float y;
```

You can also create an object by using a predefined class:

```
myClass myObject;
```

Because of the names used in this example, it is obvious that `myClass` is the class and `myObject` is the object.

Remember that each object has its own attributes (analogous to fields) and behaviors (analogous to functions or routines). A class defines the attributes and behaviors that all objects created with this class will possess. Classes are pieces of code. Objects instantiated from classes can be distributed individually or as part of a library. Because objects are created from classes, it follows that classes must define the basic building blocks of objects (data, behavior, and messages). In short, you must design a class before you can create an object.

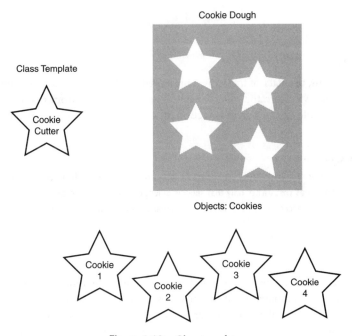

Figure 1.10   Class template.

For example, here is a definition of a Person class:

```
public class Person{

    //Attributes
    private String name;
    private String address;

    //Methods
    public String getName(){
        return name;
    }
    public void setName(String n){
        name = n;
    }

    public String getAddress(){
        return address;
```

```
    }
    public void setAddress(String adr){
        address = adr;
    }

}
```

Attributes

As you already saw, the data of a class is represented by attributes. Each class must define the attributes that will store the state of each object instantiated from that class. In the Person class example in the previous section, the Person class defines attributes for name and address.

Access Designations

When a data type or method is defined as public, other objects can directly access it. When a data type or method is defined as private, only that specific object can access it. Another access modifier, protected, allows access by related objects, which you'll learn about in Chapter 3.

Methods

As you learned earlier in the chapter, methods implement the required behavior of a class. Every object instantiated from this class has these methods. Methods may implement behaviors that are called from other objects (for example, messages) or provide the internal behavior of the class. Internal behaviors are private methods that are not accessible by other objects. In the Person class, the behaviors are getName(), setName(), getAddress(), and setAddress(). These methods allow other objects to inspect and change the values of the object's attributes. This is common design in OO systems. In all cases, access to attributes within an object should be controlled by the object—no other object should directly change an attribute of another.

Messages

Messages are the communication mechanism between objects. For example, when Object A invokes a method of Object B, Object A is sending a message to Object B. Object B's response is defined by its return value. Only the public methods, not the private methods, of an object can be invoked by another object. The following code illustrates this concept:

```
public class Payroll{

    String name;

    Person p = new Person();
```

```
String = p.setName("Joe");

... code

String = p.getName();

}
```

In this example (assuming that a `Payroll` object is instantiated), the `Payroll` object is sending a message to a `Person` object, with the purpose of retrieving the name via the `getName` method. Again, don't worry too much about the actual code, as we are really interested in the concepts. We will address the code in detail as we progress through the book.

Using UML to Model a Class Diagram

Over the years, many tools and models have been developed to assist in designing classes. One of the most popular tools today is UML. Although it is beyond the scope of this book to describe UML in fine detail, we will use UML class diagrams to illustrate the classes that we build. In fact, we have already used a class diagram in this chapter. Figure 1.11 shows the `Person` class diagram we discussed earlier in the chapter.

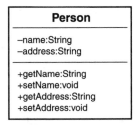

Figure 1.11   The `Person` class diagram.

Again, notice that the attributes and methods are separated (the attributes on the top, and the methods on the bottom). As we delve more deeply into OO design, these class diagrams will get much more sophisticated and convey much more information on how the different classes interact with each other.

Encapsulation

One of the primary advantages of using objects is that the object need not reveal all its attributes and behaviors. In good OO design (at least what is generally accepted as good), an object should only reveal the interfaces needed to interact with it. Details not pertinent to the use of the object should be hidden from other objects. This is called *encapsulation*. For example, an object that calculates the square of a number must provide an interface to obtain the result. However, the internal attributes and algorithms used to calculate the square need not be made available to the requesting object. Robust classes are designed with encapsulation in mind. In the next sections, we cover the concepts of interface and implementation, which are the basis of encapsulation.

Interfaces

As discussed earlier in this chapter, the interface is the fundamental means of communication between objects. Each class design specifies the interfaces for the proper instantiation and operation of objects. Any behavior that the object provides must be invoked by a message sent using one of the provided interfaces. The interface should completely describe how users of the class interact with the class. In Java, the methods that are part of the interface are designated as `public`.

Private Data

In accepted OO design, all attributes should be declared as `private`. Thus, attributes are not part of the interface. Only the `public` methods are part of the class interface. Declaring an attribute as `public` breaks the concept of data hiding.

Let's look at the example just mentioned: calculating the square of a number. In this example, the interface would consist of two pieces:

- How to instantiate a `Square` object
- How to send a value to the object and get the square of that value in return

Interfaces do not normally include attributes—only methods. As discussed earlier in the chapter, if a user needs access to an attribute, a method is created to return the attribute (a getter). If a user wants the value of an attribute, a method is called that returns the value of the attribute. In this way, the object that contains the attribute controls access to it. This is of vital importance, especially in testing and maintenance. If you control the access to the attribute, when a problem arises, you do not have to worry about tracking down every piece of code that might have changed the attribute—it can only be changed in one place (the setter).

Interfaces Versus Interfaces

It is important to note that there are interfaces to the classes as well as the methods—don't confuse the two. The interfaces to the classes are the public methods while the interfaces to the methods relate to how you call them.

Implementations

Only the public attributes and methods are considered the interface. The user should not see any part of the implementation—interacting with an object solely through class interfaces. In the previous example, for instance the Employee class, only the attributes were hidden. In many cases, there will be methods that also should be hidden and thus not part of the interface. Continuing the example of the square root from the previous section, the user does not care how the square root is calculated—as long as it is the correct answer. Thus, the implementation can change and it will not affect the user's code.

A Real-World Example of the Interface/ Implementation Paradigm

Figure 1.12 illustrates the interface/implementation paradigm using real-world objects rather than code. The toaster obviously requires electricity. To get this electricity, the cord from the toaster must be plugged into the electrical outlet, which is the interface. All the toaster needs to do to get the required electricity is to use a cord that complies with the electrical outlet specifications; this is the interface between the toaster and the electricity. The fact that the actual implementation is a coal-powered electric plant is not the concern of the toaster. In fact, for all the toaster cares, the implementation could be a nuclear power plant or a local power generator. With this model, any appliance can get electricity, as long as it conforms to the interface specification as seen in Figure 1.12.

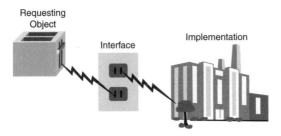

Figure 1.12   Power plant example.

A Java Example of the Interface/Implementation Paradigm

Let's explore the Square class further. Assume that you are writing a class that calculates the squares of integers. You must provide a separate interface and implementation. That is, you must provide a way for the user to invoke and obtain the square value. You must also provide the implementation that calculates the square; however, the user should not know anything about the specific implementation. Figure 1.13 shows one way to do this. Note that in the class diagram, the plus sign (+) designates public and the minus sign (-) designates private. Thus, you can identify the interface by the methods, prefaced with plus signs.

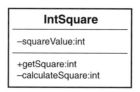

Figure 1.13 The square class.

This class diagram corresponds to the following code:

```
public class IntSquare {

    // private attribute
    private int squareValue;

    // public interface
    public int getSquare (int value) {

        SquareValue =calculateSquare(value);

        return squareValue;

    }

    // private implementation
    private int calculateSquare (int value) {

        return value*value;

    }
}
```

Note that the only part of the class that the user has access to is the public method getSquare, which is the interface. The implementation of the square algorithm is in the method calculateSquare, which is private. Also notice that the attribute SquareValue is private because users do not need to know that this attribute exists. Therefore, we have hidden the part of the implementation: The object only reveals the interfaces the user needs to interact with it, and details that are not pertinent to the use of the object are hidden from other objects.

If the implementation were to change—say, you wanted to use Java's built-in square function—you would not need to change the interface. The user would get the same functionality, but the implementation would have changed. This is very important when you're writing code that deals with data; for example, you can move data from a file to a database without forcing the user to change any application code.

Inheritance

As mentioned earlier in this chapter, one of the most powerful attributes of OO programming is code reuse. Procedural programming provides code reuse to a certain degree—you can write a procedure and then use it as many times as you want. However, OO programming goes an important step further, allowing you to define relationships between classes that facilitate not only code reuse, but also better overall design, by organizing classes and factoring in commonalties of various classes. *Inheritance* is a primary means of providing this functionality.

Inheritance allows a class to inherit the attributes and methods of another class. This allows you to create brand new classes by abstracting out common attributes and behaviors.

One of the major design issues in OO programming is to factor out commonality of the various classes. For example, say you have a Dog class and a Cat class, and each will have an attribute for eye color. In a procedural model, the code for Dog and Cat would each contain this attribute. In an OO design, the color attribute could be moved up to a class called Mammal—along with any other common attributes and methods. In this case, both Dog and Cat inherit from the Mammal class, as shown in Figure 1.14.

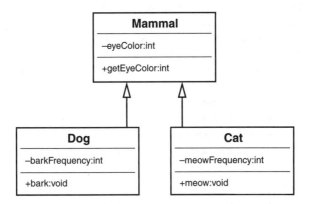

Figure 1.14   Mammal hierarchy.

The Dog and Cat classes both inherit from Mammal. This means that a Dog class actually has the following attributes:

```
eyeColor         // inherited from Mammal
barkFrequency    // defined only for Dogs
```

In the same vein, Dog object has the following methods:

```
getEyeColor    // inherited from Mammal
bark           // defined only for Dogs
```

When the Dog or the Cat object is instantiated, it contains everything in its class, as well as everything from the parent class. Thus, Dog has all the properties of its class definition, as well as the properties inherited from the Mammal class.

Superclasses and Subclasses

The superclass, or parent class, contains all the attributes and behaviors that are common to classes that inherit from it. For example, in the case of the Mammal class, all mammals have similar attributes such as eyeColor and hairColor, as well as behaviors such as generateInternalHeat and growHair. All mammals have these attributes and behaviors, so it is not necessary to duplicate them down the inheritance tree for each type of mammal. Thus, the Dog and Cat classes inherit all those common attributes and behaviors from the Mammal class. The Mammal class is considered the superclass of the Dog and the Cat subclasses, or child classes.

Inheritance provides a rich set of design advantages. When you're designing a Cat class, the Mammal class provides much of the functionality needed. By inheriting from the Mammal object, Cat already has all the attributes and behaviors that make it a true mammal. To make it more specifically a cat type of mammal, the Cat class must include any attributes or behaviors that pertain solely to a cat.

Abstraction

An inheritance tree can grow quite large. When the Mammal and Cat classes are complete, other mammals, such as dogs (or lions, tigers, and bears), can be added quite easily. The Cat class can also be a superclass to other classes. For example, it might be necessary to abstract the Cat class further, to provide classes for Persian cats, Siamese cats, and so on. Just as with Cat, the Dog class can be the parent for GermanShepherd and Poodle (see Figure 1.15). The power of inheritance lies in its abstraction and organization techniques.

Note that the classes GermanShepherd and Poodle both inherit from Dog—each contains only a single method. However, because they inherit from Dog, they also inherit from Mammal. Thus, the GermanShepherd and Poodle classes contain all the attributes and methods included in Dog and Mammal, as well as their own (see Figure 1.16).

Is-a Relationships

Consider a Shape example where Circle, Square, and Star all inherit directly from Shape. This relationship is often referred to as an is-a relationship because a circle is a shape and Square is a shape. When a subclass inherits from a superclass, it can do anything that the superclass can do. Thus, Circle, Square, and Star are all extensions of Shape.

In Figure 1.17, the name on each of the objects represents the Draw method for the Circle, Star, and Square objects, respectively. When we design this Shape system it would be very helpful to standardize how we use the various shapes. Thus, we could decide that if we want to draw a shape, no matter what shape, we will invoke a method called draw. If we adhere to this decision, whenever we want to draw a shape, only the

`Draw` method needs to be called, regardless of what the shape is. Here lies the fundamental concept of polymorphism—it is the individual object's responsibility, be it a `Circle`, `Star`, or `Square`, to draw itself.

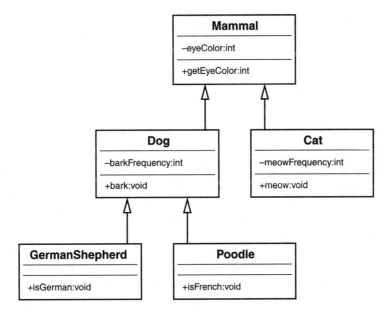

Figure 1.15 Mammal UML diagram.

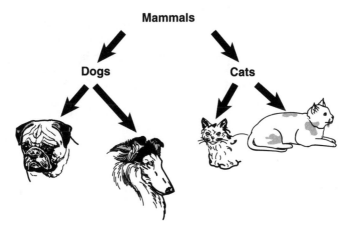

Figure 1.16 Mammal hierarchy.

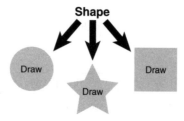

Figure 1.17   The shape hierarchy.

Polymorphism

Polymorphism literally means many shapes. Although polymorphism is tightly coupled to inheritance, it is often cited separately as one of the most powerful advantages to object-oriented technologies. When a message is sent to an object, the object must have a method defined to respond to that message. In an inheritance hierarchy, all subclasses inherit the interfaces from their superclass. However, because each subclass is a separate entity, each might require a separate response to the same message. For example, consider the Shape class and the behavior called Draw. When you tell somebody to draw a shape, the first question he asks is "What shape?" He cannot draw a shape, as it is an abstract concept (in fact, the Draw() method in the Shape code following contains no implementation). You must specify a concrete shape. To do this, you provide the actual implementation in Circle. Even though Shape has a Draw method, Circle overrides this method and provides its own Draw() method. Overriding basically means replacing an implementation of a parent with one from a child.

For example, suppose you have an array of three shapes—Circle, Square, and Star. Even though you treat them all as Shape objects, and send a Draw message to each Shape object, the end result is different for each because Circle, Square, and Star provide the actual implementations. In short, each class is able to respond differently to the same Draw method and draw itself. This is what is meant by polymorphism.
Consider the following Shape class:

```
public abstract class Shape{

    private double area;

    public abstract double getArea();

}
```

The Shape class has an attribute called area that holds the value for the area of the shape. The method getArea() includes an identifier called abstract. When a method is defined as abstract, a subclass must provide the implementation for this method; in this case, Shape is requiring subclasses to provide a getArea() implementation. Now let's create a class called `Circle` that inherits from `Shape` (the `extends` keyword signifies that `Circle` inherits from `Shape`):

```
public class Circle extends Shape{

    double radius;

    public Circle(double r) {

        radius = r;

    }

    public double getArea() {

        area = 3.14*(radius*radius);
        return (area);

    };
}
```

We introduce a new concept here called a *constructor*. The `Circle` class has a method with the same name, `Circle`. When the names are the same and no return type is provided, the method is a special method, called a constructor. Consider a constructor the entry point for the class, where the object is constructed; the constructor is a good place to perform initializations.

The `Circle` constructor accepts a single parameter, representing the radius, and assigns it to the `radius` attribute of the `Circle` class.

The `Circle` class also provides the implementation for the `getArea` method, originally defined as `abstract` in the `Shape` class.

We can create a similar class, called `Rectangle`:

```
public class Rectangle extends Shape{

    double length;
    double width;

    public Rectangle(double l, double w){
        length = l;
        width = w;
    }

    public double getArea() {
        area = length*width;
        return (area);
    };

}
```

Now we can create any number of rectangles, circles, and so on, and invoke their getArea() method. This is because we know that all rectangles and circles inherit from Shape, and all Shape classes have a getArea() method. If a subclass inherits an abstract method from a superclass, it must provide a concrete implementation of that method, or else it will be an abstract class itself (see Figure 1.18 for a UML diagram).

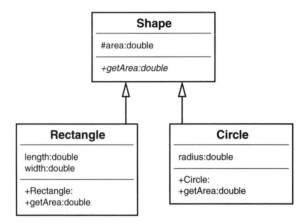

Figure 1.18   Shape UML diagram.

Thus, we can instantiate the Shape classes in this way:

```
Circle circle = new Circle(5);
Rectangle rectangle = new Rectangle(4,5);
```

Then, using a construct such as a stack, we can add these Shape classes to the stack:

```
stack.push(circle);
stack.push(rectangle);
```

What Is a Stack?
A *stack* is a data structure that is a last-in, first-out system. It is like a coin changer, where you insert coins at the top of the cylinder and, when you need a coin, you simply take one off the top, which is the last one you inserted. Pushing an item onto the stack means that you are adding an item to the top (like inserting another coin into the changer). Popping an item off the stack means that you are taking the last item off the stack (like taking the coin off the top).

Now comes the fun part. We can empty the stack, and we do not have to care about what kind of Shape classes are in it:

```
while ( !stack.empty()) {
    Shape shape = (Shape) stack.pop();
    System.out.println ("Area = " + shape.getArea());
}
```

In reality, we are sending the same message to all the shapes:

```
shape.getArea()
```

However, the actual behavior that takes place depends on the type of shape. For example, `Circle` will calculate the area for a circle, and `Rectangle` will calculate the area of a rectangle. In effect (and here is the key concept), we are sending a message to the `Shape` classes and experiencing different behavior depending on what subclass of `Shape` is being used.

Composition

It is natural to think of objects as containing other objects. A television set contains a tuner and video display. A computer contains video cards, keyboards, and drives. Although the computer can be considered an object unto itself, the drive is also considered a valid object. In fact, you could open up the computer and remove the drive and hold it in your hand. Both the computer and the drive are considered objects. It is just that the computer contains other objects—such as drives.

In this way, objects are often built, or composed, from other objects—this is composition.

Has-a Relationships

Although an inheritance relationship is considered an is-a relationship for reasons already discussed, a composition relationship is termed a has-a relationship. Using the example in the previous section, a television has-a tuner and has-a video display. A television is obviously not a tuner, so there is no inheritance relationship. In the same vein, a computer has-a video card, has-a keyboard, and has-a disk drive. The topics of inheritance, composition, and how they relate to each other is covered in great detail in Chapter 7, "Mastering Inheritance and Composition."

Conclusion

There is a lot to cover when discussing OO technologies. However, you should leave this chapter with a good understanding of the following topics:

- Encapsulation—Encapsulating the data and behavior into a single object is of primary importance in OO development. A single object contains both its data and behaviors and can hide what it wants from other objects.
- Inheritance—A class can inherit from another class and take advantage of the attributes and methods defined by the superclass.
- Polymorphism—Polymorphism means that similar objects can respond to the same message in different manners. For example, you might have a system with many shapes. However, a circle, a square, and a star are each drawn differently. Using

polymorphism, you can send each of these shapes the same message (for example, Draw), and each shape is responsible for drawing itself.

- Composition—Composition means that an object is built from other objects.

This chapter covers the fundamental OO concepts. By now you should have a good grasp of what OO concepts are all about.

2

How to Think in Terms
of Objects

IN CHAPTER 1, "INTRODUCTION TO Object-Oriented Concepts," you learned the fundamental object-oriented (OO) concepts. The rest of the book digs more deeply into these concepts. Many factors go into a good design, whether it is an OO design or not. The fundamental unit of OO design is the class. The desired end result of OO design is a robust and functional object model—a system.

As with most things in life, there is no single right or wrong way to approach a problem. There are usually many different ways to tackle the same problem. So, when attempting to design an OO solution, don't get hung up in trying to do a perfect design the first time. What you really need to do is brainstorm and let your thought process go wild. Do not try to conform to any standards or conventions when trying to solve a problem, because the whole idea is to be creative. Thus, before you start to design a system, or even a class, think the problem through and have some fun! In this chapter we explore the fine art and science of OO thinking.

The move from the procedural world to an OO world is not trivial. Changing from FORTRAN to COBOL, or even to C, requires that you learn a new language; however, making the move from COBOL to C++, C# .NET, Visual Basic .NET, or Java requires that you learn a new thought process. This is where the overused phrase *OO paradigm* rears its ugly head. When moving to an OO language, you must go through the investment of learning OO concepts and the corresponding thought process first. If this paradigm shift does not take place, one of two things will happen: Either the project will not truly be OO in nature (for example, it will use C++ without using OO constructs), or the project will be a complete object-disoriented mess.

Three important things you can do to develop a good sense of the OO thought process are covered in this chapter:

- Knowing the difference between the interface and implementation
- Thinking more abstractly
- Giving the user the minimal interface possible

We have already met some of these concepts in Chapter 1, and here we will now go into much more detail.

Knowing the Difference Between the Interface and the Implementation

As we saw in Chapter 1, one of the keys to a string OO design is to understand the difference between the interface and the implementation. Thus, when designing a class, what the user needs to know and what the user does not need to know are of vital importance. The data hiding mechanism inherent with encapsulation is the means by which nonessential data is hidden from the user.

> **Caution**
>
> Do not confuse the concept of the interface with terms like *graphical user interface (GUI)*. Although a GUI is, as its name implies, an interface, the term *interfaces*, as used here, is more general in nature and is not restricted to a graphical interface.

Remember the toaster example in Chapter 1? The toaster, or any appliance for that matter, is simply plugged into the interface, which is the electrical outlet—see Figure 2.1. All appliances have access to electricity by complying with using the correct interface: the electrical outlet. The toaster doesn't need to know anything about the implementation, or how the electricity is produced. For all the toaster cares, a coal plant or a nuclear plant could produce the electricity—the appliance does not care which, as long as the interface works.

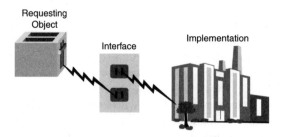

Figure 2.1 Power plant revisited.

As another example, consider an automobile. The interface between you and the car includes components such as the steering wheel, gas pedal, brake, and ignition switch. For most people, aesthetic issues aside, the main concern when driving a car is that the car starts, accelerates, stops, steers, and so on. The implementation, basically the stuff that you don't see, is of little concern to the average driver. In fact, most people would not even be able to identify certain components, such as the catalytic converter and gasket.

However, any driver would recognize and know how to use the steering wheel, because this is a common interface. By installing a standard steering wheel in the car, manufacturers are assured that the people in their target market will be able to use the system.

If, however, a manufacturer decided to install a joystick in place of the steering wheel, most drivers would balk at this, and the automobile might not be a big seller (except for some eclectic people who love bucking the trends). On the other hand, as long as the performance and aesthetics didn't change, the average driver would not notice if the manufacturer changed the engine—part of the implementation—of the automobile.

It must be stressed that the interchangeable engines must be identical in every way—as far as the driver's perceptions go. Replacing a four-cylinder engine with an eight-cylinder engine would change the rules, just as changing the current from AC to DC would affect the rules in the power plant example.

The engine is part of the implementation, and the steering wheel is part of the interface. A change in the implementation should have no impact on the driver, whereas a change to the interface might.

What Users See

Interfaces also relate directly to classes. End users do not normally see any classes—they see the GUI or command line. However, programmers *would* see the class interfaces. Class reuse means that someone has already written a class. Thus, a programmer who uses a class must know how to get the class to work properly. This programmer will combine many classes to create a system. The programmer is the one who needs to understand the interfaces of a class. Therefore, when we talk about users in this chapter, we primarily mean designers and developers—not necessarily end users. Thus, when we talk about interfaces in this context, we are talking about class interfaces, not GUIs.

Properly constructed classes are designed in two parts—the interface and the implementation.

The Interface

The services presented to an end user comprise the interface. In the best case, *only* the services the end user needs are presented. Of course, which services the user needs might be a matter of opinion. If you put 10 people in a room and ask each of them to do an independent design, you might receive 10 totally different designs—and there is nothing wrong with that. However, as a rule of thumb, the interface to a class should contain only what the user needs to know. In the toaster example, the user only needs to know that the toaster must be plugged into the interface—which in this case is the electrical outlet.

Identifying the User

Perhaps the most important issue when designing a class is identifying the audience, or users, of the class.

The Implementation

The interface services' implementation details are hidden from the user. One goal regarding the implementation should be kept in mind: A change to the implementation *should not* require a change to the user's code. This might seem a bit confusing, but this goal is at the heart of the design issue. If the interface is designed properly, a change to the implementation should not require a change to the user's code. Remember that the interface includes the syntax to call a method and return a value. If this interface does not change, the user does not care whether the implementation is changed. As long as the programmer can use the same syntax and retrieve the same value, that's all that matters.

Recall that in the toaster example, although the interface is always the electric outlet, the implementation could change from a coal power plant to a nuclear power plant without affecting the toaster. There is one very important caveat to be made here: The coal or nuclear plant must also conform to the interface specification. If the coal plant produces AC power, but the nuclear plant produces DC power, there is a problem. The bottom line is that both the user and the implementation must conform to the interface specification.

An Interface/Implementation Example

Let's create a simple (if not very functional) Oracle database reader class. We'll write some Java code that will retrieve records from the Oracle database. As we've discussed, knowing your end users is always the most important issue when doing any kind of design. You should do some analysis of the situation and conduct interviews with end users, and then list the requirements for the project. The following are some requirements we might want to use for the database reader:

- We must be able to open a connection to the database.
- We must be able to close the connection to the database.
- We must be able to position the cursor on the first record in the database.
- We must be able to position the cursor on the last record in the database.
- We must be able to find the number of records in the database.
- We must be able to determine whether there are more records in the database (that is, if we are at the end).
- We must be able to position the cursor at a specific record by supplying the key.
- We must be able to retrieve a record by supplying a key.
- We must be able to get the next record, based on the position of the cursor.

With these requirements in mind, we can make an initial attempt to design the database reader class by creating possible interfaces for these end users.

In this case, the database reader class is intended for programmers who require use of a database. Thus, the interface is essentially the application programming interface (API) that the programmer will use. These methods are, in effect, wrappers that enclose the functionality provided by the database system. Why would we do this? We will explore this question in much greater detail later in the chapter; the short answer is that we might need to customize some database functionality. For example, we might need to process the objects so that we can write them to a relational database. Writing this *middleware* is not trivial as far as design and coding go, but it is a real-life example of wrapping functionality.

Figure 2.2 shows a class diagram representing a possible interface to the `DataBaseReader` class.

```
┌─────────────────────────────────────┐
│         DataBaseReader              │
├─────────────────────────────────────┤
├─────────────────────────────────────┤
│ +open:void                          │
│ +close:void                         │
│ +goToFirst:void                     │
│ +goToLast:void                      │
│ +howManyRecords:int                 │
│ +areThereMoreRecords:boolean        │
│ +positionRecord:void                │
│ +getRecord:String                   │
│ +getNextRecord:String               │
└─────────────────────────────────────┘
```

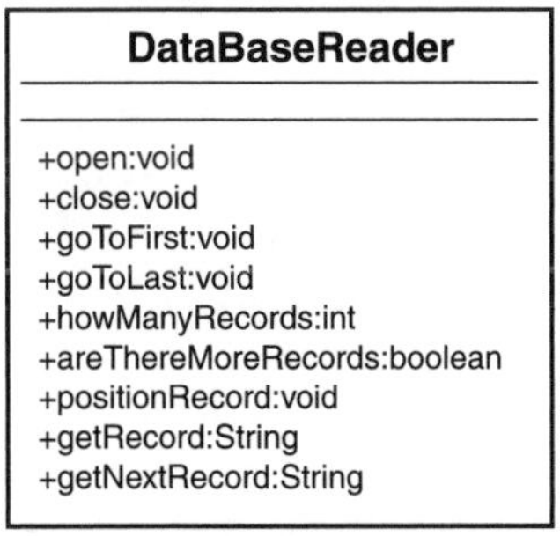

Figure 2.2   A Unified Modeling Language class diagram for the `DataBaseReader` class.

Note that the methods in this class are all public (remember that there are plus signs next to the names of methods that are public interfaces). Also note that only the interface is represented; the implementation is not shown. Take a minute to determine whether this class diagram generally satisfies the requirements outlined earlier for the project. If you find out later that the diagram does not meet all the requirements, that's okay; remember that OO design is an iterative process, so you do not have to get it exactly right the first time.

Public Interface

Remember that if a method is public, a programmer can access it, and thus, it is considered part of the class interface. Do not confuse the term *interface* with the keyword `interface` used in Java and C#—this term is discussed later.

For each of the requirements we listed, we need a corresponding method that provides the functionality we want. Now you need to ask a few questions:

- To effectively use this class, do you as a programmer need to know anything else about it?
- Do you need to know how the Oracle code actually opens the Oracle database?

- Do you need to know how the Oracle code physically positions itself over a specific record?
- Do you need to know how the Oracle code determines whether there are any more records left?

On all counts the answer is a resounding *no!* You don't need to know any of this information. All you care about is that you get the proper return values and that the operations are performed correctly. In fact, the application programmer will most likely be at least one more abstract level away from the implementation. The application will use your classes to open the database, which in turn will invoke the proper Oracle API.

Minimal Interface

Although perhaps extreme, one way to determine the minimalist interface is to initially provide the user no public interfaces. Of course, the class will be useless; however, this forces the user to come back to you and say, "Hey, I need this functionality." Thus, you add interfaces only when it is requested. Never assume that the user needs something.

Creating wrappers might seem like overkill, but there are many advantages to writing them. To illustrate, there are many middleware products on the market today. Consider the problem of mapping objects to a relational database. There are OO databases on the market today that are perfect for OO applications. However, there is one itty-bitty problem: Most companies have years of data in legacy relational database systems. How can a company embrace OO technologies and stay on the bleeding edge when its data is in a relational database?

First, you can convert all your legacy, relational data to a brand-new OO database. Anyone who has suffered the acute (and chronic) pain of any data conversion knows that this is to be avoided like the plague.

Second, you can use a middleware product to seamlessly map the objects in your application code to a relational model. This is a much better solution as long as relational databases are so prevalent. There might be an argument stating that OO databases are much more efficient for object persistence than relational databases.

Object Persistence

Object persistence refers to the concept of saving the state of an object so that it can be restored and used at a later time. An object that does not persist basically dies when it goes out of scope. For example, the state of an object can be saved in a database.

However, in the current business environment, relational-to-object mapping is a great solution. For brand-new OO applications that need to create new data stores, using an OO database might be a viable choice. However, OO databases have not gained wide acceptance.

> **Standalone Application**
> Even when creating a new OO application from scratch, it might not be easy to avoid legacy data. This is due to the fact that even a newly created OO application is most likely not a standalone application and might need to exchange information stored in relational databases (or any other data storage device, for that matter).

Let's return to the database example. Figure 2.2 shows the public interface to the class, and nothing else. Of course, when this class is complete, it will probably contain more methods, and it will certainly contain attributes. However, you as a programmer using this class do not need to know anything about these private methods and attributes. You certainly don't need to know what the code looks like within the public methods. You simply need to know how to interact with the interfaces.

What would the code for this public interface look like? Let's look at the `open()` method:

```
public void open(String Name){

        /* Some application-specific processing */

        /* call the Oracle API to open the database */

        /* Some more application-specific processing */

};
```

In this case, you, wearing your programmer's hat, realize that the `open` method requires `String` as a parameter. `Name`, which represents a database file, is passed in, but it's not important to explain how `Name` is mapped to a specific database for this example. That's all we need to know. Now comes the fun stuff—what really makes interfaces so great!

Just to annoy our users, let's change the database implementation. Last night we translated all the data from an Oracle database to an SQLAnywhere database (we endured the acute and chronic pain). It took us hours—but we did it.
Now the code looks like this:

```
public void open(String Name){

        /* Some application-specific processing

        /* call the SQLAnywhere API to open the database */

        /* Some more application-specific processing */

};
```

To our great chagrin, this morning not one user complained. Even though the implementation changed, the interface did not! As far as the user is concerned, the calls are still the same. The code change for the implementation might have required quite a bit of work (and the module with the one-line code change would have to be rebuilt), but not one line of application code that uses this `DataBaseReader` class needed to change.

Code Recompilation

Dynamically loaded classes are loaded at runtime—not statically linked into an executable file. When using dynamically loaded classes, like Java does, no user classes would have to be recompiled. However, in statically linked languages such as C++, a link is required to bring in the new class.

By separating the user interface from the implementation, we can save a lot of headaches down the road. In Figure 2.3, the database implementations are transparent to the end users, who see only the interface.

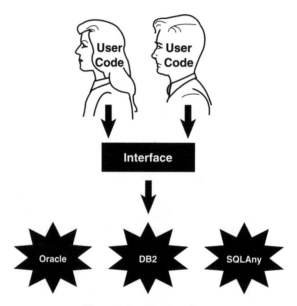

Figure 2.3   The interface.

Using Abstract Thinking when Designing Interfaces

One of the main advantages of OO programming is that classes can be reused. In general, reusable classes tend to have interfaces that are more abstract than concrete. Concrete interfaces tend to be very specific, whereas abstract interfaces are more general. However, simply stating that a highly abstract interface is more useful than a highly concrete interface, although often true, is not always the case.

It is possible to write a very useful, concrete class that is not at all reusable. This happens all the time, and there is nothing wrong with it in some situations. However, we are now in the design business, and want to take advantage of what OO offers us. So, our goal is to design abstract, highly reusable classes—and to do this we will design highly abstract user interfaces. To illustrate the difference between an abstract and a concrete interface, let's create a taxi object. It is much more useful to have an interface such as "drive me to the airport" than to have separate interfaces such as "turn right," "turn left," "start," "stop," and so on, because as illustrated in Figure 2.4, all the user wants to do is get to the airport.

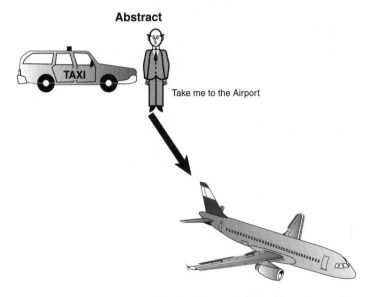

Figure 2.4   An abstract interface.

When you emerge from your hotel, throw your bags into the back seat of the taxi and get in, the cabbie will turn to you and ask, "Where do you want to go?" You reply, "Please take me to the airport." (This assumes, of course, that there is only one major airport in the city. In Chicago you would have to say, "Please take me to Midway Airport" or "Please take me to O'Hare.") You might not even know how to get to the airport yourself, and even if you did, you wouldn't want to have to tell the cabbie when to turn and which direction to turn, as illustrated in Figure 2.5. How the cabbie implements the actual drive is of no concern to you, the passenger. (Of course, the fare might become an issue at some point, if the cabbie cheats and takes you the long way to the airport.)

Now, where does the connection between abstract and reuse come in? Ask yourself which of these two scenarios is more reusable, the abstract or the not-so-abstract? To put it more simply, which phrase is more reusable: "Take me to the airport," or "Turn right, then right, then left, then left, then left"? Obviously, the first phrase is more reusable. You can use it in any city, whenever you get into a taxi and want to go to the airport. The second phrase will only work in a specific case. Thus, the abstract interface "Take me to the airport" is generally the way to go for a good, reusable OO design, whose implementation would be different in Chicago, New York, or Cleveland.

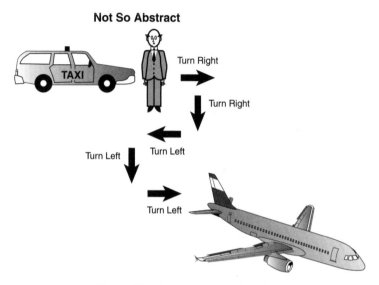

Figure 2.5   A not-so-abstract interface.

Giving the User the Minimal Interface Possible

When designing a class, the rule of thumb is to always provide the user with as little knowledge of the inner workings of the class as possible. To accomplish this, follow these simple rules:

- Give the users only what they absolutely need. In effect, this means the class has as few interfaces as possible. When you start designing a class, start with a minimal interface. The design of a class is iterative, so you will soon discover that the minimal set of interfaces might not suffice. This is fine. It is better to have to add an interface because users really need it than to give the users more interfaces than they need.

For the moment, let's use a hardware example to illustrate our software example. Imagine handing a user a PC box without a monitor or a keyboard. Obviously, the PC would be of little use. You have just provided the user with the minimal set of interfaces to the PC. Of course, this minimal set is insufficient, and it immediately becomes necessary to add interfaces.

- Public interfaces are all the users will ever see. You should initially hide the entire class from the user. Then when you start using the class, you will be forced to make certain methods public—these methods thus become the public interface.

- It is vital to design classes from a user's perspective and not from an information systems viewpoint. Too often designers of classes (not to mention any other kind of software) design the class to make it fit into a specific technological model. Even if the designer takes a user's perspective, it is still probably a technician user's perspective, and the class is designed with an eye on getting it to work from a technology standpoint, and not from ease of use for the user.

- Users are the ones who will actually use the software. Make sure when you are designing a class that you go over the requirements and the design with the people who will actually use it—not just developers. The class will most likely evolve and need to be updated when a prototype of the system is built.

Determining the Users

Let's look again at the taxi example. We have already decided that the users are the ones who will actually use the system. This said, the obvious question is who are the users?

The first impulse is to say the *customers*. This is only about half right. Although the customers are certainly users, the cabbie must be able to successfully provide the service to the customers. In other words, providing an interface that would, no doubt, please the customer, like "Take me to the airport for free," is not going to go over well with the cabbie. Thus, in reality, to build a realistic and usable interface, *both* the customer and the cabbie must be considered users.

For a software analogy, consider that users might want a programmer to provide a certain function. However, if the programmer finds the request technically impossible, it is not a reasonable request.

In short, any object that sends a message to the taxi object is considered a user (and yes, the users are objects, too). Figure 2.6 shows how the cabbie provides a service.

Looking Ahead

The cabbie is most likely an object as well.

Object Behavior

Identifying the users is only a part of the exercise. After the users are identified, you must determine the behaviors of the objects. From the viewpoint of all the users, begin identifying the purpose of each object and what it must do to perform properly. Note that many of the initial choices will not survive the final cut of the public interface. These choices are identified by gathering requirements using various methods such as UML use cases.

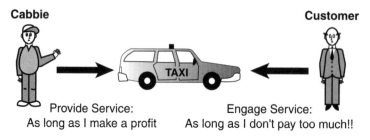

Figure 2.6 Providing services.

Environmental Constraints

In their book *Object-Oriented Design in Java*, Gilbert and McCarty point out that the environment often imposes limitations on what an object can do. In fact, environmental constraints are almost always a factor. Computer hardware might limit software functionality. For example, a system might not be connected to a network, or a company might use a specific type of printer. In the taxi example, the cab cannot drive on a road if a bridge is out, even if it provides a quicker way to the airport.

Identifying the Public Interfaces

With all the information gathered about the users, the object behaviors, and the environment, you need to determine the public interfaces for each user object. So, think about how you would use the taxi object:

- Get into the taxi.
- Tell the cabbie where you want to go.
- Pay the cabbie.
- Give the cabbie a tip.
- Get out of the taxi.

What do you need to do to use the taxi object?

- Have a place to go.
- Hail a taxi.
- Pay the cabbie money.

Initially, you think about how the object is used and not how it is built. You might discover that the object needs more interfaces, such as "Put luggage in the trunk" or "Enter into a mindless conversation with the cabbie." Figure 2.7 provides a class diagram that lists possible methods for the `Cabbie` class.

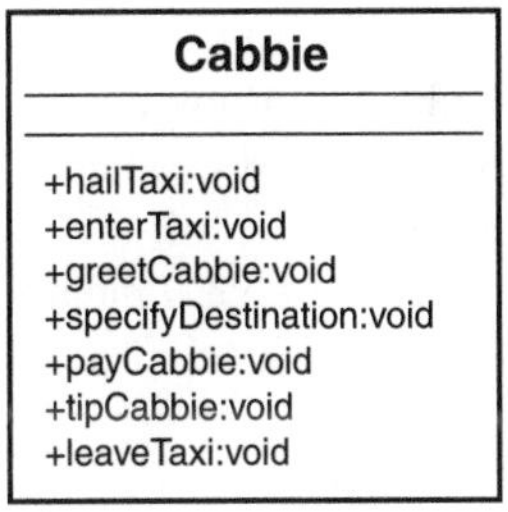

```
┌─────────────────────────────┐
│           Cabbie            │
├─────────────────────────────┤
├─────────────────────────────┤
│ +hailTaxi:void              │
│ +enterTaxi:void             │
│ +greetCabbie:void           │
│ +specifyDestination:void    │
│ +payCabbie:void             │
│ +tipCabbie:void             │
│ +leaveTaxi:void             │
└─────────────────────────────┘
```

Figure 2.7 The methods in a cabbie class.

As is always the case, nailing down the final interface is an iterative process. For each interface, you must determine whether the interface contributes to the operation of the object. If it does not, perhaps it is not necessary. Many OO texts recommend that each interface model only one behavior. This returns us to the question of how abstract we want to get with the design. If we have an interface called enterTaxi(), we certainly do not want enterTaxi() to have logic in it to pay the cabbie. If we do this, then not only is the design somewhat illogical, but there is virtually no way that a user of the class can tell what has to be done to simply pay the cabbie.

Identifying the Implementation

After the public interfaces are chosen, you need to identify the implementation. After the class is designed and all the methods required to operate the class properly are in place, the issue tends to be an either/or proposition.

Technically, anything that is not a public interface can be considered the implementation. This means that the user will never see any of the methods that are considered part of the implementation, including the method's signature (which includes the name of the method and the parameter list), as well as the actual code inside the method. The implementation is totally hidden from the user. In fact, the code within public methods is actually a part of the implementation because the user cannot see it. (The user should only see the calling structure of an interface—not the code inside it.)

This means that, theoretically, anything that is considered the implementation might change without affecting how the user interfaces with the class. This assumes, of course, that the implementation is providing the answers the user expects.

Whereas the interface represents how the user sees the object, the implementation is really the nuts and bolts of the object. The implementation contains the code that represents that state of an object.

Conclusion

In this chapter, we have explored three areas that can get you started on the path to thinking in an OO way. Remember that there is no firm list of issues pertaining to the

OO thought process. Doing things in an OO way is more of an art than a science. Try to think of your own ways to describe OO thinking.

In Chapter 3, "Advanced Object-Oriented Concepts," we'll talk about the fact that the object has a life cycle: It is born, it lives, and it dies. While it is alive, it might transition through many different states. For example, a `DataBaseReader` object is in one state if the database is open, and another state if the database is closed. How this is represented depends on the design of the class.

References

Fowler, Martin. *UML Distilled*. Addison-Wesley Longman, 1997.

Gilbert, Stephen, and Bill McCarty. *Object-Oriented Design in Java*. The Waite Group, 1998.

Meyers, Scott. *Effective C++*. Addison-Wesley, 1992.

Advanced
Object-Oriented Concepts

CHAPTERS 1, "AN INTRODUCTION TO Object-Oriented Concepts," and 2, "How to Think in Terms of Objects," cover the basics of object-oriented (OO) concepts. Before we embark on our journey to learn some of the finer design issues relating to building an OO system, we need to cover several more advanced OO concepts.

Some of these concepts might not be vital to understanding an OO design at a higher level, but they are necessary to anyone actually involved in the design and implementation of an OO system.

Constructors

Constructors are a new concept for people doing structured programming. Constructors do not normally exist in non-OO languages such as C and Basic. Earlier we spoke about special methods that are used to *construct* objects. In Java, C# and C++, as well as in other OO languages, constructors are methods that share the same name as the class and have no return type. For example, a constructor for the Cabbie class would look like this:

```
public Cabbie(){
    /* code to construct the object */
}
```

The compiler will recognize that the method name is identical to the class name and consider the method a constructor.

> **Return Value**
>
> Note again that a constructor does not have a return value. If you provide a return value, the compiler will not treat the method as a constructor.

When Is a Constructor Called?

When a new object is created, one of the first things that happens is that the constructor is called. Check out the following code:

```
Cabbie myCabbie = new Cabbie();
```

The new keyword creates a new instance of the Cabbie class, thus allocating the required memory. Then the constructor is called, passing the arguments in the parameter list. The developer must do the appropriate initialization within the constructor.

Thus, the code new Cabbie() will instantiate a Cabbie object and call the Cabbie method, which is the constructor.

What's Inside a Constructor?

Perhaps the most important function of a constructor is to initialize the memory allocated when the new keyword is encountered. In short, code included inside a constructor should set the newly created object to its initial, stable, safe state.

For example, if you have a counter object with an attribute called count, you need to set count to zero in the constructor:

```
count = 0;
```

> **Initializing Attributes**
> In structured programming, a routine named housekeeping (or initialization) is often used for initialization purposes. Initializing attributes is a common function performed within a constructor.

The Default Constructor

If you write a class and do not include a constructor, the class will still compile and you can still use it. If the class provides no explicit constructor, such as in C++, C#, and Java, a default constructor will be provided. It is important to understand that at least one constructor always exists, regardless of whether you write a constructor yourself. If you do not provide a constructor, the system will provide a default constructor for you.

The default constructor calls only the constructor of the superclass. In many cases, the super class will be part of the language framework, like the Object class in Java. For example, if a constructor is not provided for the Cabbie class, the following default constructor is inserted:

```
public Cabbie(){
    super();
}
```

In this case, if Cabbie does not explicitly inherit from another class, the Object class will be the parent class. Perhaps the default constructor might be sufficient in some cases; however, in most cases some sort of memory initialization should be performed.

Regardless of the situation, it is good programming practice to always include at least one constructor in a class. In any case, if there are attributes in the class, they should be initialized in a constructor.

Providing a Constructor

The rule of thumb is that you should *always* provide a constructor, even if you do not plan on doing anything inside it. You can provide a constructor with nothing in it and then add to it later. Although there is technically nothing wrong with using the default constructor provided by the compiler, it is always nice to know exactly what your code looks like.

Using Multiple Constructors

In many cases, an object can be constructed in more than one way. To accommodate this situation, you need to provide more than one constructor. For example, let's consider the Count class presented here:

```
public class Count {

    int count;

    public Count(){
        count = 0;
    }
}
```

On the one hand, we simply want to initialize the attribute count to count to zero. We can easily accomplish this by having a constructor initialize count to zero as follows:

```
public Count(){
    count = 0;
}
```

On the other hand, we might want to pass an initialization parameter that allows count to be set to various numbers:

```
public Count (int number){
    count = number;
}
```

This is called *overloading a method* (overloading pertains to all methods, not just constructors). Most OO languages provide functionality for overloading a method.

Overloading Methods

Overloading allows a programmer to use the same method name over and over, as long as the signature of the method is different each time. The signature consists of the method name and a parameter list (see Figure 3.1).

Thus, the following methods *all* have different signatures:

```
public void getCab();
```

```
// different parameter list
public void getCab (String cabbieName);

// different parameter list
public void getCab (int numberOfPassengers);
```

Signature

public String getRecord(int key)

Signature = getRecord   (int key)
            method name + parameter list

Figure 3.1   The components of a signature.

Signatures

Depending on the language, the signature may or may not include the return type. In Java and C#, the return type is not part of the signature. For example, the following methods would conflict even though the return types are different:

```
public void getCab (String cabbieName);
public int getCab (String cabbieName);
```

The best way to understand signatures is to write some code and run it through the compiler.

By using different signatures, you can construct objects differently depending on the constructor used.

Using UML to Model Classes

Let's return to the database reader example we used earlier in Chapter 2. Consider that we have two ways we can construct a database reader:

- Pass the name of the database and position the cursor at the beginning of the database.
- Pass the name of the database and the position within the database where we want the cursor to position itself.

Figure 3.2 shows a class diagram for the DataBaseReader class. Note that the diagram lists two constructors for the class. Although the diagram shows the two constructors, without the parameter list, there is no way to know which constructor is which. To distinguish the constructors, you can look at the corresponding code listed below.

No Return Type

Notice that in this class diagram the constructors do not have a return type. All other methods besides constructors must have return types.

```
DataBaseReader

dbName:String
startPosition:int

+DataBaseReader:
+DataBaseReader:
+open:void
+close:void
+goToFirst:void
+goToLast:void
+howManyRecords:int
+areThereMoreRecords:boolean
+positionRecord:void
+getRecord:String
+getNextRecord:String
```

Figure 3.2   The `DataBaseReader` class diagram.

Here is a code segment of the class that shows its constructors and the attributes that the constructors initialize (see Figure 3.3):

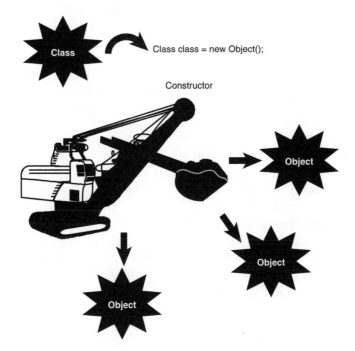

Figure 3.3   Creating a new object.

```
public class DataBaseReader {

    String dbName;
    int startPosition;

    // initialize just the name
    public DataBaseReader (String name){
        dbName = name;
      startPosition = 0;
    };

    // initialize the name and the position
    public DataBaseReader (String name, int pos){
        dbName = name;
        startPosition = pos;
    };

    .. // rest of class
}
```

Note how startPosition is initialized in both cases. If the constructor is not passed the information via the parameter list, it is initialized to a default value, like 0.

How the Superclass Is Constructed

When using inheritance, you must know how the parent class is constructed. Remember that when you use inheritance, you are inheriting everything about the parent. Thus, you must become intimately aware of all the parent's data and behavior. The inheritance of an attribute is fairly obvious. However, how a constructor is inherited is not as obvious. After the new keyword is encountered and the object is allocated, the following steps occur (see Figure 3.4):

1. The first thing that happens inside the constructor is that the constructor of the class's superclass is called. If there is no explicit call to the superclass constructor, the default is called automatically.

2. Then each class attribute of the object is initialized. These are the attributes that are part of the class definition (instance variables), not the attributes inside the constructor or any other method (local variables). In the DataBaseReader code presented earlier, the integer startPosition is an instance variable of the class.

3. Then the rest of the code in the constructor executes.

The Design of Constructors

When designing a class, it is good practice to initialize all the attributes. In some languages, the compiler provides some sort of initialization. As always, don't count on the compiler to initialize attributes! In Java, you cannot use an attribute until it is initialized.

If the attribute is first set in the code, make sure that you initialize the attribute to some valid condition—for example, set an integer to zero.

Constructing an Object

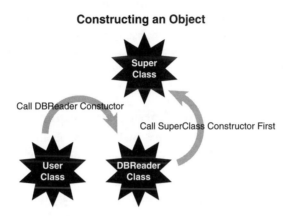

Figure 3.4   Constructing an object.

Constructors are used to ensure that the application is in a stable state (I like to call it a "safe" state). For example, initializing an attribute to zero, when it is intended for use as a denominator in a division operation, might lead to an unstable application. You must take into consideration the fact that a division by zero is an illegal operation. Initializing to zero is not always the best policy.

During the design, it is good practice to identify a stable state for all attributes and then initialize them to this stable state in the constructor.

Error Handling

It is rare for a class to be written perfectly the first time. In most, if not all, situations, things *will* go wrong. Any designer who does not plan for problems is courting danger.

Assuming that your code has the ability to detect and trap an error condition, you can handle the error in several different ways: On page 223 of their book *Java Primer Plus*, Tyma, Torok, and Downing state that there are three basic solutions to handling problems that are detected in a program: fix it, ignore the problem by squelching it, or exit the runtime in some graceful manner. On page 139 of their book *Object-Oriented Design in Java*, Gilbert and McCarty expand on this theme, but add the choice of throwing an exception:

- Ignore the problem—not a good idea!
- Check for potential problems and abort the program when you find a problem.
- Check for potential problems, catch the mistake, and attempt to fix the problem.
- Throw an exception. (Often this is the preferred way to handle the situation.)

These strategies are discussed in the following sections.

Ignoring the Problem

Simply ignoring a potential problem is a recipe for disaster. And if you are going to ignore the problem, why bother detecting it in the first place? The bottom line is that you should not ignore the problem. The primary directive for all applications is that the application should never crash. If you do not handle your errors, the application will eventually terminate ungracefully or continue in a mode that can be considered an unstable state. In the latter case, you might not even know you are getting incorrect results for some period of time.

Checking for Problems and Aborting the Application

If you choose to check for potential problems and abort the application when a problem is detected, the application can display a message indicating that you have a problem. Then the code gracefully exits and the user is left staring at the computer screen, shaking her head and wondering what just happened. Although this is a far superior option to ignoring the problem, it is by no means optimal. However, this does allow the system to clean up things and put itself in a more stable state, such as closing files.

Checking for Problems and Attempting to Recover

Checking for potential problems, catching the mistake, and attempting to recover is a far superior solution than simply checking for problems and aborting. In this case, the problem is detected by the code, and the application attempts to fix itself. This works well in certain situations. For example, consider the following code:

```
if (a == 0)
    a=1;

c = b/a;
```

It is obvious that if the `if` statement is not included in the code and a zero makes its way to the divide statement, you will get a system exception because you cannot divide by zero. By catching the exception and setting a to 1, at least the system will not crash. However, setting a to 1 might not be a proper solution. You might need to prompt the user for the proper input value.

> **A Mix of Error Handling Techniques**
>
> Despite the fact that this type of error handling is not necessarily object-oriented in nature, I believe that it has a valid place in OO design. Throwing an exception (discussed in the next section) can be expensive in terms of overhead. Thus, although exceptions are a great design choice, you will still want to consider other error handling techniques, depending on your design and performance needs.

Although this means of error checking is preferable to the previous solutions, it still has a few potentially limiting problems. It is not always easy to determine where a problem first appears. And it might take a while for the problem to be detected. In any event, it is beyond the scope of this book to explain error handling in great detail. However, it is important to design error handling into the class right from the start.

Throwing an Exception

Most OO languages provide a feature called *exceptions*. In the most basic sense, exceptions are unexpected events that occur within a system. Exceptions provide a way to detect problems and then handle them. In Java, C# and C++, exceptions are handled by the keywords `catch` and `throw`. This might sound like a baseball game, but the key here is that a specific block of code is written to handle a specific exception. This solves the problem of trying to figure out where the problem started and unwinding the code to the proper point. Here is how the code for a `try`/`catch` block looks:

```
try {

    // possible nasty code

} catch(Exception e) {

    // code to handle the exception
}
```

If an exception is thrown within the `try` block, the `catch` block will handle it. When an exception is thrown while the block is executing, the following occurs:

1. The execution of the `try` block is terminated.
2. The `catch` clauses are checked to determine whether an appropriate `catch` block for the offending exception was included. (There might be more than one `catch` clause per `try` block.)
3. If none of the `catch` clauses handle the offending exception, it is passed to the next higher-level `try` block. (If the exception is not caught in the code, the system ultimately catches it and the results are unpredictable.)
4. If a `catch` clause is matched (the first match encountered), the statements in the `catch` clause are executed.
5. Execution then resumes with the statement following the `try` block.

Again, it is beyond the scope of this book to explain exception handling in great detail. Suffice to say that exceptions are an important advantage for OO programming languages. Here is an example of how an exception is caught in Java:

```
try {

    // possible nasty code
    count = 0;
    count = 5/count;
```

```
} catch(ArithmeticException e) {

    // code to handle the exception
    System.out.println(e.getMessage());
    count = 1;

}
System.out.println("The exception is handled.");
```

Exception Granularity

You can catch exceptions at various levels of granularity. You can catch all exceptions or just check for specific exceptions, such as arithmetic exceptions. If your code does not catch an exception, the Java runtime will—and it won't be happy about it!

In this example, the division by zero (because count is equal to 0) within the try block will cause an arithmetic exception. If the exception was generated (thrown) outside a try block, the program would most likely have been terminated. However, because the exception was thrown within a try block, the catch block is checked to see whether the specific exception (in this case, an arithmetic exception) was planned for. Because the catch block contains a check for the arithmetic exception, the code within the catch block is executed, thus setting count to 1. After the catch block executes, the try/catch block is exited and the message The exception is handled. appears on the Java console (see Figure 3.5).

Figure 3.5 Catching an exception.

If you had not put ArithmeticException in the catch block, the program would likely have crashed. You can catch all exceptions by using the following code:

```
try {

    // possible nasty code

} catch(Exception e) {

    // code to handle the exception

}
```

The `Exception` parameter in the `catch` block is used to catch any exception that might be generated within a `try` block.

Bulletproof Code

It's a good idea to use a combination of the methods described here to make your program as bulletproof to your user as possible.

The Concept of Scope

Multiple objects can be instantiated from a single class. Each of these objects has its own identity and state. This is an important point. Each object is constructed separately and is allocated its own memory. However, some attributes and methods may be shared by all the objects instantiated from the same class, thus sharing the memory allocated for these class attributes and methods.

A Shared Method

A constructor is a good example of a method that is shared by all instances of a class.

Although methods generally represent the behaviors of an object, the state of the object is normally represented by attributes. There are three types of attributes:

- Local attributes
- Object attributes
- Class attributes

Local Attributes

Local attributes are local to a specific method. Consider the following code:

```
public class Number {

    public method1() {
        int count;

    }

    public method2() {

    }

}
```

The method `method1` contains a local variable called `count`. This integer is accessible only inside `method1`. The method `method2` has no idea that the integer `count` exists.

At this point, we can touch on a very important concept: scope. Attributes exist within a particular scope. In this case, the integer count exists within the scope of method1. In Java, C#, and C++, scope is delineated by curly braces ({}). In the Number class, there are several possible scopes—just start matching the curly braces.

The class itself has its own scope. Each instance of the class (that is, each object) has its own scope. Both method1 and method2 have their own scopes as well. Because count lives within method1's curly braces, when method1 is invoked, a copy of count is created. When method1 terminates, the copy of count is removed.

For some more fun, look at this code:

```
public class Number {

    public method1() {
        int count;
    }

    public method2() {
        int count;
    }

}
```

How can this be? There are two copies of an integer count in this class. Remember that method1 and method2 each has its own scope. Thus, the compiler can tell which copy of count to access simply by recognizing which method it is in. You can think of it in these terms:

```
method1.count;
```

```
method2.count;
```

As far as the compiler is concerned, the two attributes are easily differentiated, even though they have the same name. It is almost like two people having the same last name, but based on the context of their first names, you know that they are two separate individuals.

Object Attributes

There are many design situations in which an attribute must be shared by several methods within the same object. In Figure 3.6, for example, three objects have been constructed from a single class. Consider the following code:

```
public class Number {

    int count;     // available to both method1 and method2

    public method1() {
        count = 1;
    }
```

```
public method2() {
    count = 2;
}

}
```

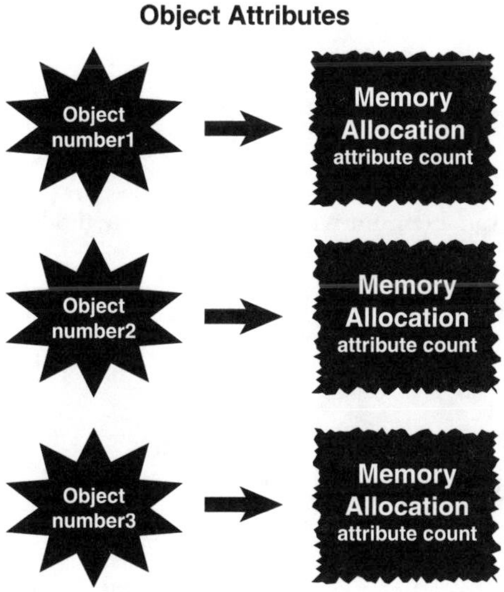

Object Attributes

Figure 3.6   Object attributes.

In this case, the class attribute count is declared outside the scope of both `method1` and `method2`. However, it is within the scope of the class. Thus, `count` is available to both `method1` and `method2`. (Basically, all methods in the class have access to this attribute.) Notice that the code for both methods is setting `count` to a specific value. There is only one copy of `count` for the entire object, so both assignments operate on the same copy in memory. However, this copy of `count` is not shared between different objects.

To illustrate, let's create three copies of the `Number` class:

```
Number number1 = new Number();
Number number2 = new Number();
Number number3 = new Number();
```

Each of these objects—`number1`, `number2`, and `number3`—is constructed separately and is allocated its own resources. There are actually three separate instances of the integer `count`. When `number1` changes its attribute `count`, this in no way affects the copy of `count` in object `number2` or object `number3`. In this case, integer `count` is an *object attribute*.

You can play some interesting games with scope. Take a look at the following code:

```
public class Number {

    int count;
```

```
public method1() {
    int count;
}

public method2() {
    int count;
}

}
```

In this case, there are actually three separate memory locations of count for each object. The object owns one copy, and method1() and method2() each own a copy of their own.

To access the object variable from within one of the methods, say method1(), you can use the following code:

```
public method1() {
    int count;

    this.count = 1;
}
```

Notice that there is some code that looks a bit weird:

```
this.count = 1;
```

The selection of the word this as a keyword is perhaps unfortunate. However, we must live with it. The use of the this keyword directs the compiler to access the object variable count, and not the local variables within the method bodies.

The this Keyword
In Java, the keyword this is a reference to the current object.

Class Attributes

As mentioned earlier, it is possible for two or more objects to share attributes. In Java, C#, and C++, you do this by making the attribute *static*:

```
public class Number {

    static int count;

    public method1() {
    }

}
```

By declaring count as static, this attribute is allocated a single piece of memory for the class. Thus, all objects of the class use the same memory location for count. Essentially, each class has a single copy, which is shared by all objects of that class (see Figure 3.7).

Class Attribute

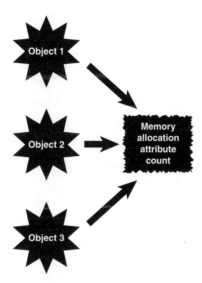

Figure 3.7   Class attributes.

There are many valid uses for class attributes; however, you must be aware of potential synchronization problems. Let's instantiate two Count objects:

```
Count Count1 = new Count();
Count Count2 = new Count();
```

For the sake of argument, let's say that the object Count1 is going merrily about its way and is using count as a means to keep track of the pixels on a computer screen. This is not a problem until the object Count2 decides to use attribute count to keep track of sheep. The instant that Count2 records its first sheep, the data that Count1 was saving is lost.

Operator Overloading

Some OO languages allow you to overload an operator. C++ is an example of one such language. Operator overloading allows you to change the meaning of an operator. For example, when most people see a plus sign, they assume it represents addition. If you see the equation

```
X = 5 + 6;
```

you expect that X would contain the value 11. And in this case, you would be correct.

However, there are times when a plus sign could represent something else. For example, in the following code:

```
String firstName = "Joe", lastName = "Smith";
```

```
String Name = firstName + " " + lastName;
```

You would expect that `Name` would contain `Joe Smith`. The plus sign here has been overloaded to perform string concatenation.

> ▐ **String Concatenation**
> *String concatenation* is when two strings are combined to create a single string.

In the context of strings, the plus sign does not mean addition of integers or floats, but concatenation of strings.

What about matrix addition? You could have code like this:

```
Matrix a, b, c;
```

```
c = a + b;
```

Thus, the plus sign now performs matrix addition, not addition of integers or floats.

Overloading is a powerful mechanism. However, it can be downright confusing for people who read and maintain code. In fact, developers can confuse themselves. In fact, it would be possible to change the operation of addition to perform subtraction. Why not? Operator overloading allows you to change the meaning of an operator. Thus, if the plus sign were changed to perform subtraction, the following code would result in an `x` value of `-1`.

```
x = 5 + 6;
```

More recent OO languages like Java and C# do not allow operator overloading.

Java does not allow the option of overloading operators. The language itself does overload the plus sign for string concatenation, but that's it. The designers of Java must have decided that operator overloading was more of a problem than it was worth. If you must use operator overloading in C++, take care not to confuse the people who will use the class by documenting and commenting properly.

Multiple Inheritance

We cover inheritance in much more detail in Chapter 7, "Mastering Inheritance and Composition." However, this is a good place to begin discussing multiple inheritance, which is one of the more powerful and challenging aspects of class design.

As the name implies, *multiple inheritance* allows a class to inherit from more than one class. In practice, this seems like a great idea. Objects are supposed to model the real world, are they not? And there are many real-world examples of multiple inheritance. Parents are a good example of multiple inheritance. Each child has two parents—that's just the way it is. So it makes sense that you can design classes by using multiple inheritance. In some OO languages, such as C++, you can.

However, this situation falls into a category similar to operator overloading. Multiple inheritance is a very powerful technique, and in fact, some problems are quite difficult to solve without it. Multiple inheritance can even solve some problems quite elegantly. However, multiple inheritance can significantly increase the complexity of a system, both for the programmer and the compiler writers.

As with operator overloading, the designers of Java and C# decided that the increased complexity of allowing multiple inheritance far outweighed its advantages, so they eliminated it from the language. In some ways, the Java and C# language construct of interfaces compensates for this; however, the bottom line is that Java and C# do not allow conventional multiple inheritance.

Behavioral and Implementation Inheritance

Java and C# interfaces are a mechanism for behavioral inheritance, whereas abstract classes are used for implementation inheritance. The bottom line is that Java and C# interfaces provide interfaces, but no implementation, whereas abstract classes may provide both interfaces and implementation. This topic is covered in great detail in Chapter 8, "Frameworks and Reuse: Designing with Interfaces and Abstract Classes."

Object Operations

Some of the most basic operations in programming become more complicated when you're dealing with complex data structures and objects. For example, when you want to copy or compare primitive data types, the process is quite straightforward. However, copying and comparing objects is not quite as simple. On page 34 of his book *Effective C++*, Scott Meyers devotes an entire section to copying and assigning objects.

Classes and References

The problem with complex data structures and objects is that they might contain references. Simply making a copy of the reference does not copy the data structures or the object that it references. In the same vein, when comparing objects, simply comparing a pointer to another pointer only compares the references—not what they point to.

The problems arise when comparisons and copies are performed on objects. Specifically, the question boils down to whether you follow the pointers or not. For example, there should be a way to copy an object. Again, this is not as simple as it might seem. Because objects can contain references, these reference trees must be followed to do a valid copy (if you truly want to do a deep copy).

Deep Versus Shallow Copies

A *deep copy* is when all the references are followed and new copies are created for all referenced objects. There might be many levels involved in a deep copy. For objects with references to many objects, which in turn might have references to even more objects, the copy itself can create significant overhead. A *shallow copy* would simply copy the reference and not follow the levels. Gilbert and McCarty have a good discussion about what shallow and deep hierarchies are on page 265 of *Object-Oriented Design in Java* in a section called "Prefer a Tree to a Forest."

To illustrate, in Figure 3.8, if you just do a simple copy of the object (called a *bitwise copy*), any object that the primary object references will not be copied—only the references will be copied. Thus, both objects (the original and the copy) will point to the same objects. To perform a complete copy, in which all reference objects are copied, you have to write the code to create all the sub-objects.

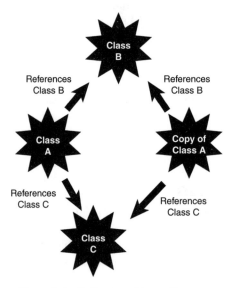

Figure 3.8   Following object references.

This problem also manifests itself when comparing objects. As with the copy function, this is not as simple as it might seem. Because objects contain references, these reference trees must be followed to do a valid comparison of objects. In most cases, languages provide a default mechanism to compare objects. As is usually the case, do not count on the default mechanism. When designing a class, you should consider providing a comparison function in your class that you know will behave as you want it to.

Conclusion

This chapter covers a number of advanced OO concepts that, although perhaps not vital to a general understanding of OO concepts, are quite necessary in higher-level OO tasks, such as designing a class. In Chapter 4, "The Anatomy of a Class," we start looking specifically at how to design and build a class.

References

Gilbert, Stephen, and Bill McCarty. *Object-Oriented Design in Java.* The Waite Group, 1998.

Tyma, Paul, Gabriel Torok, and Troy Downing. *Java Primer Plus.* The Waite Group, 1996.

Meyers, Scott. *Effective C++.* Addison–Wesley, 1992.

4

The Anatomy of a Class

WE HAVE ALREADY DISCUSSED IN great detail object-oriented (OO) concepts and the difference between the interface and the implementation. No matter how well you think out the problem of what should be an interface and what should be part of the implementation, the bottom line always comes down to how useful the class is and how it interacts with other classes. A class should never be designed in a vacuum, for as might be said, no class is an island. When objects are instantiated, they almost always interact with other objects. An object can also be used within another object, or be inherited. The following section is a bit of a dissection of a class, and the rest of the chapter offers some guidelines that you should consider when designing classes.

In this chapter we'll examine a simple class and then take it apart piece by piece. We will continue using the cabbie example presented in Chapter 2, "How to Think in Terms of Objects."

In this chapter, we'll discuss the following parts of a class:

- Class name—How the class name is identified
- Comments—How to create comments to document your code
- Attributes—How to define attributes for use in the class
- Constructors—Special methods used to properly initialize a class
- Accessors—Methods that are used to control access to private attributes
- Public interface methods—How to define public interface methods
- Private implementation methods—How to define private implementation methods

Only a Template

This class is meant for illustration purposes only. Some of the methods are not fleshed out (meaning that there is no implementation) and simply present the interface.

The Name of the Class

Figure 4.1 shows the class that will be dissected. Plain and simple, the name of the class in our example, `Cabbie`, is the name located after the keyword `class`:

```
public class Cabbie {


}
```

> **Using Java Syntax**
>
> Remember that the convention for this book is to use Java syntax. The syntax might be somewhat different in C# or C++, and totally different in other OO languages such as Smalltalk.

The class `Cabbie` name is used whenever this class is instantiated.

Comments

Regardless of the syntax of the comments used, they are vital to understanding the function of a class. In Java, C#, and C++, there are two kinds of comments.

> **The Extra Java and C# Comment Style**
>
> In Java and C#, there are actually three types of comments. In Java, the third comment type (`/** */`) relates to a form of documentation that Java provides. We will not cover this type of comment in this book. C# provides similar syntax to create XML documents.

The first comment is the old C-style comment, which uses `/*` (slash–asterisk) to open the comment and `*/` (asterisk–slash) to close the comment. This type of comment can span more than one line, and it's important not to forget to use the pair of open and close comment symbols for each comment. If you miss the closing comment (`*/`), some of your code might be tagged as a comment and overlooked by the compiler. Here is an example of this type of comment used with the `Cabbie` class:

```
/*

    This class defines a cabbie and assigns a cab

*/
```

The second type of comment is the `//` (slash–slash), which renders everything after it, to the end of the line, a comment. This type of comment spans only one line, so you don't need to remember to use a close comment symbol, but you do need to remember to confine the comment to just one line and not include any live code after the comment. Here is an example of this type of comment used with the `Cabbie` class:

```
// Name of the cabbie
```

Comments ➡️
```
/*
 This class defines a cabbie and assigns a cab
*/
public class Cabbie{
```
⬅️ Class Name

```
    //Place name of Company Here
    private static String companyName = "Blue Cab Company";

    //.Name of the Cabbie
    private String Name;

    //Car assigned to Cabbie
    private Cab myCab;
```
Attributes

```
    // Default Constructor for the Cabbie
    public Cabbie() {

        name = null;
        myCab = null;

    }

    // Name Initializing Constructor for the Cabbie
    public Cabbie(String iName, String serialNumber){

        Name = iName;
        myCab = new Cab(serialNumber);
    }
```
Constructors

```
    // Set the Name of the Cabbie
    public void setName(String iName) {
        Name = iName;
    }

    // Get the Name of the Company
    public static string getName(){
      return Name;
    }

    // Get the Name of the Cabbie
    public static String getCompanyName(){
        return companyName;
    }
```
Accessor Methods (Public Interfaces)

A Public Interface ➡️
```
    public void giveDestination(){
    }
```

```
    private void turnRight(){
    }

    private void turnLeft(){
    }

}
```
Private Implementation

Figure 4.1 Our sample class.

Attributes

Attributes represent the state of the object because they store the information about the object. For our example, the `Cabbie` class has attributes that store the name of the company, the name of the cabbie, and the cab assigned to the cabbie. For example, the first attribute stores the name of the company:

```
private static String companyName = "Blue Cab Company";
```

Note here the two keywords `private` and `static`. The keyword `private` signifies that a method or variable can be accessed only within the declaring object.

Hiding as Much Data as Possible

All the attributes in this example are private. This is in keeping with the design principle of keeping the interface design as minimal as possible. The only way to access these attributes is through the method interfaces provided (which we will explore later in this chapter).

The `static` keyword signifies that there will be only one copy of this attribute for all the objects instantiated by this class. Basically, this is a class attribute. (See Chapter 3, "Advanced Object-Oriented Concepts," for more discussion on class attributes.) Thus, even if 500 objects are instantiated from the `Cabbie` class, there will be only one copy in memory of the `companyName` attribute (see Figure 4.2).

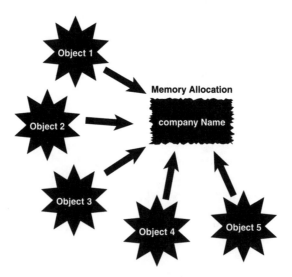

Figure 4.2   Object memory allocation.

The second attribute, `name`, is a string that holds the name of the cabbie:

```
private String name;
```

This attribute is also private so that other objects cannot access it directly. They must use the interface methods.

The `myCab` attribute is a reference to another object. The class, called `Cab`, holds information about the cab, such as its serial number and maintenance records:

```
private Cab myCab;
```

Passing a Reference

It is likely that the `Cab` object was created by another object. Thus, the object reference would be passed to the `Cabbie` object. However, for the sake of this example, the `Cab` is created within the `Cabbie` object. Likewise, for the purposes of this example, we are not really interested in the internals of the `Cab` object.

Note that at this point, only a reference to a `Cab` object is created; there is no memory allocated by this definition.

Constructors

This `Cabbie` class contains two constructors. We know they are constructors because they have the same name as the class: `Cabbie`. The first constructor is the default constructor:

```
public Cabbie() {

    name = null;
    myCab = null;

}
```

Technically, this is not a default constructor. The compiler will provide a default constructor if you do not specify a constructor for this class. By definition, the reason it is called a default constructor here is because it is a constructor with no arguments. If you provide a constructor with arguments, the system will not provide a default constructor. The rule is that the default constructor is only provided if you provide *no* constructors. In this constructor, the attributes `Name` and `myCab` are set to `null`:

```
name = null;
myCab = null;
```

The Nothingness of Null

In many programming languages, the value `null` represents a value of nothing. This might seem like an esoteric concept, but setting an attribute to nothing is a useful programming technique. Checking a variable for `null` can identify whether a value has been properly initialized. For example, you might want to declare an attribute that will later require user input. Thus, you can initialize the attribute to `null` before the user is actually given the opportunity to enter the data. By setting the attribute to `null` (which is a valid condition), you can check whether an attribute has been properly set.

As we know, it is always a good idea to initialize attributes in the constructors. In the same vein, it's a good programming practice to then test the value of an attribute to see whether it is null. This can save you a lot of headaches later if the attribute or object was not set properly. For example, if you use the myCab reference before a real object is assigned to it, you will most likely have a problem. If you set the myCab reference to null in the constructor, you can later check to see whether myCab is still null when you attempt to use it. An exception might be generated if you treat an uninitialized reference as if it were properly initialized.

The second constructor provides a way for the user of the class to initialize the Name and myCab attributes:

```
public Cabbie(String iName, String serialNumber) {

    name = iName;
    myCab = new Cab(serialNumber);

}
```

In this case, the user would provide two strings in the parameter list of the constructor to properly initialize attributes. Notice that the myCab object is actually instantiated in this constructor:

```
myCab = new Cab(serialNumber);
```

At this point, the storage for a Cab object is allocated. Figure 4.3 illustrates how a new instance of a Cab object is referenced by the attribute myCab. Using two constructors in this example demonstrates a common use of method overloading. Notice that the constructors are all defined as public. This makes sense because in this case, the constructors are obvious members of the class interface.

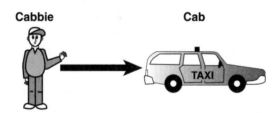

The Cabbie Object References
an Actual Cab Object

Cabbie   **Cab**

myCab = new Cab (serialNumber);

Figure 4.3   The Cabbie object referencing an actual cab object.

Accessors

In most, if not all, examples in this book, the attributes are defined as private so that a second object cannot access another object's attributes. It would be ridiculous to create an object in isolation—we want to share the appropriate information with other objects. Isn't it necessary to inspect and sometimes change another class's attribute? The answer is yes, of course. There are times when an object needs to access another object's attributes; however, it does not need to do it directly.

A class should be very protective about its attributes. For example, you do not want object A to have the capability to inspect or change the attributes of object B without object B having control. There are several reasons for this; the most important reasons really boil down to data integrity and efficient debugging.

Assume that there is a bug in the Cab class. You have tracked the problem to the Name attribute. Somehow it is getting overwritten, and garbage is turning up in some name queries. If Name were public and any class could change it, you would have to go searching through all the possible code, trying to find places that reference and change Name. However, if you let only a Cabbie object change Name, you'd only have to look in the Cabbie class. This access is provided by a type of method called an *accessor*. Sometimes accessors are referred to as getters and setters, and sometimes they're simply called get() and set(). By convention, in this book we'll name the methods with the set and get prefixes, as in the following:

```
// Set the Name of the Cabbie
public void setName(String iName) {
    name = iName;
}

// Get the Name of the Cabbie
public String getName() {
    return name;
}
```

In this snippet, a Supervisor object must ask the Cabbie object to return its name (see Figure 4.4). The important point here is that the Supervisor object can't simply retrieve the information on its own, it must ask the Cabbie object for the information. This concept is important at many levels. For example, you might have a setAge() method that checks to see whether the age entered was 0 or below. If the age is less than 0, the setAge() method can refuse to set this incorrect value. In general, the setters are used to ensure a level of data integrity.

Notice that the getCompanyName method is declared as static, as a class method; class methods are described in more detail in Chapter 3. Remember that the attribute companyName is also declared as static. A method, like an attribute, can be declared static to indicate that there is only one copy of the method for the entire class.

Objects

Actually, there isn't a physical copy of each nonstatic method for each object. Each object would point to the same physical code. However, from a conceptual level, you can think of objects as being wholly independent and having their own attributes and methods.

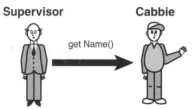

The Supervisor Object Must Ask
The Cabbie Object to Return Its Name

Supervisor   **Cabbie**

get Name()

"Can I have your name please?"

Figure 4.4 Asking for information.

The following code fragment illustrates how to define a static method, and Figure 4.5 shows how more than one object points to the same code.

Static Attributes

If an attribute is static, and the class provides a setter for that attribute, any object that invokes the setter will change the single copy. Thus, the value for the attribute will change for all objects.

```
// Get the Name of the Cabbie
public static String getCompanyName() {
    return companyName;
}
```

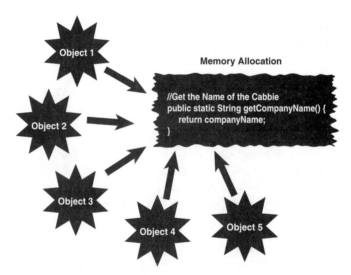

Figure 4.5 Method memory allocation.

Public Interface Methods

Both the constructors and the accessor methods are declared as public, and are part of the public interface. They are singled out because of their specific importance to the construction of the class. However, much of the *real* work is provided in other methods. As mentioned in Chapter 2, the public interface methods tend to be very abstract, and the implementation tends to be more concrete. For this class, we provide a method called giveDestination that is the public interface for the user to describe where she wants to go:

```
public void giveDestination (){

}
```

What is inside of this method is not important at this time. The main point here is that this is a public method, and it is part of the public interface to the class.

Private Implementation Methods

Although all the methods discussed so far in this chapter are defined as public, not all the methods in a class are part of the public interface. Some methods in a class are meant to be hidden from other classes. These methods are declared as private:

```
private void turnRight(){
}

private void turnLeft() {
}
```

These private methods are simply meant to be part of the implementation, and not the public interface. You might ask who invokes these methods, if no other class can. The answer is simple—you might have already surmised that these methods are called internally from the class itself. For example, these methods could be called from within the method giveDestination:

```
public void giveDestination (){

    .. some code

    turnRight();
    turnLeft();

    .. some more code

}
```

The point here is that private methods are strictly part of the implementation, and are not accessible by other classes.

Conclusion

In this chapter we have gotten inside a class and described the fundamental concepts necessary for understanding how a class is built. Although this chapter takes a practical approach to discussing classes, Chapter 5, "Class Design Guidelines," covers the class from a general design perspective.

References

Fowler, Martin. *UML Distilled*. Addison-Wesley Longman, 1997.

Gilbert, Stephen, and Bill McCarty. *Object-Oriented Design in Java*. The Waite Group, 1998.

Tyma, Paul, Gabriel Torok, and Troy Downing. *Java Primer Plus*. The Waite Group, 1996.

5

Class Design Guidelines

ONE OF THE PRIMARY GOALS OF object-oriented (OO) programming is to model real-world systems in ways similar to the ways in which people actually think. Designing classes is the object-oriented way to create these models. Rather than using a structured, or *top-down* approach, where data and behavior are separate entities, the OO approach encapsulates the data and behavior into objects that interact with each other. Don't think of a problem as a sequence of events or routines operating on separate data files. Think of how your objects model real-world objects and how they interact with other real-world objects.

These interactions occur in a way similar to the interactions between real-world objects, such as people. Thus, when creating classes, you should design them in a way that represents the true behavior of the object. Let's use the cabbie example from previous chapters. The Cab class and the Cabbie class model a real-world entity. As illustrated in Figure 5.1, the Cab and the Cabbie objects encapsulate their data and behavior, and they interact through each other's public interfaces.

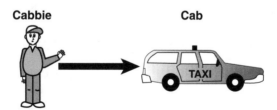

Figure 5.1 A cabbie and a cab are real-world objects.

When moving to OO programming for the first time, many people tend to still think in a structured way. One of the primary mistakes is to create a class that has behavior but no class data. In effect, they are creating a set of functions or subroutines in the structured model. This is not what you want to do, because it violates the concept of encapsulation.

As we have already discussed, OO programming supports the idea of making classes that are complete packages, encapsulating the data and behavior of a single entity. So, a class should represent a logical component, such as a taxicab.

This chapter presents several suggestions for designing solid classes. Obviously, no list such as this can be considered complete. You will undoubtedly add many guidelines to your personal list.

One of the better books pertaining to class design guidelines and suggestions is *Effective C: 50 Specific Ways to Improve Your Programs and Designs* by Scott Meyers. It offers important information about program design in a very concise manner.

Identifying the Public Interfaces

It should be clear by now that perhaps the most important issue when designing a class is to keep the public interface to a minimum. The entire purpose of building a class is to provide something useful and concise. On page 109 of their book *Object-Oriented Design in Java*, Gilbert and McCarty state that "the interface of a well-designed object describes the services that the client wants accomplished." If a class does not provide a useful service to a user, it should not have been built in the first place.

Providing the minimum public interface makes the class as concise as possible. The goal is to provide the user with the exact interface to do the job right. If the public interface is incomplete (that is, there is missing behavior), the user will not be able to do the complete job. If the public interface is not properly restricted (that is, the user has access to behavior that is unnecessary or even dangerous), problems can result in the need for debugging, and even trouble with system integrity. Creating a class is a business proposition, and as with all steps in the design process, it is very important that the users are involved with the design right from the start and through the testing phase. In this way, the utility of the class, as well as the proper interfaces, will be assured.

> **Extending the Interface**
>
> Even if the public interface of a class is insufficient for a certain application, object technology easily allows the capability to extend and adapt this interface by means of inheritance. In short, if designed with inheritance in mind, a new class can inherit from an existing class and create a new class with an extended interface.

To illustrate, consider the cabbie example once again. If other objects in the system need to get the name of a cabbie, the `Cabbie` class must provide a public interface to return its name; this is the `getName()` method. Thus, if a `Supervisor` object needs a name from a `Cabbie` object, it must invoke the `getName()` method from the `Cabbie` object. In effect, the supervisor is asking the cabbie for its name (see Figure 5.2).

Users of your code need to know nothing about its internal workings. All they need to know is how to create and use the object. Give them a way to get in, but hide the details.

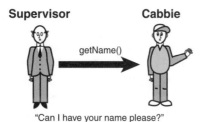

Figure 5.2   The public interface specifies how the objects interact.

Hiding the Implementation

The need for hiding the implementation has been covered in great detail. Whereas identifying the public interface is a design issue that revolves around the users of the class, the implementation should not involve the users at all. Of course, the implementation must provide the services that the user needs, but how these services are actually performed should not be made apparent to the user. A class is most useful if the implementation can change without affecting the users. In short, a change to the implementation should not necessitate a change in application code.

In the cabbie example, the `Cabbie` class might have behavior pertaining to how it eats breakfast. However, the cabbie's supervisor does not need to know what the cabbie has for breakfast. Thus, this behavior is part of the implementation of the `Cabbie` object and should not be available to other objects in this system (see Figure 5.3). Gilbert and McCarty state that the prime directive of encapsulation is that "all fields shall be private." In this way, none of the fields in a class is accessible from other objects.

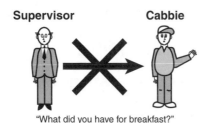

Figure 5.3   Objects don't need to know some implementation details.

Designing Robust Constructors (and Perhaps Destructors)

When designing a class, one of the most important design issues involves how the class will be constructed. Constructors are discussed in Chapter 3, "Advanced Object-

Oriented Concepts." Revisit this discussion if you need a refresher on guidelines for designing constructors.

First and foremost, a constructor should put an object into a safe state. This includes issues such as attribute initialization and memory management. Scott Meyers discusses some of these issues in the section "Constructors, Destructors and Assignment Operators" of *Effective C++*. You also need to make sure the object is constructed properly in the default condition. It is normally a good idea to provide a constructor to handle this default situation.

In languages that include destructors, it is of vital importance that the destructors include proper clean-up functions. In most cases, this clean-up pertains to releasing system memory that the object acquired at some point. Java and C# reclaim memory automatically with a garbage collection mechanism. In languages such as C++, the developer must include code in the destructor to properly free up the memory that the object acquired during its existence. If this function is ignored, a memory leak will result.

Memory Leaks

When an object fails to properly release the memory that it acquired during an object's life cycle, the memory is lost to the entire operating system as long as the application that created the object is executing. For example, suppose multiple objects of the same class are created and then destroyed, perhaps in some sort of loop. If these objects fail to release their memory when they go out of scope, this memory leak slowly depletes the available pool of system memory. At some point, it is possible that enough memory will be consumed that the system will have no available memory left to allocate. This means that any application executing in the system would be unable to acquire any memory. This could put the application in an unsafe state and even lock up the system.

Designing Error Handling into a Class

As with the design of constructors, designing how a class handles errors is of vital importance. Error handling is discussed in detail in Chapter 3.

It is almost certain that every system will encounter unforeseen problems. Thus, it is not a good idea to simply ignore potential errors. The developer of a good class (or any code, for that matter) anticipates potential errors and includes code to handle these conditions when they are encountered.

The rule of thumb is that the application should never crash. When an error is encountered, the system should either fix itself and continue, or exit gracefully without losing any data that's important to the user.

Documenting a Class and Using Comments

The topic of comments and documentation comes up in every book and article, in every code review, and in every discussion you have about good design. Unfortunately, comments and good documentation are often not taken seriously, or even worse, they are ignored.

Most developers know that they should thoroughly document their code, but they don't usually want to take the time to do it. The bottom line is that a good design is practically impossible without good documentation practices. At the class level, the scope might be small enough that a developer can get away with shoddy documentation. However, when the class gets passed to someone else to extend and/or maintain, or it becomes part of a larger system (which is what should happen), a lack of proper documentation and comments can be lethal.

Many people have said all this before. One of the most crucial aspects of a good design, whether it's a design for a class or something else, is to carefully document the process. Languages such as Java and C# provide special comment syntax to facilitate the documentation process. Check out Chapter 4, "The Anatomy of a Class" for the appropriate syntax.

Building Objects with the Intent to Cooperate

In Chapter 6, "Designing with Objects," we discuss the issues involved in designing a system. We can safely say that almost no class lives in isolation. In most cases, there is no reason to build a class if it is not going to interact with other classes. This is simply a fact in the life of a class. A class will service other classes; it will request the services of other classes, or both. In later chapters we will discuss various ways that classes interact with each other.

In the cabbie example, the cabbie and the supervisor are not standalone entities; they interact with each other at various levels (see Figure 5.4).

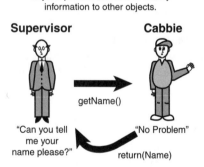

Figure 5.4 Objects should request information.

When designing a class, make sure you are aware of how other objects will interact with it.

Designing with Reuse in Mind

Objects can be reused in different systems, and code should be written with reuse in mind. For example, when a `Cabbie` class is developed and tested, it can be used anywhere you need a cabbie. To make a class usable in various systems, the class must be designed with reuse in mind. This is where much of the thought is required in the design process. Attempting to figure out all the possible scenarios in which a `Cabbie` object must operate is not a trivial task.

Designing with Extensibility in Mind

Adding new features to a class might be as easy as extending an existing class, and adding a few new methods and modifying the behavior of others. It is not necessary to rewrite everything. This is where inheritance comes into play. If you have just written a `Person` class, you must consider the fact that you might later want to write an `Employee` class, or a `Vendor` class. Thus, having `Employee` inherit from `Person` might be the best strategy; in this case, the `Person` class is said to be *extensible*. You do not want to design `Person` so that it contains behavior that prevents it from being extended by classes such as `Employee` or `Vendor` (assuming, of course, that in your design you really intend for other classes to extend `Person`). For example, you would not want to code functionality into an `Employee` class that is specific to supervisory functions. If you did, and then a class that does not require supervisory functionality inherited from `Employee`, you would have a problem.

This point touches on the abstraction guideline discussed earlier. `Person` should contain only the data and behaviors that are specific to a person. Other classes can then subclass it and inherit appropriate data and behaviors.

What Attributes and Methods Can Be Static?

It is important to decide what attributes and methods can be declared as static. Revisit the discussions in Chapter 3 on using the `static` keyword to understand how to design these into your classes.

Making Names Descriptive

Earlier we discussed the use of proper documentation and comments. Following a naming convention for your classes, attributes, and methods is a similar subject. There are many naming conventions, and the convention you choose is not as important as choosing one and sticking to it. However, when you choose a convention, make sure that when you create classes, attributes, and method names, you not only follow the convention, but make the names descriptive. When someone reads the name, he should be able to tell from the name what the object represents.

Good Naming

Make sure that a naming convention makes sense. Often, people go overboard and create conventions that might make sense to them, but are totally incomprehensible to others. Take care when forcing other to conform to a convention. Make sure that the conventions are sensible and that everyone involved understands the intent behind them.

Making names descriptive is a good development practice that applies to more than just OO development.

Abstracting Out Nonportable Code

If you are designing a system that must use nonportable code (that is, the code will only run on a specific hardware platform), you should abstract this code out of the class. By abstracting out, we mean isolating the nonportable code in its own class. For example, if you are writing code to access a serial port, you should create a wrapper class to deal with it. Your class should then send a message to the wrapper class to get the information or services it needs. Do not put the system–dependent code into your primary class (see Figure 5.5).

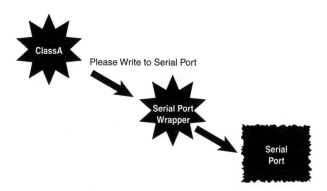

Figure 5.5   A serial port wrapper.

If the class moves to another hardware system, the way to access the serial port changes, or you want to go to a parallel port, the code in your primary class does not have to change. The only place the code needs to change is in the wrapper class.

Providing a Way to Copy and Compare Objects

Chapter 3 discusses the issue of copying and comparing objects. It is important to understand how objects are copied and compared. You might not want, or expect, a simple bitwise copy or compare operation. You must make sure that your class behaves as expected, and this means you have to spend some time designing how objects are copied and compared.

Keeping the Scope as Small as Possible

Keeping the scope as small as possible goes hand-in-hand with abstraction and hiding the implementation. The idea is to localize attributes and behaviors as much as possible. In this way, maintaining, testing, and extending a class are much easier.

Keeping Scope as Small as Possible

Minimizing the scope of global variables is a good programming style, and not specific to OO programming.

For example, if you have a method that requires a temporary attribute, keep it local. Consider the following code:

```
public class Math {

    int temp=0;

    public int swap (int a, int b) {

        temp = a;
        a=b;
        b=temp;

        return temp;

    }

}
```

What is wrong with this class? The problem is that the attribute `temp` is only needed within the scope of the `swap()` method. There is no reason for it to be at the class level. Thus, you should move `temp` within the scope of the `swap()` method:

```
public class Math {

    public int swap (int a, int b) {

        int temp=0;

        temp = a;
        a=b;
        b=temp;
```

```
      return temp;

   }

}
```

This is what is meant by keeping the scope as small as possible.

A Class Should Be Responsible for Itself

In a training class based on their book, *Java Primer Plus*, Tyma, Torok and Downing propose the class design guideline that all objects should be responsible for acting on themselves whenever possible. Consider trying to print a circle.

First, let's use a non-OO example. The print command finds `Circle` and prints it (see Figure 5.6):

```
print(circle);
```

Choose a Shape and Print

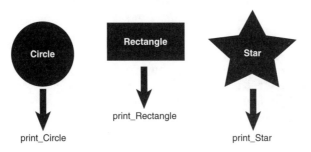

Figure 5.6   A non-OO example of a print scenario.

`print`, `draw`, and other functions need to have a `case` statement (or something like an `if/else` structure) to determine what to do for the given shape passed. In this case, a separate print routine for each shape could be called.

Every time you add a new shape, all the functions need to add the shape to their `case` statement.

Now let's look at an OO example. By using polymorphism and grouping the `Circle` into a `Shape` category, `Shape` figures out that it is a `Circle` and knows how to print itself (see Figure 5.7):

```
Shape.print(); // Shape is actually a Circle
```

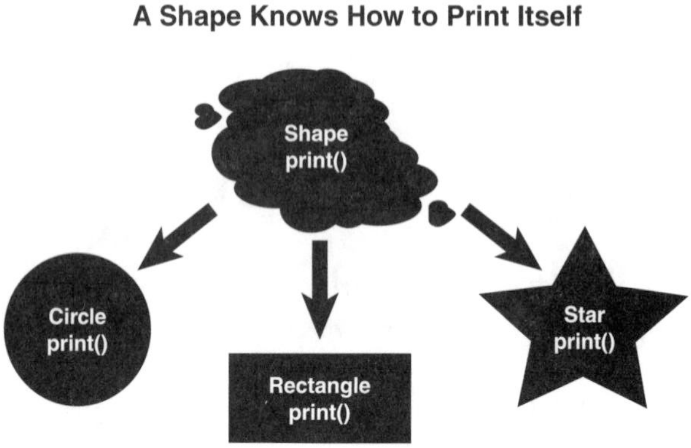

A Shape Knows How to Print Itself

Figure 5.7   An OO example of a print scenario.

Designing with Maintainability in Mind

Designing useful and concise classes promotes a high level of maintainability. Just as you design a class with extensibility in mind, you should also design with future maintenance in mind.

The process of designing classes forces you to organize your code into many (ideally) manageable pieces. Separate pieces of code tend to be more maintainable than larger pieces of code (at least that's the idea). One of the best ways to promote maintainability is to reduce interdependent code—that is, changes in one class have no or minimal effects on other classes.

Highly Coupled Classes

Classes that are highly dependent on one another are considered *highly coupled*. Thus, if a change made to one class forces a change to another class, these two classes are considered highly coupled. Classes that have no such dependencies have a very low degree of coupling. For more information on coupling, refer to *The Object Primer* by Scott Ambler.

This means that changes should only be made to the implementation of an object. Changes to the public interface should be avoided at all costs. Any changes to the public interface will cause ripple effects throughout all the systems that use the interface.

For example, if a change were made to the getName() method of the Cabbie class, every single place in all systems that use this interface must be changed and recompiled. Simply finding all these method calls is a daunting task.

To promote a high level of maintainability, keep the coupling level of your classes as low as possible.

Using Iteration

As in most design and programming functions, using an iterative process is recommended. This dovetails well into the concept of providing minimal interfaces. A good testing plan quickly uncovers any areas where insufficient interfaces are provided. In this way, the process can iterate until the class has the appropriate interfaces. This testing process is not simply confined to coding. Testing the design with walkthroughs and other design review techniques is very helpful. Testers' lives are more pleasant when iterative processes are used, because they are involved in the process early and are not simply handed a system that is thrown over the wall at the end of the development process.

Testing the Interface

The minimal implementations of the interface are often called *stubs*. (Gilbert and McCarty have a good discussion on stubs in *Object-Oriented Design in Java*.) By using stubs, you can test the interfaces without writing any *real* code. In the following example, rather than connect to an actual database, stubs are used to verify that the interfaces are working properly (from the user's perspective—remember that interfaces are meant for the user). Thus, the implementation is really not necessary at this point. In fact, it might cost valuable time and energy to complete the implementation at this point, because the design of the interface will affect the implementation, and the interface is not yet complete.

In Figure 5.8, note that when a user class sends a message to the `DataBaseReader` class, the information returned to the user class is provided by code stubs, and not by the actual database. (In fact, the database most likely does not exist yet.) When the interface is complete and the implementation is under development, the database can then be connected and the stubs disconnected.

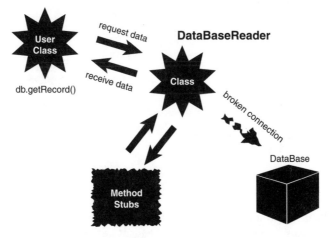

Figure 5.8 Using stubs.

Here is a code example that uses an internal array to simulate a working database (albeit a simple one):

```
public class DataBaseReader {

    String db[] = { "Record1",
        "Record2",
        "Record3",
        "Record4",
        "Record5"};

    boolean DBOpen = false;
    int pos;

    public void open(String Name){
        DBOpen = true;
    };
    public void close(){
        DBOpen = false;
    };
    public void goToFirst(){
        pos = 0;
    };
    public void goToLast(){
        pos = 4;
    };
    public int howManyRecords(){
        int numOfRecords = 5;

        return numOfRecords;
    };
    public String getRecord(int key){

        /* DB Specific Implementation */
        return db[key];
    };
    public String getNextRecord(){

        /* DB Specific Implementation */
        return db[pos++];
    };

}
```

Notice how the methods simulate the database calls. The strings within the array represent the records that will be written to the database. When the database is successfully integrated into the system, it will then be substituted for the array.

> **Keeping the Stubs Around**
>
> When you are done with the stubs, don't delete them. Keep them in the code for possible use later. In fact, in a well-designed program, your test stubs should be integrated into the design and kept in the program for later use. In short, design the testing right into the class!

As you find problems with the interface design, make changes and repeat the process until you are satisfied with the result.

Using Object Persistence

Object persistence is another issue that must be addressed in many OO systems. *Persistence* is the concept of maintaining the state of an object. When you run a program, if you don't save the object in some manner, the object simply dies, never to be recovered. These transient objects might work in some applications, but in most business systems, the state of the object must be saved for later use. In his book *The Object Primer*, Scott Ambler devotes an entire section to this topic.

> **Object Persistence**
>
> Although the topic of object persistence and the topics in the next section might not be considered true design guidelines, I believe that they must be addressed when designing classes. Thus, I introduced them here to stress that they must be addressed early on when designing classes.

In its simplest form, an object can persist by being serialized and written to a flat file. Although it is true that an object theoretically can persist in memory as long as it is not destroyed, we will concentrate on storing persistent objects on some sort of storage device. There are three primary storage devices to consider:

- Flat filesystem—You can store an object in a flat file by serializing the object. This has very limited use.

- Relational database—Some sort of middleware is necessary to convert an object to a relational model.

- OO database—This is the logical way to make objects persistent, but most companies have all their data in legacy systems and are just starting to explore object databases. Even brand-new OO applications must usually interface with legacy data.

Serializing and Marshaling Objects

We have already discussed the problem of using objects in environments that were originally designed for structured programming. The middleware example, where we wrote objects to a relational database, is one good example. We also touched on the problem of writing an object to a flat file or sending it over a network.

To send an object over a wire (for example, to a file, over a network), the system must deconstruct the object (flatten it out), send it over the wire, and then reconstruct it on the other end of the wire. This process is called *serializing* an object. (For an in-depth discussion on object serialization, refer to *Java 1.1 Developers Guide* by Jamie Jaworski.) The act of actually sending the object across a wire is called *marshaling* an object. A serialized object, in theory, can be written to a flat file and retrieved later, in the same state in which it was written.

The major issue here is that the serialization and deserialization must use the same specifications. It is sort of like an encryption algorithm. If one object encrypts a string, the object that wants to decrypt it must use the same encryption algorithm. Java provides an interface called `Serializable` that provides this translation.

Conclusion

This chapter presents many guidelines that can help you in designing classes. This is by no means a complete list of guidelines. You will undoubtedly come across additional guidelines as you go about your travels in OO design.

This chapter deals with design issues as they pertain to individual classes. However, we have already seen that a class does not live in isolation. Classes must be designed to interact with other classes. A group of classes that interact with each other is part of a system. Ultimately, these systems provide value to end users. Chapter 6 covers the topic of designing complete systems.

References

Gilbert, Stephen, and Bill McCarty. *Object-Oriented Design in Java.* The Waite Group, 1998.

Meyers, Scott. *Effective C++.* Addison-Wesley, 1992.

Tyma, Paul, Gabriel Torok, and Troy Downing. *Java Primer Plus.* The Waite Group, 1996.

Ambler, Scott. *The Object Primer.* Cambridge University Press, 1998.

Jaworski, Jamie. *Java 1.1 Developers Guide.* Sams Publishing, 1997.

6

Designing with Objects

WHEN YOU USE A SOFTWARE PRODUCT, you expect it to behave as advertised. Unfortunately, not all products live up to expectations. The problem is that when most products are produced, the majority of time and effort go into the engineering phase, and not into the design phase.

Object-oriented (OO) design has been touted as a robust and flexible software development approach. The truth is that you can create a very bad OO design just as easily as you can create a very bad non–OO design. Don't be lulled into a sense of security just because you are using a state-of-the-art OO design tool. You have to pay attention to the design and invest the proper time and effort into it to create the best product.

Design Guidelines

Whereas Chapter 5, "Class Design Guidelines," concentrated on designing good classes, this chapter focuses on designing good systems. (A *system* can be defined as classes that interact with each other.) Proper design practices have evolved throughout the history of software development, and there is no reason you should not take advantage of the blood, sweat, and tears of your software predecessors, whether they used OO technologies or not.

One fallacy is that there is one true design methodology. This is not the case. There is no right or wrong way to create a design. There are many design methodologies available today, and they all have their proponents. However, the primary issue is not which design method to use, but simply whether to use a method at all. This can be expanded to the entire software development process. Many organizations do not follow a standard software development process. The most important factor in creating a good design is to find a process that you and your organization can feel comfortable with. It makes no sense to implement a design process that no one will follow.

Most books that deal with object-oriented technologies offer very similar strategies for designing systems. In fact, except for some of the object-oriented specific issues involved, much of the strategy is applicable to non–OO systems as well.

Generally, a solid OO design process will include the following steps:

- Doing the proper analysis
- Developing a statement of work that describes the system
- Gathering the requirements from this statement of work
- Developing a prototype for the user interface
- Identifying the classes
- Determining the responsibilities of each class
- Determining how the various classes interact with each other
- Creating a high-level model that describes the system to be built

We are most interested in the last item on this list. This system, or object model, is made up of class diagrams and class interactions. This model should represent the system faithfully and be easy to understand and modify. We also need a notation for the model. This is where the Unified Modeling Language (UML) comes in. As you know, UML is not a design process, but a modeling language.

The Ongoing Design Process

Despite the best intentions and planning, in all but the most trivial cases, the design is an ongoing process. Even after a product is in testing, design changes will pop up. It is up to the project manager to draw the line that says when to stop changing a product and adding features.

It is important to understand that many design methodologies are available. One methodology, called the waterfall model, advocates strict boundaries between the various phases. In this case, the design phase is completed before the implementation phase, which is completed before the testing phase, and so on. In practice, the waterfall model has been found to be unrealistic. Currently there are other design models, such as rapid prototyping, that promote a true iterative process. In these models, some implementation is attempted prior to completing the design phase as a type of proof-of-concept. Despite the recent aversion to the waterfall model, the goal behind the model is understandable. Coming up with a complete and thorough design before starting to code is a sound practice. You do not want to be in the release phase of the product and then decide to iterate through the design phase again. Iterating across phase boundaries is unavoidable; however, you should keep these iterations to a minimum (see Figure 6.1).

Simply put, the reasons to identify requirements early and keep design changes to a minimum are as follows:

- The cost of a requirement/design change in the design phase is relatively small.
- The cost of a design change in the implementation phase is significantly higher.
- The cost of a design change in the deployment phase is astronomical.

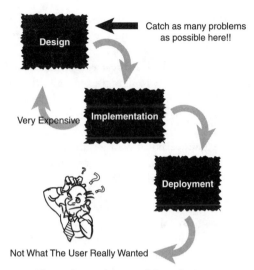

Figure 6.1   The waterfall method.

Similarly, you would not want to start the construction of your dream house before the architectural design was complete. If I said that the Golden Gate Bridge or the Empire State Building were constructed without any design, you would find the statement absolutely crazy. Yet, you would most likely not find it crazy if I told you that the software you were using might not have had a thorough design, and in fact, might not have been thoroughly tested.

That said, it may well be impossible to thoroughly test software. But that does not mean that we shouldn't try. Bridges and software might not be directly comparable; however, software must strive for the same level of engineering excellence as the "harder" engineering disciplines such as bridge building. Poor-quality software can be lethal—it's not just wrong numbers on payroll checks. For example, inferior software in medical equipment can kill and maim people.

Safety Versus Economics

Would you want to cross a bridge that has not been inspected and tested? As is unfortunately the case with many software packages, the users are left with the responsibility of doing the majority of the testing. This is very costly for both the users and the software provider. Unfortunately, short-term economics often seem to be the primary factor in making project decisions.

Because customers seem to be willing to pay the price and put up with software of poor quality, software providers find that it is cheaper in the long run to let the customers test the product rather than do it themselves. In the short term this might be true, but in the long run it costs far more than the software provider realizes. Ultimately, the software provider's reputation will be damaged.

Some major computer software companies are infamous for using the beta test phase to let the customers do testing—testing that should have been done before the beta even reached the customers. Although this strategy damages the company's reputation, many customers are willing to take the risk of using pre-release software simply because they are anxious to get the functionality the product promises.

After the software is released, problems that have not been caught and fixed prior to release become much more expensive. To illustrate, consider the dilemma automobile companies face when they are confronted with a recall. If a defect in the automobile is identified and fixed before it is shipped (ideally before it is manufactured), it is much cheaper than if all delivered automobiles have to be recalled and fixed one at a time. Not only is this scenario very expensive, but it damages the reputation of the company. In an increasingly competitive market, high-quality software, support services, and reputation are *the* competitive advantage (see Figure 6.2).

> **Software Engineering**
>
> Although it might be acceptable to compare automobiles, bridges, and software when discussing quality, the legal implications of these topics cannot be compared, at least not yet. The legal issues regarding software are currently being defined and revised. Currently disclaimers such as "we are not responsible for anything that this software does or causes to happen" abound. Some other industries do not have this luxury. As the software legal process evolves and matures, software manufacturers may well have to contend with these issues. (As a standard disclaimer, in no way does this book attempt to offer any legal advice.)

The Competitive Advantage

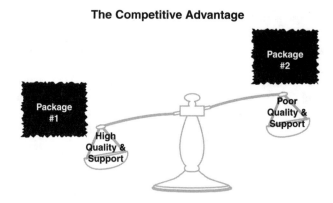

Figure 6.2   The competitive advantage.

The following sections provide brief summaries of the items listed previously as being part of the design process. Later in the chapter, we will work through an example that explains in greater detail each of these items.

Performing the Proper Analysis

There are a lot of variables involved in building a design and creating a software product. The users must work hand-in-hand with the developers at all stages. In the analysis phase, the users and the developers must do the proper research and analysis to determine the statement of work, the requirements of the project, and whether to actually do the project. The third point might seem a bit surprising, but it is important. During the analysis phase, there must not be any hesitation to terminate the project if there is a valid reason to do so. Too many times pet project status or some political inertia keeps a project going, regardless of the obvious warning signs that cry out for project cancellation. Assuming that the project is viable, the primary focus of the analysis phase is for everyone to learn the systems (both the old and the proposed new one) and determine the system requirements.

Safety Versus Economics

Many of these practices are not specific to OO. They are general to structures software practices as well.

Developing a Statement of Work

The *statement of work* is a text document that describes the system. Although determining the requirements is the ultimate goal of the analysis phase, requirements are not in a format that a nondeveloper usually sees. The statement of work is a document that should give anyone who reads it a complete understanding of the system. Regardless of how it is written, the statement of work must represent the complete system and be clear about how the system will look and feel.

The statement of work contains everything that must be known about the system. Many customers create a *request-for proposal (RFP)* to a vendor, which is similar to the statement of work. A customer creates an RFP that totally describes the system they want built and sends it to multiple vendors. The vendors then use this document, and whatever analysis they need to do, to determine whether they should bid on the project, and if so, what price to charge.

Gathering the Requirements

The *requirements document* describes what the users want the system to do. Even though the level of detail of the requirements document does not need to be of a highly technical nature, the requirements must be specific enough to represent the true nature of the user's needs for the end product. The requirements document must be of sufficient detail for the user to make educated judgments about the completeness of the system. It must also be of specific detail for a design group to use the document to proceed with the design phase.

Whereas the statement of work is a document written in paragraph form, the requirements are usually represented as a summary statement or presented as bulleted items. Each individual bulleted item represents one specific requirement of the system. The requirements are distilled from the statement of work. This process is shown later in the chapter.

In many ways, these requirements are the most important part of the system. The statement of work might contain irrelevant material; however, the requirements are the final representation of the system that must be implemented. All future documents in the software development process will be based on the requirements.

Developing a Prototype of the User Interface

One of the best ways to make sure users and developers understand the system is to create a *prototype*. A prototype can be just about anything; however, most people consider the prototype to be a simulated user interface. By creating actual screens and screen flows, it is easier for people to get an idea of what they will be working with and what the system will feel like. In any event, a prototype will almost certainly not contain all the functionality of the final system.

Most prototypes are created with an integrated development environment (IDE). However, drawing the screens on a whiteboard or even on paper might be all that is needed. Visual Basic is a good environment for prototyping. Remember that you are not necessarily creating business logic (the logic/code behind the interface that actually does the work) when you build the prototype, although it is possible to do so. The look and feel of the user interface are the major concerns at this point. Having a good prototype can help immensely when finding classes.

Identifying the Classes

After the requirements are recorded, the process of identifying classes can begin. From the requirements, one way of identifying classes is to highlight all the nouns. These are objects, such as people, places, and things. Don't be too fussy about getting all the classes right the first time. You might end up eliminating classes, adding classes, and changing classes at various stages throughout the design. It is important to get something down first. Take advantage of the fact that the design is an iterative process. As in other forms of brainstorming, get something down initially, with the understanding that the final result might look nothing like the initial pass.

Determining the Responsibilities of Each Class

You need to determine the responsibilities of each class you have identified. What must the class store and what operations must it perform? For example, an `Employee` object would be responsible for calculating payroll and transferring the money to the appropriate account. It might also be responsible for storing the various payroll rates and the account numbers of various banks.

Determining How the Classes Interact with Each Other

Most classes do not exist in isolation. Although a class must fulfill certain responsibilities, many times it will have to interact with another class to get something it wants. This is where the messages between classes come in. One class can send a message to another class when it needs information from that class, or if it wants the other class to do something for it.

Creating a Class Model to Describe the System

When all the classes are determined and the class responsibilities and collaborations are listed, a class model that represents the complete system can be built. The class model shows how the various classes interact within the system.

In this book, we are using UML to model the system. Several tools on the market use UML and provide a good environment for creating and maintaining UML class models. As we develop the example in the next section, we will see how the class diagrams fit into the big picture and how modeling large systems would be virtually impossible without some sort of good modeling notation and modeling tool.

Case Study: A Blackjack Example

The rest of this chapter is dedicated to a case study pertaining to the design process covered in the previous sections. Walking through a case study seems to be a standard exercise in many object-oriented books that deal with OO design.

My first recollection of such an exercise was a graduate course that I took in which we followed an example in the book *Designing Object-Oriented Software* by Wrifs-Brock, Wilkerson, and Weiner. The modeling technique was called CRC modeling, which will be described later in this section. The case study was that of an automated teller machine (ATM) system. The iterative process of identifying the classes and responsibilities using CRC modeling was an eye-opening experience. The books *The Object Primer* by Scott Ambler and *Object-Oriented Design in Java* by Gilbert and McCarty both go through similar exercises using CRC modeling and use cases.

Let's start an example that we will expand on throughout this chapter.

Because we want to have some fun, instead of creating a payroll system or an ATM system, let's create a program that simulates a game of blackjack. We will assume that the statement of work has already been completed. In fact, let's say that a customer has come to you with a proposal that includes a very well-written statement of work and a rule book about how to play blackjack.

According to the statement of work, the basic goal is to design a software system that will simulate the game of blackjack (see Figure 6.3). Remember, we will not describe how to implement this game—we are only going to design the system. Ultimately, this will culminate in the discovery of the classes, along with their responsibilities and collaborations. After some intense analysis, we have determined the requirements of the system. In this case, we will use a requirements summary statement; however, we could have presented the requirements as bullets. Because this is a small system, a requirements summary statement might make more sense. However, in most large systems, a database of the requirements (in bulleted list format) would be more appropriate. Here is the requirements summary statement:

Figure 6.3   A winning blackjack hand.

Requirements Summary Statement

The intended purpose of this software application is to implement a game of blackjack. In the game of blackjack, one or more individuals play against the dealer (or house). Although there might be more than one player, each player plays only against the dealer, and not any of the other players.

From a player's perspective, the goal of the game is to draw cards from the deck until the sum of the face value of all the cards equals 21 or as close to 21 as possible, without exceeding 21. If the sum of the face value of all the cards exceeds 21, the player loses. If the sum of the face value of the first two cards equals 21, the player is said to have blackjack. The dealer plays the game along with the players. The dealer must deal the cards, present a player with additional cards, show all or part of a hand, calculate the value of all or part of a hand, calculate the number of cards in a hand, determine the winner, and start a new hand.

A card must know what its face value is and be able to report this value. The suit of the card is of no importance (but it might be for another game in the future). All cards must be members of a deck of cards. This deck must have the functionality to deal the next card, as well as report how many cards remain in the deck.

During the game, a player can request that a card be dealt to his hand. The player must be able to display the hand, calculate the face value of the hand, and determine the number of cards in the hand. When the dealer asks the player whether to deal another card or to start a new game, the player must respond.

Each card has its own face value (suit does not factor into the face value). Aces count as 1 or 11. Face cards (Jack, Queen, King) each count as 10. The rest of the cards represent their face values.

The rules of the game state that if the sum of the face value of the player's cards is closer to 21 than the sum of the face value of the dealer's cards, the player wins an amount equal to the bet that was made. If the player wins with a blackjack, the player wins 3:2 times the bet made (assuming that the dealer does not also have blackjack). If the sum of the face value of the player's cards exceeds 21, the bet is lost. Blackjack (an ace and a face card or a 10) beats other combinations of 21.

If the player and the dealer have identical scores and at least 17, it is considered a draw and the player retains the bet.

As already mentioned, you could also have presented the requirements in bullet form, as we did for the `DataBaseReader` class in Chapter 2, "How to Think in Terms of Objects."

We want to take the perspective of the user. Because we are not interested in the implementation, we'll concentrate on the interface. Think back to the black-box example from Chapter 1, "What an Object Really Is." We only care about *what* the system does, not *how* it does it.

The next step is to study the requirements summary statement and start identifying the classes. Before we actually start this process, let's define how we are going to model and track the classes that we ultimately identify.

Using CRC Cards

Discovering classes is not a trivial process. In the blackjack example we are working on, there will be relatively few classes, because this is intended as an example. However, in most business systems, there could be dozens of classes—perhaps 100 or more. There must be a way to keep track of the classes as well as their interactions. One of the most popular methods for identifying and categorizing classes is to use *class-responsibility-collaboration cards (CRC)*. Each CRC card represents a single class's data attributes, responsibilities, and collaborations.

One of the more endearing qualities of CRC cards is that they are non-electronic (although I'm sure that there are computer applications around that simulate CRC cards). CRC cards are, quite literally, a collection of standard index cards.

You need to create three sections on each card:

- The name of the class
- The responsibilities of the class
- The collaborations of the class

The use of CRC cards conjures up scenes of dimly lit rooms, partially filled boxes of pizza, pop cans, and multitudes of index cards strewn around the room. Although this might be partially true, using CRC cards is a good technique because many of the people involved with the design will not be developers. They might not even have much computer experience. Thus, using the index cards to discover classes is a technique that everyone can understand. Figure 6.4 shows the format of a CRC card.

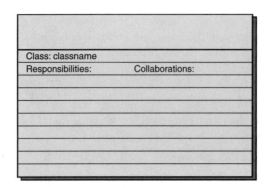

Figure 6.4   The format of a CRC card.

Identifying the Blackjack Classes

Remember that, in general, classes correspond to nouns, which are objects—people, places, and things. If you go through the requirements summary statement and highlight all the nouns, you have a good list from which you can start gleaning your objects.

Nouns

Although it is true that nouns generally indicate classes, nouns are not the only places where classes are found.

As stated earlier, you shouldn't get too hung up in getting things right the first time. Not all the classes that you identify from the list of nouns, or elsewhere, will make it through to the final cut. On the other hand, some classes might make the final cut that were not in your original list. Start feeling comfortable with the iterative process throughout the design. And as always, make sure that you realize that there are always many ways to skin a cat. We have already stated that if you put 10 people in different rooms, they will come up with 10 different designs, and they might all be equally good. In most cases, although the designs might be different, ideally there will be significant overlap. Of course, when working with a team, the final design will have to be a consensus, iterating and evolving to a common solution.

Let's identify some nouns from our blackjack example:

If the **player** and the **dealer** have identical scores and at least 17, it is considered a draw and the player retains the bet.

Now let's make a list of the possible objects(classes):

- Game
- Blackjack
- Dealer
- House

- Players
- Player
- Cards
- Card
- Deck
- Hand
- Face value
- Suit
- Winner
- Ace
- Face card
- King
- Queen
- Jack
- Game
- Bet

Can you find any other possible classes that were missed? There might well be some classes that you feel should be in the list but are not. There might also be classes that you feel should not have made the list. In any event, we now have a starting point, and we can begin the process of fine-tuning the list of classes. This is an iterative process, and although we have 19 potential classes, our final class list might be a lot shorter.

Again, remember that this is just the initial pass. You will want to iterate through this a number of times and make changes. You might even find that you left an important object out, or that you need to split one object into two objects. Now let's explore each of the possible classes:

- `Game`—*Blackjack* is the name of the game. Thus, we will treat this in the same way we treated the noun *game*.
- ~~Blackjack~~—In this case, *game* might be considered a noun, but the game is actually the system itself, so we will eliminate this as a potential class.
- `Dealer`—Because we cannot do without a dealer, we will keep this one (as a note, we could abstract out the stuff pertaining to people in general, but we won't in this example). It might also be possible to avoid a dealer class altogether, thus having the dealer simply be an instance of the player class. However, there are enough additional attributes of a dealer that we should probably keep this class.
- ~~House~~—This one is easy because it is just another name for the dealer, so we strike it.

- ~~Players~~ and `player`—We need players, so we have to have this class. However, we want the class to represent a single player and not a group of players, so we strike `players` and keep `player`.

- ~~Cards~~ and `card`—This one follows the same logic as `player`. We absolutely need cards in the game, but we want the class to represent a single card, so we strike `cards` and keep `card`.

- `Deck`—Because there are a lot of actions required by a `deck` (like shuffling and drawing), we decide that this is a good choice for a class.

- `Hand`—This class represents a gray area. Each player will have a hand. In this game, we will require that a player has a single hand. So it would be possible for a player to keep track of the cards without having to have a `hand` object. However, because it is theoretically possible for a player to have multiple hands, and because we might want to use the concept of a hand in other card games, we will keep this class. Remember that one of the goals of a design is to be extensible. If we create a good design for the blackjack game, perhaps we can reuse the classes later for other card games.

- ~~Face value~~—The face value of the card is best represented as an attribute in the `card` class, so let's strike this as a class.

- ~~Suit~~—Again, this is a gray area. For the blackjack game, we do not need to keep track of the suit. However, there are card games that need to keep track of the suit. Thus, to make this class reusable, we should track it. However, the suit is not a good candidate for a class. It should be an attribute of a card, so we will strike it as a class.

- ~~Ace~~—This could better be represented as an attribute of the `card` class, so let's strike it as a class.

- ~~Face Card~~—This could better be represented as attribute of the `card` class, so let's strike it as a class.

- ~~King~~—This could better be represented as attribute of the `card` class, so let's strike it as a class.

- ~~Queen~~—This could better be represented as attribute of the `card` class, so let's strike it as a class.

- `Bet`—This class presents a dilemma. Technically you could play blackjack without a bet; however, the requirements statement clearly includes a bet in the description. The bet could be considered an attribute of the player in this case, but there are many other games where a player does not need to have a bet. In short, a bet is not a logical attribute of a player. Also, abstracting out the bet is a good idea because we might want to bet various things. You can bet money, chips, your watch, your horse, or even the title to your house. Even though there might be many valid arguments not to make the bet a class, in this case we will.

We are left with six classes, as shown in Figure 6.5.

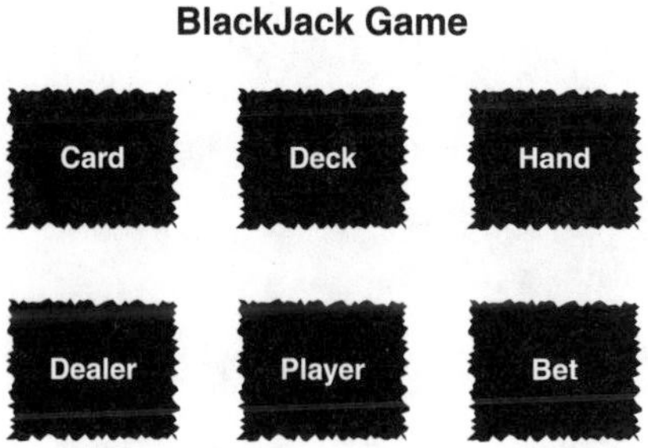

BlackJack Game

Figure 6.5   The initial blackjack classes.

Design Decisions

The dealer could be a specific type of player, and perhaps inherit from a player class. However, this would be a design decision.

Identifying the Classes' Responsibilities

Responsibilities relate to actions. You can generally identify responsibilities by selecting the verbs from the summary of the requirements. From this list you can glean your responsibilities. However, keep in mind the following:

Verbs

Although it is true that verbs generally correlate with responsibilities, verbs are not the only places where responsibilities are found.

- Not all verbs in the requirements summary will ultimately end up as responsibilities.
- You might need to combine several verbs to find an actual responsibility.
- Some responsibilities ultimately chosen will not be in the original requirements summary.
- Because this is an iterative process, you need to keep revising and updating both the requirements summary and the responsibilities.
- If two or more classes share a responsibility, each class will have the responsibility.

Let's take an initial stab at identifying the verbs, which will lead us down the path toward uncovering the responsibilities of our classes:

If the player and the dealer have identical scores and at least 17, then it is considered a draw and the player retains the bet.

Now let's make a list of the possible responsibilities for our classes:

- `Card`
    - Know its face value

- Know its suit
- Know its value
- Know whether it is a face card
- Know whether it is an ace
- Know whether it is a joker

- Deck
  - Shuffle
  - Deal the next card
  - Know how many cards are left in the deck
  - Know whether there is a full deck to begin

- Hand
  - Know how many cards are in the hand
  - Know the value of the hand
  - Show the hand

- Dealer
  - Deal the cards
  - Shuffle the deck
  - Give a card to a player
  - Show the dealer's hand
  - Calculate the value of the dealer's hand
  - Know the number of cards in the dealer's hand
  - Request a card (hit or hold)
  - Determine the winner
  - Start a new hand

- Player
  - Request a card (hit or hold)
  - Show the player's hand
  - Calculate the value of the player's hand
  - Know how many cards are in the hand
  - Know whether the hand value is over 21
  - Know whether the hand value is equal to 21 (and if it is a blackjack)
  - Know whether the hand value is below 21

- `Bet`
    - Know the type of bet
    - Know the value of the current bet
    - Know how much the player has left to bet
    - Know whether the bet can be covered

Remember that this is just the initial pass. You will want to iterate through this a number of times and make changes. You might even find that you've left an important responsibility out, or that you need to split one responsibility into two responsibilities. Now let's explore the possible responsibilities. We are left with the following classes and responsibilities:

`Card`

- Know its face value

    The card definitely needs to know this. Internally, this class must track the value of the card. Because this is an implementation issue, we don't want to phrase the responsibility in this way. From an interface perspective, let's call this *display face value*.

- Know its suit

    For the same reason as with face value, we will keep this responsibility, and rename it *display name* (which will identify the suit). However, we don't need this for blackjack. We will keep it for potential reuse purposes.

- ~~Know whether it is a face card.~~

    We could have a separate responsibility for face cards, aces, and jokers, but the report value responsibility can probably handle this. Strike this responsibility.

- ~~Know whether it is an ace.~~

    Same as above—let's strike this responsibility.

- ~~Know whether it is a joker.~~

    Same as above, but notice that the joker was never mentioned in the requirements statement. This is a situation where we can add a responsibility to make the class more reusable. However, the responsibility for the joker goes to the report value, so let's strike this responsibility

---

Class Design

What to do with the jokers presents an interesting OO design issue. Should there be two separate classes—a superclass representing a regular deck of cards (sans jokers) and a subclass representing a deck of cards with the addition of the jokers? From an OO purist's perspective, having two classes might be the right approach. However, having a single class with two separate constructors might also be a valid approach.

What happens if you have decks of cards that use other configurations (such as no aces or no jacks)? Do we create a separate class for each, or do we handle them in the main class?

This is another design issue that has no right or wrong answer.

Deck

- Shuffle

  We definitely need to shuffle the deck, so let's keep this one.

- Deal the next card

  We definitely need to deal the next card, so let's keep this one.

- Know how many cards are left in the deck

  At least the dealer needs to know whether there are any cards left, so let's keep this one.

- Know whether there is a full deck to begin.

  The deck must know whether it includes all the cards. However, this might be strictly an internal implementation issue; in any event, let's keep this one for now.

Hand

- Know how many cards are in the hand

  We definitely need to know how many cards are in a hand, so let's keep this one. However, from an interface perspective, let's rename this *report the number of cards in the hand*.

- Know the value of the hand

  We definitely need to know the value of the hand, so let's keep this one. However, from an interface perspective, let's rename this *report the value of the hand*.

- Show the hand

  We need to be able to see the contents of the hand.

Dealer

- Deal the cards

  The dealer must be able to deal the initial hand, so let's keep this one.

- Shuffle the deck

  The dealer must be able to shuffle the deck, so let's keep this one. Actually, should we make the dealer request that the deck shuffle itself? Possibly.

- Give a card to a player

  The dealer must be able to add a card to a player's hand, so let's keep this one.

- Show the dealer's hand

We definitely need this functionality, but this is a general function for all players, so perhaps the hand should show itself and the dealer should request this. Let's keep it for now.

- Calculate the value of the dealer's hand

  Same as above. But the term *calculate* is an implementation issue in this case. Let's rename it *show the value of the dealer's hand*.

- Know the number of cards in the dealer's hand

  Is this the same as *show the value of the dealer's hand*? Let's keep this for now, but rename it *show the number of cards in the dealers hand*.

- Request a card (hit or hold)

  A dealer must be able to request a card. However, because the dealer is also a player, is there a way that we can share the code? Although this is possible, for now we are going to treat a dealer and a player separately. Perhaps in another iteration through the design, we can use inheritance and factor out the commonality.

- Determine the winner

  This depends on whether we want the dealer to calculate this or the game object. For now, let's keep it.

- Start a new hand

  Same as the previous functionality.

Player

- Request a card (hit or hold)

  A player must be able to request a card, so let's keep this one.

- Show the player's hand

  We definitely need this functionality, but this is a general function for all players, so perhaps the hand should show itself and the dealer should request this. Let's keep this one for now.

- Calculate the value of the player's hand

  Same as above. But the term *calculate* is an implementation issue in this case. Let's rename this *show the value of the player's hand*.

- Know how many cards are in the hand

  Is this the same as *show the player's hand*? Let's keep this for now, but rename it *show the number of cards in the player's hand*.

- Know whether the hand value is over 21, equal to 21 (including a blackjack), or below 21.

  Who should make this determination? These are based on the specific rules of the game. The player definitely needs to know this to make a decision about whether to request a card. In fact, the dealer needs to do this, too. This could be handled in *report the value of the hand.*

Bet

- Know the type of bet

  At this point, we will keep this for future reuse; however, for this game, we will require that the type of the bet is always money.

- Know the value of the current bet

  We need this to keep track of the value of the current bet. The player and the dealer need to know this. We will assume that the dealer (that is, the house) has an unlimited amount to bet.

- Know how much the player has left to bet

  In this case, the bet can also act as the pool of money that the player has available. In this way, the player cannot make a bet that exceeds his resources.

- Know whether the bet can be covered

  This is a simple response that allows the dealer (or the house) to determine whether the player can cover the bet.

As we iterate through the design process, we decide that we really do not want to have a separate bet class. If we need to, we can add it later. The decision needs to be based on two issues:

- Do we really need the class now or for future classes?
- Will it be easy to add later without a major redesign of the system?

After careful consideration, we decide that the class is not needed, and most probably will not be needed later. We make an assumption that the payment method for all future bets will be money. This is not necessarily a proper design decision. I can think of many reasons that we might want to have a bet object. There might be some behavior that should be encapsulated in a bet object. However, for now, we will scrap the bet object and make the dealer and players handle their own bets.

UML Use Cases: Identifying the Collaborations

To identify the collaborations, we need to study the responsibilities and determine what other classes the object interacts with. In short, what other classes does this object need to fulfill all its required responsibilities and complete its job? As you examine the collaborations, you might find that you have missed some necessary classes, or that some classes you initially identified are not needed:

- To help discover collaborations, use-case scenarios can be used. A *use case* is a transaction or sequence of related operations that the system performs in response to a user request or event.

- For each use case, identify the objects and the messages that it exchanges.

You might want to create collaboration diagrams to document this step. Obviously, there can be an infinite number of scenarios. The purpose of this part of the process is not to document all possible scenarios, which is an impossible task. The real purpose of creating use-case scenarios is to help you refine the choice of your classes and their responsibilities. By examining the collaborations, you might identify an important class that you missed. If this is the case, you can simply add another CRC card. You might also discover that one of the classes you originally chose is not as important as you once thought, so you can strike it and remove the CRC card from consideration. CRC cards help you discover classes, whereas use-case scenarios help you discover collaborations.

For example, let's consider a single possible scenario. In this case, we have a dealer and a single player.

- Dealer shuffles deck
- Player makes bet
- Dealer deals initial cards
- Player adds cards to player's hand
- Dealer adds cards to dealer's hand
- Hand returns value of player's hand to player
- Hand returns value of dealer's hand to dealer
- Dealer asks player whether player wants another card
- Dealer deals player another card
- Player adds the card to player's hand
- Hand returns value of player's hand to player
- Dealer asks player whether player wants another card
- Dealer gets the value of the player's hand
- Dealer sends or requests bet value from players
- Player adds to/subtracts from player's bet attribute

Let's determine some of the collaborations. Assume that we have a main application that contains all the objects (that is, we do not have a Game class). As part of our design, we have the dealer start the game. Figures 6.6 through 6.15 present some collaboration diagrams pertaining to this initial design.

Figure 6.6   Start the game.

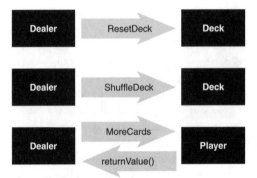

Figure 6.7   Shuffle and initially deal.

Figure 6.8   Get the hand value.

Figure 6.9   Get a card.

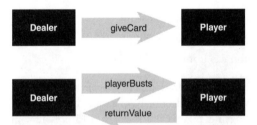

Figure 6.10   Deal a card and check to see whether the player busts.

Figure 6.11   Return the value of the hand.

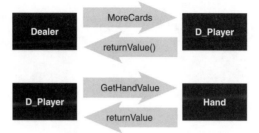

Figure 6.12   Does the dealer want more cards?

Intangibles

Be aware that there are more issues than the value of a player's hand involved in deciding whether to take another card. A player at a real blackjack table might go with a gut feel or how the dealer's hand looks. Although we might not be able to take gut feelings into consideration, we can attend to the issue of what the dealer's hand currently shows.

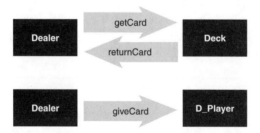

Figure 6.13   If requested, give the dealer a card.

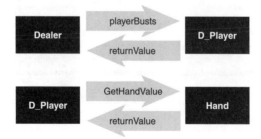

Figure 6.14   Does the dealer bust?

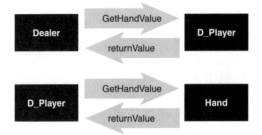

Figure 6.15   Do either the dealer or the player stand?

First Pass at CRC Cards

Now that we have identified the initial classes and the initial collaborations, we can complete the CRC cards for each class. It is important to note that these cards represent the initial pass only. In fact, although it is likely that many of the classes will survive the subsequent passes, the final list of classes and their corresponding collaborations might look nothing like what was gleaned from the initial pass. This exercise is meant to explain the process and create an initial pass, not to come up with a final design. Completing the design is a good exercise for you to undertake at the end of this chapter. Figures 6.16 through 6.20 present some CRC cards pertaining to this initial design.

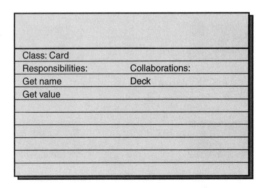

Figure 6.16   A CRC card for the Card class.

UML Class Diagrams: The Object Model

After you have completed the initial design using CRC cards, transfer the information contained on the CRC cards to class diagrams (see Figure 6.21). Note that this class diagram represents one possible design—it does not represent the initial pass of classes created during the previous exercise. The class diagrams go beyond the information on the CRC cards and might include such information as method parameters and return types.

(Note that the UML diagrams in this book do not include method parameters.) Check out the options for the modeling tool that you have to see how information is presented. You can use the detailed form of the class diagram to document the implementation.

Class: Deck	
Responsibilities:	Collaborations:
Reset deck	Dealer
Get deck size	Card
Get next card	
Shuffle Deck	
Show deck.	

Figure 6.17   A CRC card for the Deck class.

Class: Dealer	
Responsibilities:	Collaborations:
Start a new game.	Hand
Get a card.	Player
	Deck

Figure 6.18   A CRC card for the Dealer class.

Class: Player	
Responsibilities:	Collaborations:
Want more cards?	Hand
Get a card.	Dealer
Show hand.	
Get value of hand.	

Figure 6.19   A CRC card for the Player class.

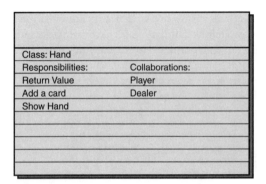

Class: Hand	
Responsibilities:	Collaborations:
Return Value	Player
Add a card	Dealer
Show Hand	

Figure 6.20   A CRC card for the Hand class.

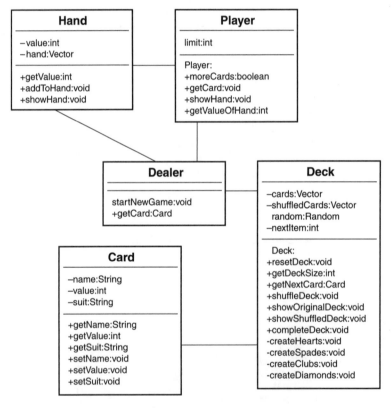

Figure 6.21   A UML diagram for the blackjack program.

Remember that the purpose of this exercise is to identify the classes and their interfaces. All the methods listed are public. Now a light bulb should be going off in your head.

Even though the search for the interfaces does not lead directly to private attributes and even private methods, the process is helpful in determining these as well. As you iterate through the CRC process, note what attributes and private methods each class will require.

Prototyping the User Interface

As our final step in the OO design process, we must create a prototype of our user interface. This prototype will provide invaluable information to help navigate through the iterations of the design process. As Gilbert and McCarty in *Object-Oriented Design in Java* aptly point out, "to a system user, the user interface is the system." There are several ways to create a user interface prototype. You can sketch the user interface simply drawing it on paper or a whiteboard. You can use a special prototyping tool, or even a language environment like Visual Basic, which is often used for rapid prototyping. Or you can use the IDE from your favorite development tool to create the prototype.

However you develop the user interface prototype, make sure that the users have the final say on the look and feel.

Conclusion

This chapter covers the design process for complete systems. It focuses on combining several classes to build a system. This system is represented by UML class diagrams. The example in this chapter shows the first pass at creating a design and is not meant to be a finished design. Many iterations may be required to get the system model to the point where you are comfortable with it.

Implementing Some Blackjack Code

I recently came across a complete implementation of a blackjack game in the book *Java 1.1 Developers Guide* by Jamie Jaworski. If you would like to actually get your hands dirty and write some code to implement another blackjack design, you might want to pick up this good, compressive Java book.

In the next several chapters, we will explore in more detail the relationships between classes. Chapter 7, "Mastering Inheritance and Composition," covers the concepts of inheritance and composition and how they relate to each other.

References

Gilbert, Stephen, and Bill McCarty. *Object-Oriented Design in Java.* The Waite Group, 1998.

Jaworski, Jamie. *Java 1.1 Developers Guide.* Sams Publishing, 1997.

Wrifs-Brock, R., B. Wilkerson, and L. Weiner. *Designing Object-Oriented Software.* Prentice-Hall, 1990.

Ambler, Scott. *The Object Primer*. Cambridge University Press, 1998.

Weisfeld, Matt and John Ciccozzi. "Software by Committee," *Project Management Journal*, volume 5, number 1. Pages 30–36, September, 1999.

7

Mastering Inheritance and Composition

INHERITANCE AND COMPOSITION PLAY major roles in the design of object-oriented (OO) systems. In fact, many of the most difficult and interesting design decisions come down to deciding between inheritance and composition.

Both inheritance and composition are mechanisms for reuse. *Inheritance*, as its name implies, involves inheriting attributes and behaviors from other classes. In this case, there is a true parent/child relationship. The child (or subclass) inherits directly from the parent (or superclass). Inheritance represents the is-a relationship that was introduced in Chapter 1, "Introduction to Object-Oriented Concepts." For example, a dog **is a** mammal.

Composition involves using other classes to build more complex classes. There is no parent/child relationship in this case. Basically, complex objects are composed of other objects. Composition represents a has-a relationship. For example, a car **has an** engine. Both the engine and the car are standalone objects. However, the car is a complex object that contains (has an) engine object. In fact, a child object might itself be composed of other objects; for example, the engine might include cylinders.

A Real-World Example
It might be helpful to explain the differences between is-a and has-a relationships based on terms from the relational database world. Is-a represents a hierarchical relationship between entity types (tables), whereas has-a represents a referential relationship.

When OO technologies first entered the mainstream, inheritance was all the rage. The fact that you could design a class once and then inherit functionality from it was considered the foremost advantage to using OO technologies. Reuse was the name of the game, and inheritance was the ultimate expression of reuse.

However, over the past several years the luster of inheritance has dulled a bit. In fact, if you listen to some people, inheritance should be avoided like the plague. It is interesting that inheritance, the once-shining star of OO technologies, has now become, in some circles, a sort of pariah. In their book *Java Design*, Peter Coad and Mark Mayfield have a complete chapter titled "Design with Composition Rather Than Inheritance." In fact, many object-based platforms do not even support true inheritance. Platforms such as the MS COM model are based on interface inheritance. Interface inheritance is covered in great detail in Chapter 8, "Frameworks and Reuse: Designing with Interfaces and Abstract Classes."

The good news is that the discussions about whether to use inheritance or composition are a natural progression toward some seasoned middle ground. As in all philosophical debates, there are fanatical people on both sides of the argument. Fortunately, as is normally the case, these heated discussions have led to a more sensible understanding of how to utilize the technologies.

For reasons that we will discuss later in this chapter, some people believe that inheritance should be avoided and composition should be the design method of choice. The argument is fairly complex and subtle. In actuality, both inheritance and composition are valid class design techniques, and they each have their proper place in the OO developer's toolkit.

The fact that inheritance is often misused and overused is more a result of a lack of understanding of what inheritance is all about than a fundamental flaw in using inheritance as a design strategy.

The bottom line is that inheritance and composition are both important techniques in building OO systems. Designers and developers simply need to take the time to understand the strengths and weaknesses of both and to use each in the proper contexts.

Inheritance

Inheritance was defined in Chapter 1 as a system in which children inherit attributes and behavior from a parent class. However, there is more to inheritance, and in this chapter we will explore inheritance in greater detail.

Chapter 1 states that you can determine an inheritance relationship by following a simple rule: If Class B is a Class A, then this is a good candidate for inheritance.

> **Is-a**
> One of the primary rules of OO design is that public inheritance is represented by an is-a relationship.

Let's revisit the mammal example used in Chapter 1. To present a very simple example, let's concentrate on a `Dog` class. A dog has several behaviors that make it distinctly a dog, as opposed to a cat. For this example, let's specify two: A dog barks and a dog pants. So we can create a `Dog` class that has these two behaviors, along with two attributes (see Figure 7.1).

Now, let's say that you want to create a `GoldenRetriever` class. You could create a brand new class that contains the same behaviors that the `Dog` class has. However, we could make the following, and quite reasonable, definition: A Golden Retriever is-a dog. Because of this relationship, we can inherit the attributes and behaviors from `Dog` and use it in our new `GoldenRetriever` class (see Figure 7.2).

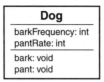

Figure 7.1   A class diagram for the Dog class.

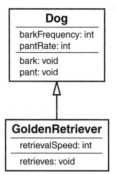

Figure 7.2   The GoldenRetriever class inherits from the Dog class.

The GoldenRetriever class now contains its own behavior as well as all the more general behaviors of a dog. This provides us with some significant benefits. First, when we wrote the GoldenRetriever class, we did not have to reinvent the wheel by writing the bark and pant methods over again. Not only does this save some coding time, but it saves testing and maintenance time as well. The bark and pant methods are written only once and, assuming that they were properly tested when the Dog class was written, they do not need to be heavily tested again (but it does need to be tested).

Now let's take full advantage of our inheritance structure and create a second class under the Dog class: a class called LhasaApso. Whereas retrievers are bred for retrieving, Lhasa Apsos are bred for use as guard dogs. These dogs are not attack dogs, they have acute senses, and when they sense something unusual, they start barking. So we can create our LhasaApso class and inherit from the Dog class just as we did with the GoldenRetriever class (see Figure 7.3).

Testing New Code

In our example with the GoldenRetriever class, the bark and pant methods should be written, tested, and debugged when the Dog class is written. Theoretically, this code is now robust and ready to reuse in other situations. However, the fact that you do not need to rewrite the code does not mean it should not be tested. Although it is unlikely, there might be some characteristic of a retriever that somehow breaks the code. The bottom line is that you should always test new code. Each new inheritance relationship creates a new context for using inherited methods. A complete testing strategy should take into account each of these contexts.

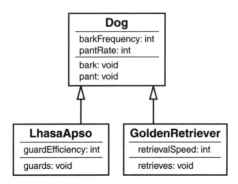

Figure 7.3   The LhasaApso class inherits from the Dog class.

Another primary advantage of inheritance is that the code for bark() and pant() is in a single place. Let's say there is a need to change the code in the bark() method. When you change it in the Dog class, you do not need to change it in the LhasaApso class and the GoldenRetriever class.

Do you see a problem here? This inheritance model appears to work great. However, can you be certain that all dogs have the behavior contained in the Dog class?

In his book *Effective C++*, Scott Meyers gives a great example of a dilemma with design using inheritance. Consider a class for a bird. One of the most recognizable characteristics of a bird is, of course, that it can fly. So we create a class called Bird with a fly method. You should immediately understand the problem. What do we do with a penguin, or an ostrich? They are birds, but they can't fly. You could override the behavior locally, but the method would still be called fly. And it would not make sense to have a method called fly for a bird that does not fly, but only waddles.

In our dog example, we have designed in the fact that all dogs can bark. However, there are dogs that do not bark. The Basenji breed is a barkless dog. These dogs do not bark, but they do yodel. So, should we reevaluate our design? What would this design look like? Figure 7.4 is an example that shows a more correct way to model the hierarchy of the Dog class.

Generalization and Specialization

Consider the object model of the Dog class hierarchy. We started with a single class, called Dog, and we factored out some of the commonality between various breeds of dogs. This concept, sometimes called *generalization-specialization*, is yet another important consideration when using inheritance. The idea is that as you make your way down the inheritance tree, things get more specific. The most general case is at the top of the tree. In our Dog inheritance tree, the class Dog is at the top and is the most general category. The various breeds—the GoldenRetriever, LhasaApso, and Basenji classes—are the most specific. The idea of inheritance is to go from the general to the specific by factoring out commonality.

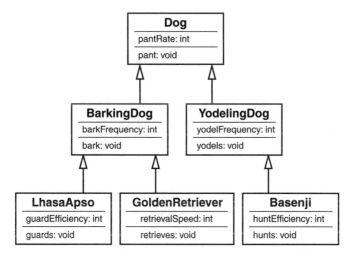

Figure 7.4   The Dog class hierarchy.

In the Dog inheritance model, we started factoring out common behavior by understanding that although a retriever has some different behavior from that of a LhasaApso, the breeds do share some common behaviors—for example, they both pant and bark. Then we realized that all dogs do not bark—some yodel. Thus, we had to factor out the barking behavior into a separate BarkingDog class. The yodeling behavior went into a YodelingDog class. However, we still realized that both barking dogs and barkless dogs still shared some common behavior—all dogs pant. Thus, we kept the Dog class and had the BarkingDog and the YodelingDog classes inherit from Dog. Now Basenji can inherit from YodelingDog, and LhasaApso and GoldenRetriever can inherit from BarkingDog.

Design Decisions

In theory, factoring out as much commonality as possible is great. However, as in all design issues, sometimes it really is too much of a good thing. Although factoring out as much commonality as possible might represent real life as closely as possible, it might not represent your model as closely as possible. The more you factor out, the more complex your system gets. So you have a conundrum: Do you want to live with a more accurate model, or a system with less complexity? You have to make this choice based on your situation, for there are no hard guidelines to make the decision.

What Computers Are Not Good At

Obviously a computer model can only approximate real-world situations. Computers are good at number crunching, but are not as good at more abstract operations.

For example, breaking up the Dog class into BarkingDog and the YodelingDog models real life better than assuming that all dogs bark, but it does add a bit of complexity.

> **Model Complexity**
>
> At this level of our example, adding two more classes does not make things so complex that it makes the model untenable. However, in larger systems, when these kinds of decisions are made over and over, the complexity quickly adds up. In larger systems, keeping things as simple as possible is usually the best practice.

There will be instances in your design when the advantage of a more accurate model does not warrant the additional complexity. Let's assume that you are a dog breeder and that you contract out for a system that tracks all your dogs. The system model that includes barking dogs and yodeling dogs works fine. However, suppose that you simply do not breed any yodeling dogs—never have and never will. Perhaps you do not need to include the complexity of differentiating between yodeling dogs and barking dogs. This will make your system less complex, and it will provide the functionality that you need.

Deciding whether to design for less complexity or more functionality is really a balancing act. The primary goal is always to build a system that is flexible without adding so much complexity that the system collapses under its own weight. Current and future costs are also a major factor in these decisions. Although it might seem appropriate to make a system more complete and flexible, this added functionality might barely add any benefit. In short, the return on investment is just not there. For example, would you extend the design of your Dog system to include other canines, such as hyenas and foxes (see Figure 7.5)?

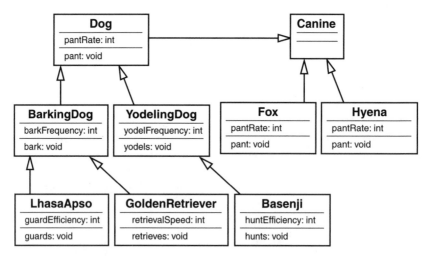

Figure 7.5   An expanded canine model.

Although this design might be prudent if you were a zookeeper, the extension of the Canine class is probably not necessary if you are breeding and selling domesticated dogs. So as you can see, there are always tradeoffs when creating a design.

> **Making Design Decisions with the Future in Mind**
>
> You might at this point say, "Never say never." Although you might not breed yodeling dogs now, sometime in the future you might want to do so. If you do not design for the possibility of yodeling dogs now, it will be much more expensive to change the system later to include them. This is yet another design decision that you have to make. You could possibly override the bark() method to make it yodel; however, this is not intuitive, as some people will expect a method called bark() to actually bark.

Composition

It is natural to think of objects as containing other objects. A television set contains a tuner and video display. A computer contains video cards, keyboards, and floppy drives. The computer can be considered an object unto itself, and the floppy drive is also considered a valid object. You could open up the computer and remove the floppy drive and hold it in your hand. In fact, you could take the floppy drive to another computer and install it; because it works in multiple computers, the fact that it is a standalone object is reinforced.

The classic example of object composition is the automobile. Many books, training classes, and articles seem to use the automobile as the essence of object composition. Besides the original interchangeable manufacture of the rifle, most people think of the automobile assembly line created by Henry Ford as the quintessential example of interchangeable parts. Thus, it seems natural that the automobile has become a primary reference point for designing OO software systems.

For example, most people would think it natural for a car to contain an engine. In fact, a car contains many objects besides an engine, including wheels, a steering wheel, and a stereo. Whenever a particular object is composed of other objects, and those objects are included as object fields, the new object is known as a *compound*, an *aggregate*, or a *composite object* (see Figure 7.6).

> **Aggregation, Association, and Composition**
>
> From my perspective, there are really only two ways to reuse classes—with inheritance or composition. In Chapter 9, "Building Objects," we will discuss composition in more detail; specifically, aggregation and association. In this book, I consider aggregation and association to be types of composition.

Representing Composition with UML

To represent the fact that the car object contains a steering wheel object, UML uses the notation shown in Figure 7.7.

> **Aggregation, Association, and UML**
>
> In this book, aggregations are represented in UML by lines with a diamond, such as an engine as part of a car. Associations are represented by just the line (no diamond), such as a standalone keyboard servicing a separate computer box.

A Car has a Steering Wheel

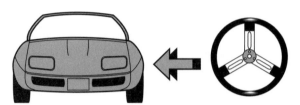

Figure 7.6 An example of composition.

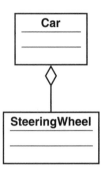

Figure 7.7 Representing composition in UML.

Note that the line connecting the Car class to the SteeringWheel class has a diamond shape on the Car side of the line. This signifies that a Car *contains* (has-a) SteeringWheel.

Let's expand this example. Let's say that none of the objects used in this design use inheritance in any way. All the object relationships are strictly composition, and there are multiple levels of composition. Of course, this is a simplistic example, and there are many, many more object and object relationships in designing a car. However, this design is simply meant to be a simple illustration of what composition is all about.

Let's say that a car is composed of an engine, a stereo system, and a door.

How Many Doors and Stereos?

Note that a car normally has more than one door. Some have two, and some have four. You might even consider a hatchback a fifth door. In the same vein, it is not necessarily true that all cars have a stereo system. A car could have no stereo system or it could have one. I have even seen a car with two separate stereo systems. These situations are discussed in detail in Chapter 9. For the sake of this example, just pretend that a car has only a single door (perhaps a special racing car) and a single stereo system.

The fact that a car is made up of an engine, a stereo system, and a door is easy to understand because most people think of cars in this way. However, it is important to keep in mind when designing software systems, just like automobiles, that objects are made up of other objects. In fact, the number of nodes and branches that can be included in this tree structure of classes is virtually unlimited.

Figure 7.8 shows the object model for the car, with the engine, stereo system, and door included.

Note that all three objects that make up a car are themselves composed of other objects. The engine contains pistons and spark plugs. The stereo contains a radio and a cassette. The door contains a handle. Also note that there is yet another level. The radio contains a tuner. We could have also added the fact that a handle contains a lock; the cassette contains a fast forward button, and so on. Additionally, we could have gone one level beyond the tuner and created an object for a dial. The level and complexity of the object model is, obviously, up to the designer.

Model Complexity

As with the inheritance problem of the barking and yodeling dogs, using too much composition can also lead to more complexity. There is a fine line between creating an object model that contains enough granularity to be sufficiently expressive, and a model that is so granular that it is difficult to understand and maintain.

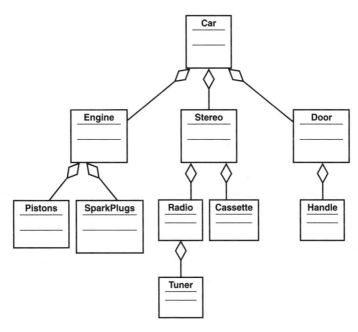

Figure 7.8   The Car class hierarchy.

Why Encapsulation Is Fundamental to OO

Encapsulation is really the fundamental concept of OO. Whenever the interface/implementation paradigm is covered, we are really talking about encapsulation. The basic question is what in a class should be exposed and what should not be exposed. This encapsulation pertains equally to data and behavior. When talking about a class, the primary design decision revolves around encapsulating both the data and the behavior into a well-written class.

Stephen Gilbert and Bill McCarty define encapsulation as "the process of packaging your program, dividing each of its classes into two distinct parts: the interface and the implementation." This is the message that has been presented over and over again in this book.

But what does encapsulation have to do with inheritance, and how does it apply with regard to this chapter? This has to do with an OO paradox. Encapsulation is so fundamental to OO that it is one of OO design's cardinal rules. Inheritance is also considered one of the three primary OO concepts. However, in one way, inheritance actually breaks encapsulation! How can this be? Is it possible that two of the three primary concepts of OO are incompatible with each other? Well, let's explore this possibility.

How Inheritance Weakens Encapsulation

As already stated, encapsulation is the process of packaging classes into the public interface and the private implementation. In essence, a class hides everything that is not necessary for other classes to know about.

Peter Coad and Mark Mayfield make a case that when using inheritance, encapsulation is inherently weakened within a class hierarchy. They talk about a specific risk: Inheritance connotes strong encapsulation with other classes, but weak encapsulation between a superclass and its subclasses.

The problem is that if you inherit an implementation from a superclass and then change that implementation, the change *ripples through* the class hierarchy. This rippling effect potentially affects all the subclasses. At first, this might not seem like a major problem; however, as we have seen, a rippling effect such as this can cause unanticipated problems. For example, testing can become a nightmare. In Chapter 6, "Designing with Objects," we talked about how encapsulation makes testing systems easier. In theory, if you create a class called Cabbie (see Figure 7.9) with the appropriate public interfaces, any change to the implementation of Cabbie should be transparent to all other classes. If the other classes were directly dependent on the implementation of the Cabbie class, testing would become more difficult, if not untenable.

Keep Testing

Even with encapsulation, you would still want to retest the classes that use Cabbie to verify that no problem has been introduced by the change.

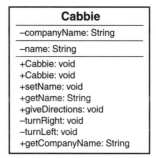

Figure 7.9   A UML diagram of the `Cabbie` class.

If you then create a subclass of `Cabbie` called `PartTimeCabbie`, and `PartTimeCabbie` inherits the implementation from `Cabbie`, changing the implementation of `Cabbie` directly affects the `PartTimeCabbie` class.

For example, consider the UML diagram in Figure 7.10. `PartTimeCabbie` is a subclass of `Cabbie`. Thus, `PartTimeCabbie` inherits the public implementation of `Cabbie`, including the method `giveDirections()`. If the method `giveDirections` is changed in `Cabbie`, it will have a direct impact on `PartTimeCabbie` and any other classes that might later be subclasses of `Cabbie`. In this subtle way, changes to the implementation of `Cabbie` are not necessarily encapsulated within the `Cabbie` class.

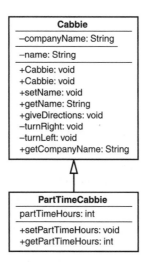

Figure 7.10   A UML diagram of the `Cabbie`/`PartTimeCabbie` classes.

To reduce the risk posed by this dilemma, it is important that you stick to the strict is-a condition when using inheritance. If the subclass were truly a specialization of the superclass, changes to the parent would likely affect the child in ways that are natural and expected. To illustrate, if a `Circle` class inherits implementation from a `Shape` class, and a change to the implementation of `Shape` breaks `Circle`, then `Circle` was not truly a `Shape` to begin with.

How can inheritance be used improperly? Consider a situation in which you want to create a window for the purposes of a graphical user interface (GUI). One impulse might be to create a window by making it a subclass of a rectangle class:

```
class Rectangle {

}

class Window extends Rectangle {

}
```

In reality a GUI window is much, much more than a rectangle. It is not really a specialized version of a rectangle, as is a square. A true window might contain a rectangle (in fact many rectangles); however, it is really not a true rectangle. In this approach, a `Window` class should not inherit from `Rectangle`, but it should contain `Rectangle` classes.

```
class Window {

    Rectangle menubar;
    Rectangle statusbar;
    Rectangle mainview;

}
```

A Detailed Example of Polymorphism

Many people consider polymorphism the cornerstone of OO design. Designing a class for the purpose of creating totally independent objects is what OO is all about. In a well-designed system, an object should be able to answer all the important questions about it. As a rule, an object should be responsible for itself. This independence is one of the primary mechanisms of code reuse.

As stated in Chapter 1, polymorphism literally means *many shapes*. When a message is sent to an object, the object must have a method defined to respond to that message. In an inheritance hierarchy, all subclasses inherit the interfaces from their superclass. However, because each subclass is a separate entity, each might require a separate response to the same message.

To review the example in Chapter 1, consider a class called `Shape`. This class has a behavior called `Draw`. However, when you tell somebody to draw a shape, the first question they ask is likely to be, "What shape?" Simply telling a person to draw a shape is too abstract (in fact, the `Draw` method in `Shape` contains no implementation). You must specify which shape you mean. To do this, you provide the actual implementation in `Circle` and other subclasses. Even though `Shape` has a `Draw` method, `Circle` overrides this method and provides its own `Draw` method. Overriding basically means replacing an implementation of a parent with your own.

Object Responsibilty

Let's revisit the `Shape` example from Chapter 1 (see Figure 7.11).

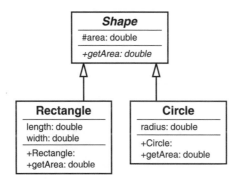

Figure 7.11   The `Shape` class hierarchy.

Polymorphism is one of the most elegant uses of inheritance. Remember that a `Shape` cannot be instantiated. It is an abstract class because it has an abstract method, `getArea()`. Chapter 8 explains abstract classes in great detail.

However, `Rectangle` and `Circle` can be instantiated because they are concrete classes. `Rectangle` and `Circle` are both shapes; however, they obviously have some differences. Because `Rectangle` and `Circle` are both shapes, their area can be calculated. Yet, the formula to calculate the area is different for each. Thus, the area formulas cannot be placed in the `Shape` class.

This is where polymorphism comes in. The premise of polymorphism is that you can send messages to various objects, and they will respond according to their object type. For example, if you send the message `getArea` to a `Circle` class, you will invoke a completely different method than if you send the same `getArea` message to a `Rectangle` class. This is because both `Circle` and `Rectangle` are responsible for themselves. If you ask `Circle` to return its area, it knows how to do this. If you want a circle to draw itself, it can do this, too. A `Shape` object could not do this even if it could be instantiated. Notice that in the UML diagram, the `getArea` method in the `Shape` class is italicized. This designates that the method is abstract.

As a very simple example, imagine that there are four classes: the abstract class `Shape`, and concrete classes `Circle`, `Rectangle`, and `Star`. Here is the code:

```
public abstract class Shape{

    public abstract void draw();
```

```
}

public class Circle extends Shape{

    public void draw() {

        System.out.println("I am drawing a Circle");

    }
}

public class Rectangle extends Shape{

    public void draw() {

        System.out.println("I am drawing a Rectangle");

    }
}

public class Star extends Shape{

    public void draw() {

        System.out.println("I am drawing a Star");

    }
}
```

Notice that there is only one method for each class: draw. Here is the important point regarding polymorphism and an object being responsible for itself: The concrete classes themselves have responsibility for the drawing function. The Shape class does not provide the code for drawing; the Circle, Rectangle, and Star classes do this for themselves. Here is some code to prove it:

```
public class TestShape {

    public static void main(String args[]) {

        Circle circle = new Circle();
        Rectangle rectangle = new Rectangle();
        Star star = new Star();

        circle.draw();
        rectangle.draw();
        star.draw();
```

```
        }

}
```

Compiling This Code

If you want to compile this Java code, make sure that you set `classpath` to the current directory:

```
javac -classpath . Shape.java
javac -classpath . Circle.java
javac -classpath . Rectangle.java
javac -classpath . Star.java
javac -classpath . TestShape.java
```

Actually, when you compile a Java class (in this case `TestShape`) and it requires another class (let's say `Circle`), the javac compiler will attempt to compile all the required classes. Thus, the following line will actually compile all the files in this example.

```
javac -classpath . TestShape.java
```

The test application `TestShape` creates three classes: `Circle`, `Rectangle`, and `Star`. To actually draw these classes, `TestShape` simply asks the individual classes to draw themselves:

```
circle.draw();
rectangle.draw();
star.draw();
```

When you execute `TestShape`, you get the following results:

```
C:\>java TestShape
I am drawing a Circle
I am drawing a Rectangle
I am drawing a Star
```

This is polymorphism at work. What would happen if you wanted to create a new shape, say `Triangle`? Simply write the class, compile it, test it, and use it. The base class `Shape` does not have to change—nor does any other code:

```
public class Triangle extends Shape{

    public void draw() {

        System.out.println("I am drawing a Triangle");

    }
}
```

A message can now be sent to `Triangle`. And even though `Shape` does not know how to draw a triangle, the `Triangle` class does:

```
public class TestShape {

    public static void main(String args[]) {

        Circle circle = new Circle();
        Rectangle rectangle = new Rectangle();
        Star star = new Star();
        Triangle triangle = new Triangle ();

        circle.draw();
        rectangle.draw();
        star.draw();
        triangle.draw();

    }

}
```

```
C:\>java TestShape
I am drawing a Circle
I am drawing a Rectangle
I am drawing a Star
I am drawing a Triangle
```

To see the real power of polymorphism, you can actually pass the shape to a method that has absolutely no idea what shape is coming.

```
public class TestShape {

    public static void main(String args[]) {

        Circle circle = new Circle();
        Rectangle rectangle = new Rectangle();
        Star star = new Star();

        drawMe(circle);
        drawMe(rectangle);
        drawMe(star);

    }

    static void drawMe(Shape s) {
        s.draw();
    }

}
```

In this case, the Shape object can be passed to the method drawMe, and the drawMe method can handle any valid Shape—even one you add later. You can run this version of TestShape just like the previous one.

Conclusion

This chapter gives a basic overview of what inheritance and composition are and how they are different. Many well-respected OO designers have stated that composition should be used whenever possible, and inheritance should be used only when necessary.

However, this is a bit simplistic. I believe that the idea that composition should be used whenever possible hides the real issue, which might simply be that composition is more appropriate in more cases than inheritance—not that it should be used whenever possible. The fact that composition might be more appropriate in most cases does not mean that inheritance is evil. Use both composition and inheritance, but only in their proper contexts.

In earlier chapters, the concepts of abstract classes and Java interfaces arose several times. In Chapter 8, we will explore the concept of development contracts and how abstract classes and Java interfaces are used to satisfy these contracts.

References

Coad, Peter, and Mark Mayfield. *Java Design*. Object International, 1999.

Meyers, Scott. *Effective C++*. Addison-Wesley, 1992.

Gilbert, Stephen, and Bill McCarty. *Object-Oriented Design in Java*. The Waite Group, 1998.

8

Frameworks and Reuse: Designing with Interfaces and Abstract Classes

Chapter 7, "Mastering Inheritance and Composition," explains how inheritance and composition play major roles in the design of object-oriented (OO) systems. This chapter expands on this theme and introduces the concepts of a Java interface and an abstract class.

Java interfaces and abstract classes are a powerful mechanism for code reuse, providing the foundation for a concept we will call *contracts*. This chapter covers the topics of code reuse, frameworks, contracts, Java interfaces, and abstract classes. At the end of the chapter, we'll work through an example of how all these concepts can be applied to a real-world situation.

Code: To Reuse or Not to Reuse?

You have probably heard people singing the praises of code reuse since you took your first computer class or wrote your first line of code. Some people consider code reuse to be the savior of the software development community. Since the dawn of computer software, the concept of reusing code has been reinvented several times. The OO paradigm is no different. One of the major advantages touted by OO proponents is that you can write code once, and then reuse it to your heart's content.

This is true to a certain degree. As with all design approaches, the utility and the reusability of code depends on how well it was designed and implemented. OO design does not hold the patent on code reuse. There is nothing stopping anyone from writing very robust and reusable code in a non–OO language. Certainly, there are countless numbers of routines and functions, written in structured languages such as COBOL and C, that are of high quality and quite reusable.

Thus, it is clear that following the OO paradigm is not the only way to develop reusable code. However, the OO approach does provide several mechanisms for facilitating the development of reusable code. One way to create reusable code is to create frameworks. In this chapter, we focus on using interfaces and abstract classes to create frameworks and encourage reusable code.

What Is a Framework?

Hand-in-hand with the concept of code reuse is the concept of *standardization*, which is sometimes called *plug-and-play*. The idea of a framework revolves around these plug-and-play and reuse principles. One of the classic examples of a framework is a desktop application. Let's take an office suite application as an example. The document editor that I am currently using (Microsoft Word) has a menu bar that includes multiple menu options. These options are similar to those in the presentation package (Microsoft PowerPoint) and the spreadsheet software (Microsoft Excel) that I also have open. In fact, the first six menu items (File, Edit, View, Insert, Format, and Tools) are the same in all three programs. Not only are the menu options similar, but the first toolbar looks remarkably alike as well (New, Open, Save, and so on). Below the toolbars is the document area—whether it be for a document, a presentation, or a spreadsheet. The common framework makes it easier to learn various applications within the office suite. It also makes a developer's life easier by allowing maximum code reuse.

The fact that all these menu bars have a similar look and feel is obviously not an accident. In fact, when you develop in most integrated development environments, on a certain platform like Microsoft Windows, for example, you get certain things without having to create them yourself. When you create a window in a Windows environment, you get elements like the main title bar and the file close button in the top-right corner. When you double-click on the main title bar, the screen always minimizes/maximizes. When you click on the close button in the top-right corner, the application always terminates. This is all part of the framework. Figure 8.1 is a screenshot of a word processor. Note the menu bars, toolbars, and other elements that are part of the framework. A word processing framework generally includes operations such as creating documents; opening documents; saving documents; cutting, copying, and pasting text; searching through documents; and so on. To use this framework, a developer must use a predetermined interface to create an application. This predetermined interface conforms to the standard framework, which has two obvious advantages. First, as we have already seen, the look and feel are consistent, and the end users do not have to learn a new framework. Second, a developer can take advantage of code that has already been written and tested (and this testing issue should not be underestimated). Why write code to create a brand new Open dialog when one already exists and has been thoroughly tested? In a business setting, when time is critical, people do not want to have to learn new things unless it is absolutely necessary.

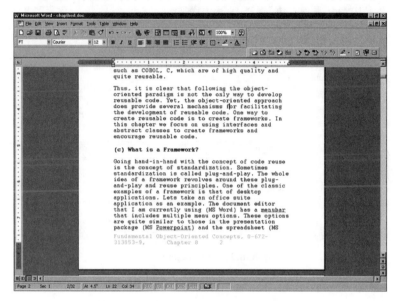

Figure 8.1   A word processing framework.

You might next wonder how you use the dialog box provided by the framework. The answer is simple: You follow the rules that the framework provides you. And where might you find these rules? The rules for the framework are found in the documentation. The person or persons who wrote the class, classes, or class libraries should have provided documentation on how to use the public interfaces of the class, classes, or class libraries (at least we hope). In many cases, this takes the form of the application programming interface (API).

For example, to create an applet in Java, you would bring up the API documentation for the `Applet` class and take a look at the public interfaces it presents. Figure 8.2 shows a part of the Java API. By using these APIs, you can create a valid Java applet and conform to required standards. If you follow these standards, your applet will be set to run in Java-enabled browsers.

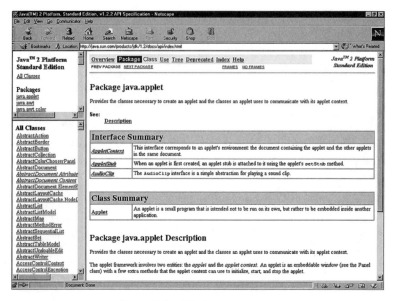

Figure 8.2   API documentation.

What Is a Contract?

In the context of this article, we will consider a *contract* to be any mechanism that requires a developer to comply with the specifications of an Application Programming Interface (API). Often, an API is referred to as a framework. The online dictionary Dictionary.com (`http:www.dictionary.com`) defines a contact as "an agreement between two or more parties, especially one that is written and enforceable by law."

   This is exactly what happens when a developer uses an API—with the project man-ager or business owner representing the law.   When using contracts, the developer is required to comply with the rules defined in the framework. This includes issues like method names, number of parameters, and so on. In short, standards are created to facili-tate good coding practices.

The Term *Contract*

The term *contract* is widely used in many aspects of business, including software development. Do not con-fuse the concept here with other possible software design concepts called contracts.

Enforcement is vital, because it is always possible for a developer to break a contract. Without enforcement, a rogue developer could decide to reinvent the wheel and write her own code rather than use the code provided by the framework. There is little benefit to a standard if people routinely disregard or circumvent it. In Java and the .NET lan-guages, the two ways to implement contracts are to use abstract classes and interfaces.

C#

For this chapter, I use C# as the .NET representative. However, these concepts apply to all .NET languages, such as Visual Basic .NET.

Abstract Classes

One way a contract is implemented is via an abstract class. An *abstract class* is a class that contains one or more methods that do not have any implementation provided. Suppose that you have an abstract class called Shape. It is abstract because you cannot instantiate it. If you ask someone to draw a shape, the first thing they will most likely ask you is "What kind of shape?" Thus, the concept of a shape is abstract. However, if someone asks you to draw a circle, this does not pose quite the same problem, because a circle is a concrete concept. You know what a circle looks like. You also know how to draw other shapes, such as rectangles.

How does this apply to a contract? Let's assume that we want to create an application to draw shapes. Our goal is to draw every kind of shape represented in our current design, as well as ones that might be added later. There are two conditions we must adhere to.

First, we want all shapes to use the same syntax to draw themselves. For example, we want every shape implemented in our system to contain a method called draw(). Thus, seasoned developers implicitly know that to draw a shape you simply invoke the draw() method, regardless of what the shape happens to be. Theoretically, this reduces the amount of time fumbling through manuals and cuts down on syntax errors.

Second, remember that it is important that every class be responsible for its own actions. Thus, even though the class must provide a method called draw(), the class must provide its own implementation of the code. For example, a class called Circle and a class called Rectangle both have a draw() method; however, the Circle class obviously has code to draw a circle, and as expected, the Rectangle class has code to draw a rectangle. When we ultimately create classes called Circle and Rectangle, which are subclasses of Shape, these classes must implement their own version of Draw (see Figure 8.3).

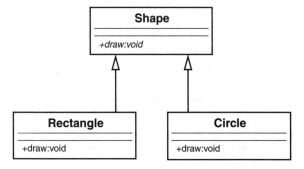

Figure 8.3   An abstract class hierarchy.

In this way, we have a Shape framework that is truly polymorphic. The Draw method can be invoked for every shape in the system, and invoking each shape produces a different result. Invoking the `Draw` method on a `Circle` object draws a circle, and invoking the `Draw` method on a `Rectangle` object draws a rectangle. In essence, sending a message to an object evokes a different response, depending on the object. This is the essence of polymorphism.

```
circle.draw();        // draws a circle
rectangle.draw();     // draws a rectangle
```

Let's look at some code to illustrate how `Rectangle` and `Circle` conform to the `Shape` contract. Here is the code for the `Shape` class:

```
public abstract class Shape {

    public abstract void draw();

}
```

Note that the class does not provide any implementation for `draw()`; basically there is no code and this is what makes the method abstract (providing code would make the method concrete). There are two reasons why there is no implementation. First, `Shape` does not know what to draw, so we could not implement the `draw()` method even if we wanted to.

Second, we want the subclasses to provide the implementation. Let's look at the `Circle` and `Rectangle` classes:

```
public class Circle extends Shape {

    public void Draw() {System.out.println ("Draw a Circle"};

}

public class Rectangle extends Shape {

    public void Draw() {System.out.println ("Draw a Rectangle"};

}
```

Note that both `Circle` and `Rectangle` extend (that is, inherit from) `Shape`. Also notice that they provide the actual implementation (in this case, the implementation is obviously trivial). Here is where the contract comes in. If `Circle` inherits from `Shape` and fails to provide a `draw()` method, `Circle` won't even compile. Thus, `Circle` would fail in its attempt to satisfy the contract with `Shape`. A project manager can require that programmers creating shapes for the application must inherit from `Shape`. By doing this, all shapes in the application will have a `draw()` method that performs in an expected manner.

Circle

If Circle does indeed fail to implement a draw() method, Circle will be considered abstract. Thus, yet another subclass must inherit from Circle and implement a draw() method. This subclass would then become the concrete implementation of both Shape and Circle.

Although the concept of abstract classes revolves around abstract methods, there is nothing stopping Shape from actually providing some implementation. (Remember that the definition for an abstract class is that it contains one or more abstract methods—this implies that an abstract class can provide concrete methods as well.) For example, although Circle and Rectangle implement the draw() method differently, they share the same mechanism for setting the color of the shape. So, the Shape class can have a color attribute and a method to set the color. This setColor() method is an actual concrete implementation, and would be inherited by both Circle and Rectangle. The only methods that a subclass must implement are the ones that the superclass declares as abstract. These abstract methods are the contract.

Caution

Be aware that in the cases of Shape, Circle, and Rectangle, we are dealing with a strict inheritance relationship, as opposed to an interface, which we will discuss in the next section. Circle is a Shape, and Rectangle is a Shape. This is an important point because contracts are not meant to be used in cases of composition or has-a relationships.

Some languages, such as C++, use only abstract classes to implement contracts. Java and C#, however, have another mechanism that implements a contract: an interface.

Interfaces

Before defining an interface, it is important to note that C++ does not have a construct called an interface. For C++, an abstract class provides the functionality of an interface. The obvious question is this: If an abstract class can provide the same functionality as an interface, why do Java and C# bother to provide interfaces?

Interface Terms

The term *interface* used in earlier chapters is a term generic to OO programming, and refers to the public interface to a class. The term *Java interface* refers to a language construct that is specific to Java. It is important not to get the two terms confused. (Actually, interfaces are not specific to only Java; other OO languages use them as well.)

For one thing, C++ supports multiple inheritance, whereas Java and C# do not. Although Java and C# classes can inherit from only one parent class, they can implement many interfaces. Using more than one abstract class constitutes multiple inheritance; thus Java and C# cannot go this route. Although this explanation might specify the need for Java and C# interfaces, it does not really explain what an interface is. Let's explore what function an interface performs.

No Replacement for Multiple Inheritance

Because of these considerations, interfaces are often thought to be a workaround for the lack of multiple inheritance. This is not technically true. Interfaces are a separate design technique, and although they can be used to design applications that could be done with multiple inheritance, they do not replace the concept of multiple inheritance.

As with abstract classes, interfaces are a powerful way to enforce contracts for a framework. Before we get into any conceptual definitions, it's helpful to see an actual interface UML diagram and the corresponding code. Consider an interface called `Nameable`, as shown in Figure 8.4.

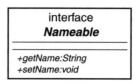

Figure 8.4   A UML diagram of a Java interface.

Note that `Nameable` is identified in the UML diagram as an interface, which distinguishes it from a regular class (abstract or not). Also note that the interface contains two methods, `getName()` and `setName()`. Here is the corresponding code:

```
public interface Nameable {

    String getName();
    void setName (String aName);

}
```

In the code, notice that `Nameable` is not declared as a class, but as an interface. Because of this, both methods, `getName()` and `setName()`, are considered abstract and there is no implementation provided. An interface, unlike an abstract class, can provide **no** implementation. As a result, any class that implements an interface must provide the implementation for all methods. (In Java, a class inherits from an abstract class, whereas a class implements an interface.)

Implementation Versus Definition Inheritance

Sometimes inheritance is referred to as *implementation inheritance*, and interfaces are called *definition inheritance.*

Tying It All Together

If both abstract classes and interfaces provide abstract methods, what is the real difference between the two? As we saw before, an abstract class provides both abstract and concrete methods, whereas an interface provides only abstract methods. Why is there such a difference?

Assume that we want to design a class that represents a dog, with the intent of adding more mammals later. The logical move would be to create an abstract class called `Mammal`:

```
public abstract class Mammal {

    public void generateHeat() {System.out.println("Generate heat");};

    public abstract void makeNoise();

}
```

This class has a concrete method called `generateHeat()`, and an abstract method called `makeNoise()`. The method `generateHeat()` is concrete, because all mammals generate heat. The method `makeNoise()` is abstract, because each mammal will make noise differently.

Let's also create a class called `Head` that we will use in a composition relationship:

```
public class Head {

    String size;

    public String getSize() {

        return size;

    }

    public void setSize(String aSize) { size = aSize;};

}
```

`Head` has two methods: `getSize()` and `setSize()`. Although composition might not shed much light on the difference between abstract classes and interfaces, using composition in this example does illustrate how composition relates to abstract classes and interfaces in the overall design of an object-oriented system. I feel that this is important because the example is more complete. Remember that there are two ways to build object relationships: the *is-a* relationship, represented by inheritance, and the *has-a* relationship, represented by composition. The question is: where does the interface fit in?

Compiling This Code

If you want to compile this Java code, make sure that you set `classpath` to the current directory:

```
javac -classpath . Nameable.java
javac -classpath . Mammal.java
javac -classpath . Head.java
javac -classpath . Dog.java
```

To answer this question and tie everything together, let's create a class called `Dog` that is a subclass of `Mammal`, implements `Nameable`, and has a `Head` object (see Figure 8.5).

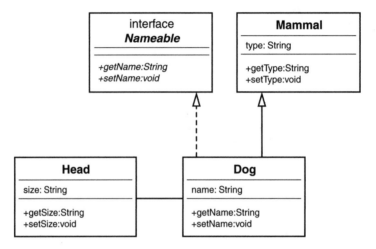

Figure 8.5 A UML diagram of the sample code.

In a nutshell, Java and C# build objects in three ways: inheritance, interfaces, and composition. Note the dashed line in Figure 8.5 that represents the interface. This example illustrates when you should use each of these constructs. When do you choose an abstract class? When do you choose an interface? When do you choose composition? Let's explore further.

You should be familiar with the following concepts:

- `Dog` is a `Mammal`, so the relationship is inheritance.
- `Dog` implements `Nameable`, so the relationship is an interface.
- `Dog` has a `Head`, so the relationship is composition.

The following code shows how you would incorporate an abstract class and an interface in the same class.

```
public class Dog extends Mammal implements Nameable {

    String name;
```

```
Head head;

public void makeNoise(){System.out.println("Bark");};

public void setName (String aName) {name = aName;};
public String getName () {return (name);};

}
```

After looking at the UML diagram, you might come up with an obvious question: Even though the dashed line from Dog to Nameable represents an interface, isn't it still inheritance? At first glance, the answer is not simple. Although interfaces are a special type of inheritance, it is important to know what *special* means. Understanding these *special* differences are key to a strong object-oriented design.

Although inheritance is a strict is-a relationship, an interface is not. For example:

- A dog is a mammal.
- A reptile is not a mammal

Thus, a Reptile class could not inherit from the Mammal class. However, an interface transcends the various classes. For example:

- A dog is nameable.
- A lizard is nameable.

The key here is that classes in a strict inheritance relationship must be related. For example, in this design, the Dog class is directly related to the Mammal class. A dog is a mammal. Dogs and lizards are not related at the mammal level because you can't say that a lizard is a mammal. However, interfaces can be used for classes that are not related. You can name a dog just as well as you can name a lizard. This is the key difference between using an abstract class and using an interface.

The abstract class represents some sort of implementation. In fact, we saw that Mammal provided a concrete method called generateHeat(). Even though we do not know what kind of mammal we have, we know that all mammals generate heat. However, an interface models only behavior. An interface *never* provides any type of implementation, only behavior. The interface specifies behavior that is the same across classes that conceivably have no connection. Not only are dogs nameable, but so are cars, planets, and so on.

The Compiler Proof

Can we prove or disprove that interfaces have a true is-a relationship? In the case of Java, we can let the compiler tell us. Consider the following code:

```
Dog D = new Dog();
Head H = D;
```

When this code is run through the compiler, the following error is produced:

```
Test.java:6: Incompatible type for Identifier. Can't convert Dog to Head.
➥Head H = D;
```

Obviously, a dog is not a head. However, as expected, the following code works just fine:

```
Dog D = new Dog();
Mammal M = D;
```

This is a true inheritance relationship, and it is not surprising that the compiler parses this code cleanly, because a dog is a mammal.

Now we can perform the true test of the interface. Is an interface an actual is-a relationship? The compiler thinks so:

```
Dog D = new Dog();
Nameable N = D;
```

This code works fine. So, we can safely say that a dog is a nameable entity. This is a simple but effective proof that both inheritance and interfaces constitute an is-a relationship.

> **Nameable Interface**
>
> An interface specifies certain behavior, but not the implementation. By implementing the Nameable interface, you are saying that you will provide nameable behavior by implementing methods called getName and setName. How you implement these methods is up to you. All you have to do is to provide the methods.

Making a Contract

The simple rule for defining a contract is to provide an unimplemented method, via either an abstract class or an interface. Thus, when a subclass is designed with the intent of implementing the contract, it must provide the implementation for the unimplemented methods in the parent class or interface.

As stated earlier, one of the advantages of a contract is to standardize coding conventions. Let's explore this concept in greater detail by providing a good example of what happens when coding standards are not used. In this case, there are three classes: Planet, Car, and Dog. Each class implements code to name the entity. However, because they are all implemented separately, each class has different syntax to retrieve the name. Consider the following code for the Planet class:

```
public class Dog extends Mammal implements Nameable {

    String name;

    Head head;
public class Planet
```

```
    String planetName;

    public void getplanetName() {return planetName;};

}
```

Likewise, the `Car` class might have code like this:
```
public class Car

    String carName;

    public String getCarName() { return carName;};

}
```

And the `Dog` class might have code like this:
```
public class Dog

    String dogName;

    public String getDogName() { return dogName;};

}
```

The obvious problem here is that anyone using these classes would have to look at the documentation (what a horrible thought!) to figure out how to retrieve the name in each of these cases. Even though looking at the documentation is not the worst fate in the world, it would be nice if all the classes used in a project (or company) would use the same naming convention—it would make life a bit easier. This is where the `Nameable` interface comes in.

The idea would be to make a contract for any type of class that needs to use a name. As users of various classes move from one class to the other, they would not have to figure out the current syntax for naming an object. The `Planet` class, the `Car` class, and the `Dog` class would all have the same naming syntax.

To implement this lofty goal, we can create an interface (we can use the `Nameable` interface that we used previously). The convention is that all classes must implement `Nameable`. In this way, the users only have to remember a single interface for all classes when it comes to naming conventions:

```
public interface Nameable {

    public String getName();
    public void setName(String aName);

}
```

The new classes, Planet, Car, and Dog, should look like this:

```
public class Planet implements Nameable

    String planetName;

    public String getName() {return planetName;};
    public void setName(String myName) { planetName = myName;};

}

public class Car implements Nameable

    String carName;

    public String getName() {return carName;};
    public void setName(String myName) { carName = myName;};

}

public class Dog implements Nameable

    String dogName;

    public String getName() {return dogName;};
    public void setName(String myName) { dogName = myName;};

}
```

In this way, we have a standard interface, and we've used a contract to ensure that it is the case.

There is one little issue that you might have thought about. The idea of a contract is great as long as everyone plays by the rules, but what if some shady individual doesn't want to play by the rules (the rogue programmer)? The bottom line is that there is nothing to stop someone from breaking the standard contract; however, in some cases, doing so will get them in deep trouble.

On one level, a project manager can insist that everyone use the contract, just like team members must use the same variable naming conventions and configuration management system. If a team member fails to abide by the rules, he could be reprimanded, or even fired.

Enforcing rules is one way to ensure that contracts are followed, but there are instances in which breaking a contract will result in unusable code. Consider the Java interface Runnable. Java applets implement the Runnable interface because it requires that any class implementing Runnable must implement a run() method. This is important because the browser that calls the applet will call the run() method within Runnable. If the run() method does not exist, things will break.

System Plug-in-Points

Basically, contracts are "plug-in points" into your code. Anyplace where you want to make parts of a system abstract, you can use a contract. Instead of coupling to objects of specific classes, you can connect to any object that implements the contract. You need to be aware of where contracts are useful; however, you can overuse them. You want to identify common features such as the `Nameable` interface, as discussed in this chapter. However, be aware that there is a trade-off when using contracts. They might make code reuse more of a reality, but they make things somewhat more complex.

An E-Business Example

It's sometimes hard to convince a decision maker, who may have no development background, of the monetary savings of code reuse. However, when reusing code, it is pretty easy to understand the advantage to the bottom line. In this section, we'll walk through a simple but practical example of how to create a workable framework using inheritance, abstract classes, interfaces and composition.

An E-Business Problem

Perhaps the best way to understand the power of reuse is to present an example of how you would reuse code. In this example, we'll use inheritance (via interfaces and abstract classes) and composition. Our goal is to create a framework that will make code reuse a reality, reduce coding time, and reduce maintenance—all the typical software development wish-list items.

Let's start our own Internet business! It should be easy, if everyone else is doing it. Let's assume that we have a client, a small pizza shop called Papa's Pizza. Despite the fact that it is a small, family-owned business, Papa realizes that the Web is the wave of the future. Papa wants his customers to access his Web site, find out what Papa's Pizza is all about, and order pizzas right from the comfort of their Java-enabled browsers.

> **Be Aware**
>
> Although we will state many of the requirements for this example, the code used will only implement a very small subset of the functionality. Obviously, we cannot implement the entire Web site here. We are only concerned with illustrating how abstract classes and Java interfaces are used to create a framework, and to take advantage of code reuse.

At the site we develop, customers will be able to bring up the Web site, select the products they want to order, and select a delivery mechanism and time for delivery. They can either eat their food at the restaurant, pick up the order, or have the order delivered. For example, a customer decides at 3:00 that he wants to order a pizza dinner (with salads, breadsticks, and drinks), to be delivered to his home at 6:00. Let's say the customer is at work (on a break, of course). He gets on the Web and selects the pizzas, including size, toppings, and crust; the salads, including dressings; breadsticks; and drinks. He chooses the delivery option, and requests that the food be delivered to his home at 6:00. Then he pays for the order by credit card, gets a confirmation number, and exits. Within a few minutes he gets an email confirmation as well. We will set up accounts so that when people bring up the site, they will get a greeting reminding them of who they are, what their favorite pizza is, and what new pizzas have been created this week.

When the system is finally complete, it is deemed a total success. For the next several weeks, Papa's customers happily order pizzas and other food and drinks over the Internet. During this rollout period, Papa's brother-in-law, who owns a donut shop called Dad's Donuts, pays Papa a visit. Papa shows Dad the system, and Dad falls in love with it. The next day, Dad calls our company and asks us to develop a Web-based system for his donut shop. This is great, and exactly what we had hoped for. Now, how can we leverage the code that we used for the pizza shop in the system for the donut shop?

And how many more small businesses, besides Papa's Pizza and Dad's Donuts, could take advantage of our framework to get on the Web? If we can develop a good, solid framework, then we will be able to efficiently deliver Web-based systems at lower costs than we were able to do before. There will also be an added advantage that the code will have been tested and implemented previously, so debugging and maintenance should be greatly reduced.

The Non-Reuse Approach

There are many reasons the concept of code reuse has not been as successful as some software developers would like. First, many times reuse is not even considered when developing a system. Second, even when reuse is entered into the equation, the issues of schedule constraints, limited resources, and budgetary concerns often short-circuit the best intentions.

In many instances, code ends up highly coupled to the specific application for which it was written. This means that the code within the application is highly dependent on other code within the same application.

A lot of code reuse is the result of simply using cut, copy, and paste operations. While one application is open in a text editor, you would copy code and then paste it into another application. Sometimes certain functions or routines can be used without any change. As is unfortunately many times the case, even though most of the code may remain identical, a small bit of code must change to work in a specific application.

For example, consider two totally separate applications, as represented by the UML diagram in Figure 8.6.

In this example, the applications testDonutShop and testPizzaShop are totally independent code modules. The code is kept totally separate, and there is no interaction between the modules. However, these applications might use some common code. In fact, some code might have been copied verbatim from one application to another. At some point, someone involved with the project might decide to create a library of these shared pieces of code to use in these and other applications. In many well-run and disciplined projects, this approach works well. Coding standards, configuration management, change management, and so on are all very well run. However, in many instances, this discipline breaks down.

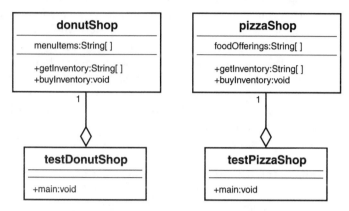

Figure 8.6   Applications on divergent paths.

Anyone who is familiar with the software development process knows that when bugs crop up and time is being wasted, there is the temptation to put some fixes or additions into a system that are specific to the application currently in distress. This might fix the problem for the distressed application, but could have unintended, possibly harmful, implications for other applications. Thus, in situations like these, the initially shared code can diverge, and separate code bases must be maintained.

For example, one day Papa's Web site crashes. He calls us in a panic, and one of our developers is able to track down the problem. The developer fixes the problem, knowing that the fix works, but is not quite sure why. The developer also does not know what other areas of the system the fix might inadvertently affect. So the developer makes a copy of the code, strictly for use in the Papa's Pizza system. This is affectionately named Version 2.01papa. Because the developer does not yet totally understand the problem, and because Dad's system is working fine, the code is not migrated to the donut shop's system.

Tracking Down a Bug
The fact that the bug turned up in the pizza system does not mean that it will also turn up in the donut system. Even though the bug caused a crash in the pizza shop, the donut shop might never encounter it. It may be that the fix to the pizza shop's code is more dangerous to the donut shop than the original bug.

The next week Dad calls up in a panic, with a totally unrelated problem. A developer fixes it, again not knowing how the fix will affect the rest of the system, makes a separate copy of the code, and calls it Version 2.03dad. This scenario gets played out for all the sites we now have in operation. There are now a dozen or more copies of the code, with various versions for the various sites. This becomes a mess. We have multiple code paths and have crossed the point of no return. We can never merge them again. (Perhaps we could, but from a business perspective, this would be costly.)

Our goal is to avoid the mess of the previous example. Although many systems must deal with legacy issues, fortunately for us, the pizza and donut applications are brand-new systems. Thus, we can use a bit of foresight and design this system in a reusable manner. In this way, we will not run into the maintenance nightmare just described. What we want to do is factor out as much commonality as possible. In our design, we will focus on all the common business functions that exist in a Web-based application. Instead of having multiple application classes like testPizzaShop and testDonutShop, we can create a design that has a class called Shop that all the applications will use.

Notice that testPizzaShop and testDonutShop have similar interfaces, getInventory and buyInventory. We will factor out this commonality and require that all applications that conform to our Shop framework implement getInventory and buyInventory methods. This requirement to conform to a standard is sometimes called a contract. By explicitly setting forth a contract of services, you isolate the code from a single implementation. In Java, you can implement a contract by using an interface or an abstract class. Let's explore how this is accomplished.

An E-Business Solution

Now let's show how to use a contract to factor out some of the commonality of these systems. In this case, we will create an abstract class to factor out some of the implementation, and an interface (our familiar Nameable) to factor out some behavior.

Our goal is to provide customized versions of our Web application, with the following features:

- An interface, called Nameable, which is part of the contract.
- An abstract class called Shop, which is also part of the contract.
- A class called CustList, which we use in composition.
- A new implementation of Shop for each customer we service.

The UML Object Model

The newly created Shop class is where the functionality is factored out. Notice in Figure 8.7 that the methods getInventory and buyInventory have been moved up the hierarchy tree from DonutShop and PizzaShop to the abstract class Shop. Now, whenever we want to provide a new, customized version of Shop, we simply plug in a new implementation of Shop (such as a grocery shop). Shop is the contract that the implementations must abide by:

```
public abstract class Shop {

    CustList customerList;
```

```
public void CalculateSaleTax() {

    System.out.println("Calculate Sales Tax");

};

public abstract String[] getInventory();

public abstract void buyInventory(String item);

}
```

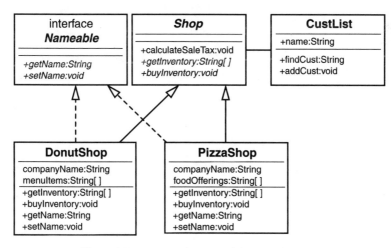

Figure 8.7 A UML diagram of the Shop system.

To show how composition fits into this picture, the Shop class has a customer list. Thus, the class CustList is contained within Shop:

```
public class CustList {

    String name;

    public  String findCust() {return name;}
    public  void addCust(String Name){}

}
```

To illustrate the use of an interface in this example, an interface called Nameable is defined:

```java
public interface Nameable {

    public abstract String getName();
    public abstract void setName(String name);

}
```

We could potentially have a large number of different implementations, but all the rest of the code (the application) is the same. In this small example, the code savings might not look like a lot. But in a large, real-world application, the code savings is significant. Let's take a look at the donut shop implementation:

```java
public class DonutShop extends Shop implements Nameable {

    String companyName;

    String[] menuItems = {
        "Donuts",
        "Muffins",
        "Danish",
        "Coffee",
        "Tea"
    };

    public String[] getInventory() {

        return menuItems;

    }

    public void buyInventory(String item) {

        System.out.println("\nYou have just purchased " + item);

    }

    public String getName(){

        return companyName;
    }

    public void setName(String name){

        companyName = name;
    }
}
```

The pizza shop implementation looks very similar:

```java
public class PizzaShop extends Shop implements Nameable {

    String companyName;


    String[] foodOfferings = {
        "Pizza",
        "Spaghetti",
        "Garden Salad",
        "Anitpasto",
        "Calzone"
    };

    public String[] getInventory() {

        return foodOfferings;

    }

    public void buyInventory(String item) {

        System.out.println("\nYou have just purchased " + item);

    }

    public String getName(){

        return companyName;
    }

    public void setName(String name){

        companyName = name;
    }

}
```

Unlike the initial case, where there is a large number of customized applications, we now have only a single primary class (Shop) and various customized classes (PizzaShop, DonutShop). There is no coupling between the application and any of the customized classes. The only thing the application is coupled to is the contract (Shop). The contract specifies that any implementation of Shop must provide an implementation for two methods, getInventory and buyInventory. It also must provide an implementation for getName and setName that relates to the interface Nameable that is implemented.

Although this solution solves the problem of highly coupled implementations, we still have the problem of deciding which implementation to use. With the current strategy, we would still have to have separate applications. In essence, you have to provide one application for each Shop implementation. Even though we are using the Shop contract, we still have the same situation as before we used the contract:

```
DonutShop myShop= new DonutShop();
```

```
PizzaShop myShop = new PizzaShop ();
```

How do we get around this problem? We can create objects dynamically. In Java, we can use code like this:

```
String className = args[0];
```

```
Shop  myShop;
```

```
myShop = (Shop)Class.forName(className).newInstance();
```

In this case, you set className by passing a parameter to the code. (There are other ways to set className, such as by using a system property.)

Let's look at Shop using this approach. (Note that there is no exception handling, and nothing else besides object instantiation.)

```
class TestShop {

    public static void main (String args[]) {

        Shop shop = null;

        String className = args[0];

        System.out.println("Instantiate the class:" + className + "\n");


        try {

         // new pizzaShop();
            shop = (Shop)Class.forName(className).newInstance();

        } catch (Exception e) {

            e.printStackTrace();
        }

        String[] inventory = shop.getInventory();
```

```
// list the inventory

for (int i=0; i<inventory.length; i++) {
   System.out.println("Argument" + i + " = " + inventory[i]);
}


// buy an item

shop.buyInventory(Inventory[1]);

   }

}
```

Compiling this Code

If you who want to compile this Java code, make sure to set `classpath` to the current directory:

```
javac -classpath . Nameable.java
javac -classpath . Shop.java
javac -classpath . CustList.java
javac -classpath . DonutShop.java
javac -classpath . PizzaShop.java
javac -classpath . TestShop.java
```

To run the code to test the pizza shop application, execute the following command:

```
java -classpath . TestShop PizzaShop
```

In this way, we can use the same application code for both `PizzaShop` and `DonutShop`. If we add a `GroceryShop` application, we only have to provide the implementation and the appropriate string to the main application. No application code needs to change.

Conclusion

When designing classes and object models, it is vitally important to understand how the objects are related to each other. This chapter discusses the primary topics of building objects: inheritance, interfaces, and composition. In this chapter, you have learned how to build reusable code by designing with contracts.

In Chapter 9, "Building Objects," we complete our OO journey and explore how objects that might be totally unrelated can interact with each other.

References

Coad, Peter, and Mark Mayfield. *Java Design*. Object International, 1999.

Meyers, Scott. *Effective C++*. Addison-Wesley, 1992.

9

Building Objects

THE PREVIOUS TWO CHAPTERS cover the topics of inheritance and composition. In Chapter 7, "Mastering Inheritance and Composition," we learned that inheritance and composition represent the primary ways to build objects. In Chapter 8, "Frameworks and Reuse: Designing with Interfaces and Abstract Classes," we learned that there are varying degrees of inheritance and how inheritance, interfaces, abstract classes, and composition all fit together.

This chapter covers the issue of how objects are related to each other in an overall design. You might say that this topic was already introduced, and you would be correct. Both inheritance and composition represent ways that objects interact. However, inheritance and composition have one significant difference in the way objects are built. When inheritance is used, the end result is, at least conceptually, a single class that incorporates all of the behaviors and attributes of the inheritance hierarchy. When composition is used, several different classes are used to build the target class.

Although it is true that inheritance is a relationship between two classes, what is really happening is that a wholly new class is created. Let's revisit the example of the Person and Employee classes (see Figure 9.1).

Although there are indeed two classes here, the relationship is not interaction—it is inheritance. Basically, an employee is a person. An Employee object does not send a message to a Person object. An Employee object does need the services of a Person object. This is because an Employee object is a Person object.

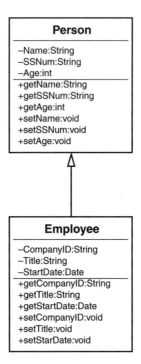

Figure 9.1   An inheritance relationship.

However, composition is a different situation. Composition represents an interaction between distinct objects. So, although Chapter 8 primarily covers the different flavors of inheritance, this chapter delves into the various flavors of composition and how objects interact with each other.

Composition Relationships

We have already seen that composition represents a part of a whole. Although the inheritance relationship is stated in terms of is-a, composition is stated in terms of has-a. We know intuitively that a car "has-a" steering wheel (see Figure 9.2).

Is-a and Has-a

Please forgive my grammar: For consistency, I will stick with "has a engine," even though "has an engine" might be grammatically correct. I do this because I want to simply state the rules as "is-a" and "has-a."

The reason for using composition is that it combines systems into less complex parts. This is a common way for people to approach problems. Studies show that even the best of us can keep, at most, seven chunks of data in our short-term memory at one time. Thus we like to use abstract concepts. Instead of saying that we have a large unit with a steering wheel, four tires, an engine, and so on, we say that we have a car. This makes it easier for us to communicate and keep things clear in our heads.

A Car has a Steering Wheel

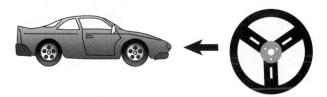

Figure 9.2   A composition relationship.

Composition also helps in other ways, such as making parts interchangeable. If all steering wheels are the same, it does not matter which steering wheel goes with which car. In software development, interchangeable parts mean reuse. In Chapters 7 and 8 of their book *Object-Oriented Design in Java*, Stephen Gilbert and Bill McCarty present many examples of associations and composition in much more detail. I highly recommend referencing this material for a more in-depth look into these subjects. Here we address some of the more fundamental points of these concepts and explore some variations of their examples.

Building in Phases

Another major advantage in using composition is that systems and subsystems can be built independently, and perhaps more importantly, tested and maintained independently.

There is no question that today's software systems are quite complex. To build quality software, you must follow one overriding rule to be successful: Keep things as simple as possible. For large software systems to work properly and be easily maintained, they must be broken up into smaller, more manageable parts. How do you accomplish this? In a 1962 article titled "The Architecture of Complexity," Nobel Prize winner Herbert Simon noted the following thoughts regarding stable systems:

- **"Stable complex systems usually take the form of a hierarchy, where each system is built from simpler subsystems, and each subsystem is built from simpler subsystems still."**—You might already be familiar with this principle because it forms the basis for functional decomposition, the method behind procedural software development. In object-oriented design, you apply the same principles to composition—building complex objects from simpler pieces.

- **"Stable, complex systems are nearly decomposable."**—This means you can identify the parts that make up the system and can tell the difference between interactions between the parts and inside the parts. Stable systems have fewer links between their parts than they have inside their parts. Thus, a modular stereo system, with simple links between the speakers, turntable, and amplifier, is inherently more stable than an integrated system, which isn't easily decomposable.

- **"Stable complex systems are almost always composed of only a few different kinds of subsystems, arranged in different combinations."**—Those subsystems, in turn, are generally composed of only a few different kinds of parts.

- **"Stable systems that work have almost always evolved from simple systems that worked."**—Rather than build a new system from scratch—reinventing the wheel—the new system builds on the proven designs that went before it.

In our stereo example (see Figure 9.3), suppose the stereo system was totally integrated and was not built from components (that is, that the stereo system was one big black-box system). In this case, what would happen if the CD player broke and became unusable? You would have to take in the entire system for repair. Not only would this be more complicated and expensive, but you would not have the use of any of the other components.

This concept becomes very important to languages such as Java and those included in the .NET architecture. Because Java objects are dynamically loaded, decoupling the design is quite important. For example, if you distribute a Java application and one of the class files needs to be re-created (for bug fixes or maintenance), you would only be required to redistribute that particular class file. If everything was in one file, the entire application would need to be redistributed.

Suppose the system is broken up into components rather than a single unit. In this case, if the CD player broke, you could disconnect the CD player and simply take it in for repair. (Note that all the components are connected by patch cords.) This would obviously be less complicated and less expensive, and it would take less time than having to deal with a single, integrated unit. As an added benefit, you could still use the rest of the system. You could even buy another CD player because it is a component. The repairperson could then plug your broken CD player into his repair systems to test and fix it. All in all, the component approach works quite well. Composition is one of the primary weapons that you, as a software designer, have in your arsenal to fight software complexity.

One major advantage of using components is that you can use components that were built by other developers, or even third-party vendors. However, using a software component from another source requires a certain amount of trust. Third-party components must come from a reliable source, and you must feel comfortable that the software is properly tested, not to mention that it must perform the advertised functions properly. There are still many who would rather build their own than trust components built by others.

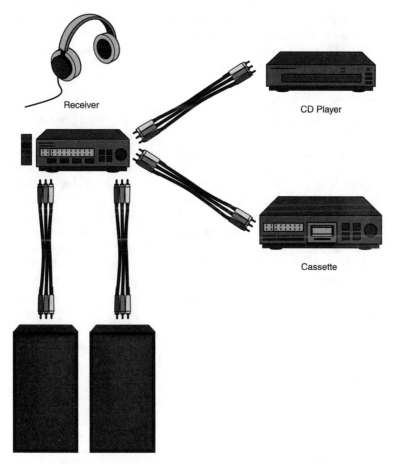

Figure 9.3 Building, testing, and verifying a complete
system one step at a time.

Types of Composition

Generally, there are two types of composition: association and aggregation. In both cases, these relationships represent collaborations between the objects. The stereo example we just used to explain one of the primary advantages of composition actually represents an association.

Is Composition a Form of Association?

Composition is another area in OO technologies where there is a question of which came first, the chicken or the egg. Some texts say that composition is a form of association, and some say that an association is a form of composition. In any event, in this book, we consider inheritance and composition the two primary ways to build classes. Thus, in this book, an association is a form of composition.

All forms of composition include a has-a relationship. However, there are subtle differences between associations and aggregations based on how you visualize the parts of the whole. In an aggregation, you normally see only the whole, and in associations, you normally see the parts that make up the whole.

Aggregations

Perhaps the most intuitive form of composition is aggregation. Aggregation means that a complex object is composed of other objects. A TV set is a clean, neat package that you use for entertainment. When you look at your TV, you see a single TV. Most of the time, you do not stop and think about the fact that the TV contains some transistors, a picture tube, a tuner, and so on. Sure, you see a switch to turn the set on and off, and you certainly see the picture tube. However, this is not the way people normally think of TVs. When you go into an appliance store, the salesperson does not say, "Let me show you this aggregation of transistors, a picture tube, a tuner, and so on." The salesperson says, "Let me show you this TV."

Similarly, when you go to buy a car, you do not pick and choose all the individual components of the car. You do not decide what sparkplugs to buy or what door handles to buy. You go to buy a car. Of course, you do choose some options, but for the most part, you choose the car as a whole, a complex object made up of many other complex and simple objects (see Figure 9.4).

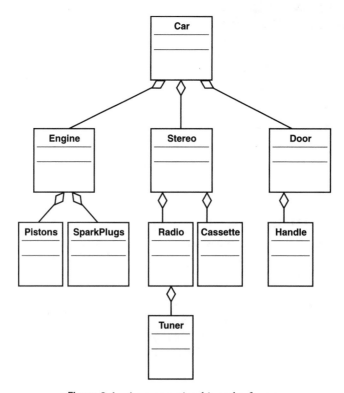

Figure 9.4   An aggregation hierarchy for a car.

Associations

Although aggregations represent relationships where you normally only see the whole, associations present both the whole and the parts. As stated in the stereo example, the various components are presented separately and connect to the whole by use of patch cords (the cords that connect the various components). Each one of the stereo components has a user interface that is manipulated independently. We can look back at the example in Chapter 2, "How to Think in Terms of Objects," at the example of designing for minimal interfaces.

Using a computer system as an example (see Figure 9.5), the whole is the computer system. The components are the monitor, keyboard, mouse, and main box. Each is a separate object, but together they represent the whole of the computer system. The main computer is using the keyboard, the mouse, and the monitor to delegate some of the work. In other words, the computer box needs the service of a mouse, but does not have the capability to provide this service by itself. Thus, the computer box requests the service from a separate mouse via the specific port and cable connecting the mouse to the box.

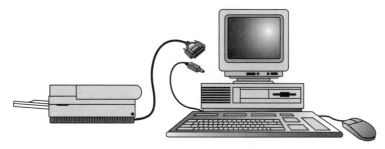

Figure 9.5   Associations.

Aggregation Versus Association

An aggregation is a complex object composed of other objects. An association is used when one object wants another object to perform a service for it.

Using Associations and Aggregations Together

One thing you might have noticed in all the examples is that the dividing lines between what is an association and what is an aggregation are blurred. Suffice it to say that many of your most interesting design decisions will come down to whether to use associations or aggregations.

For example, the computer system example used to describe association also contains some aggregation. Although the interaction between the computer box, the monitor, the keyboard, and the mouse is association, the computer box itself represents aggregation. You see only the computer box, but it is actually a complex system made up of other objects, including chips, motherboards, video cards, and so on.

Consider that an `Employee` object might be composed of an `Address` object and a `Spouse` object. You might consider the `Address` object as an aggregation (basically a part of the `Employee` object), and the `Spouse` object as an association. To illustrate, suppose both the employee and the spouse are employees. If the employee is fired, the spouse is still in the system, but the association is broken.

Similarly, in the stereo example, the relationship between the receiver, the speakers, and the CD player is association; however, each of these components are complex objects that are made up of other objects.

In the car example, although the engine, sparkplugs, and doors represent composition, the stereo also represents an association relationship.

No One Right Answer

As usual, there isn't a single absolutely correct answer when it comes to making a design decision. Design is not an exact science. Although we can make general rules to live by, these rules are not hard and fast.

Avoiding Dependencies

When using composition, it is desirable to avoid making objects highly dependent on one another. One way to make objects very dependent on each other is to mix domains. In the best of all worlds, an object in one domain should not be mixed with an object in another domain. We can return again to the stereo example to explain this concept.

By keeping the receiver and the CD player in separate domains, the stereo system is easier to maintain. For example, if the CD component breaks, you can send the CD player off to be repaired individually. In this case, the CD player and the cassette player have separate domains. This provides flexibility such as buying the CD player and the cassette player from separate manufacturers. So, if you decide you want to swap out the CD player with a brand from another manufacturer, you can.

Sometimes there is a certain convenience in mixing domains. A good example of this pertains to the existence of TV/VCR combinations. Granted, it is convenient to have both in the same module. However, if the TV breaks, the VCR is unusable—at least as part of the unit it was purchased in.

In fact, anyone who has kids and has discovered the wonder of the TV/VCR combination can attest to this dilemma. On long trips, we can take the unit into the car and let the kids watch their favorite videos, thus keeping the incessant chanting of "Are we there yet?" to a minimum. When we are not traveling, which is most of the time, the TV part of the unit is used in the exercise room to pass the time while doing our daily workouts. Unfortunately, on at least two occasions over the years, the VCR part of the unit has broken. This has forced us to take the entire unit to the repair shop. Because the TV is integrated with the VCR, the TV part is obviously unavailable for use while the unit is out for repair. Thus, our exercise time does not pass as quickly. If the TV and VCR were separate components, we could at least use the TV while the VCR is out for repair.

You need to determine whether you want convenience or stability. There is no right answer. It all depends on the application and the environment. In the case of the TV/VCR combination, we decided that the convenience of the integrated unit (for use in travel) far outweighed the risk of lower unit stability (see Figure 9.6).

More Convenient/Less Stable

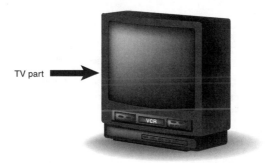

TV part

Figure 9.6   Convenience versus stability.

Mixing Domains

The convenience of mixing domains is a design decision. If the power of having a TV/VCR combination outweighs the risk and potential downtime of the individual components, the mixing of domains may well be the preferred design choice.

Cardinality

Gilbert and McCarty describe cardinality as the number of objects that participate in an association and whether the participation is optional or mandatory. To determine cardinality, ask the following questions:

- Which objects collaborate with which other objects?
- How many objects participate in each collaboration?
- Is the collaboration optional or mandatory?

For example, let's consider the following example. We are creating an `Employee` class that inherits from `Person`, and has relationships with the following classes:

- `Division`
- `JobDescription`
- `Spouse`
- `Child`

What do these classes do? Are they optional? How many does an `Employee` need?

- `Division`
  - This object contains the information relating to the division that the employee works for.
  - Each employee must work for a division, so the relationship is mandatory.
  - The employee works for one, and only one, division.
- `JobDescription`
  - This object contains a job description, most likely containing information such as salary grade and salary range.
  - Each employee must have a job description, so the relationship is mandatory.
  - The employee can hold various jobs during the tenure at a company. Thus, an employee can have many job descriptions. These descriptions can be kept as a history if an employee changes jobs, or it is possible that an employee might hold two different jobs at one time. For example, a supervisor might take on an employee's responsibilities if the employee quits and a replacement has not yet been hired.
- `Spouse`
  - In this simplistic example, the `Spouse` class contains only the anniversary date.
  - An employee can be married or not married. Thus, a spouse is optional.
  - An employee can have only one spouse.
- `Child`
  - In this simple example, the `Child` class contains only the string `FavoriteToy`.
  - An employee can have children or not have children.
  - An employee can have no children or an infinite number of children (wow!). You could make a design decision as to the upper limit of the number of children that the system can handle.

To sum up, Table 9.1 represents the cardinality of the associations of the classes we just considered.

Table 9.1 **Cardinality of Class Associations**

Optional/Association	Cardinality	Mandatory
`Employee/Division`	1	Mandatory
`Employee/JobDescription`	1...n	Mandatory
`Employee/Spouse`	0...1	Optional
`Employee/Child`	0...n	Optional

Cardinality Notation

The notation of 0...1 means that an employee can have either zero or one spouse. The notation of 0...n means that an employee can have any number of children from zero to an unlimited number. The *n* basically represents infinity.

Figure 9.7 shows the class diagram for this system. Note that in this class diagram, the cardinality is indicated along the association lines. Refer to Table 9.1 to see whether the association is mandatory.

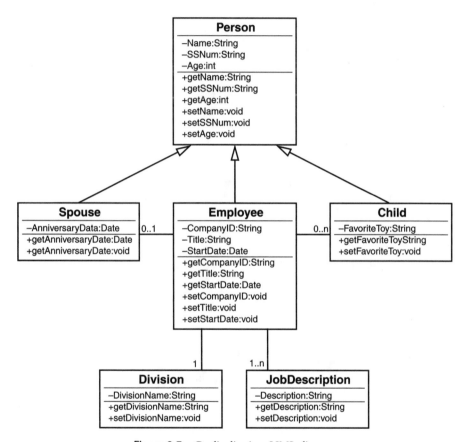

Figure 9.7   Cardinality in a UML diagram.

Multiple Object Associations

How do we represent an association that might contain multiple objects (like 0 to many children) in code? Here is the code for the `Employee` class:

```java
import java.util.Date;

public class Employee extends Person{

        private String CompanyID;
        private String Title;
        private Date StartDate;

        private Spouse spouse;
        private Child[] child;
        private Division division;
        private JobDescription[] jobDescriptions;

        public String getCompanyID() {return CompanyID;}
        public String getTitle() {return Title;}
        public Date getStartDate() {return StartDate;}

        public void setCompanyID(String CompanyID) {}
        public void setTitle(String Title) {}
        public void setStartDate(int StartDate) {}

}
```

Note that the classes that have a one-to-many relationship are represented by arrays in the code:

```java
private Child[] child;
private JobDescription[] jobDescriptions;
```

Optional Associations

One of the most important issues when dealing with associations is to make sure that your application is designed to check for optional associations. This means that your code must check to see whether the association is `null`.

Suppose in the previous example, your code assumes that every employee has a spouse. However, if one employee is not married, the code will have a problem (see Figure 9.8). If your code does indeed expect a spouse to exist, it may well fail and leave the system in an unstable state. The bottom line is that the code must check for a `null` condition, and must handle this as a valid condition.

For example, if no spouse exists, the code must not attempt to invoke a spouse method. This could lead to an application failure. Thus, the code must be able to process an `Employee` object that has no spouse.

Object Mary

OOPS!! Mary has no spouse

Must check all optional associations for null!!!

Figure 9.8   Checking all optional associations.

Tying It All Together: An Example

Let's work on a simple example that will tie the concepts of inheritance, interfaces, composition, associations, and aggregations together into a single, short system diagram.

Consider the example used in Chapter 8, with one addition: We will add an Owner class that will take the dog out for walks.

Recall that the Dog class inherits directly from the Mammal class. The solid arrow represents this relationship between the Dog class and the Mammal class in Figure 9.9. The Nameable class is an interface that Dog implements, which is represented by the dashed arrow from the Dog class to the Nameable interface.

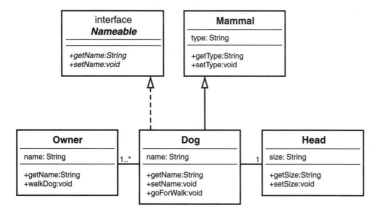

Figure 9.9   A UML diagram for the Dog example.

In this chapter, we are mostly concerned with associations and aggregations. The relationship between the Dog class and the Head class is considered aggregation because the head is actually part of the dog. The cardinality on the line connecting the two class diagrams specifies that a dog can have only a single head.

The relationship between the Dog class and the Owner class is association. The owner is clearly not part of the dog, or vice versa, so we can safely eliminate aggregation. However, the dog does require a service from the owner—the act of taking him on a walk. The cardinality on the line connecting the Dog and Owner classes specifies that a dog can have one or more owners (for example, a wife and husband can both be considered owners, with shared responsibility for walking the dog).

These relationships—inheritance, interfaces, composition, associations, and aggregations—represent the bulk of the design work you will encounter when designing OO systems.

Conclusion

In this chapter, we have explored some of the finer points of composition and its two primary types: aggregation and association. Whereas inheritance represents a new kind of already-existing object, composition represents the interactions between various objects.

The last three chapters have covered the basics of inheritance and composition. Using these concepts and your skills in the software development process, you are on your way to designing solid classes and object models.

References

Gilbert, Stephen, and Bill McCarty. *Object-Oriented Design in Java*. The Waite Group, 1998.

Coad, Peter, and Mark Mayfield. *Java Design*. Object International, 1999.

Meyers, Scott. *Effective C++*. Addison-Wesley, 1992.

10

Creating Object Models with UML

I BELIEVE VERY STRONGLY THAT LEARNING THE FUNDAMENTAL OO CONCEPTS should come before learning any specific modeling tools. Thus, the placement of this chapter was somewhat problematic. In many ways, this chapter could go first, because UML diagrams are present throughout the book, including Chapter 1. Finally, it was decided to place this chapter at the end of the "conceptual" chapters, which I consider Chapters 1–9. The remaining chapters cover more application issues rather than concepts.

This chapter is a brief overview of the Unified Modeling Language (UML) notation used in this book. It is not a comprehensive tutorial on UML because that would require an entire book unto itself, and there are many such books. For several good sources, see the references at the end of this chapter. Because this book deals with fundamentals, the UML that is used only scratches the surface of what UML actually offers.

In this book, the UML notation we are concerned with concerns modeling object-oriented systems or, as I like to call it, object-modeling. This notation includes object-models and class diagrams. Many components of UML are not used in this book. For example, because this book is concerned with object-models, UML constructs such as State Chart Diagrams and Activity Diagrams are not covered.

Each of those topics could warrant a complete chapter or more. Again, the purpose of this chapter is to provide a quick overview of object models and class diagrams so that if you are unfamiliar with class diagrams, you can pick up the basics quickly, and the examples in the book will be more meaningful.

What Is UML?

UML, as its name implies, is a modeling language. The UML User Guide defines UML as "a graphical language for visualizing, specifying, constructing and documenting the artifacts of a software-intensive system." UML gives you a standard way to write the system's blueprints. In a nutshell, UML offers a way to graphically represent and manipulate an object-oriented (OO) software system. It is not only the representation of the design of a system, but a tool to assist in this design.

UML is actually a synthesis of different modeling languages developed independently by Grady Booch, James Rumbaugh, and Ivar Jacobson, affectionately called the Three Amigos. The software company Rational brought the three modeling languages together under one roof—thus the name Unified Modeling Language. As stated above, object modeling is simply one part of UML.

However, it is important not to link UML and OO development too closely. In his article "What the UML Is—and Isn't," Craig Larman states:

Yet unfortunately, in the context of software engineering and the UML diagramming language, acquiring the skills to read and write UML notation seems to sometimes be equated with skill in object-oriented analysis and design. Of course, this is not so, and the latter is much more important than the former. Therefore, I recommend seeking education and educational materials in which intellectual skill in object-oriented analysis and design is paramount rather than UML notation or the use of a case tool.

Although UML is very important, it is much more important to learn the OO skills first. Learning UML before learning OO concepts is similar to learning how to read an electrical diagram without first knowing anything about electricity.

The Structure of a Class Diagram

A class diagram is constructed of three different parts: the class name, the attributes, and the methods (constructors are considered methods). The class diagram is essentially a rectangle that separates these three parts with horizontal lines. The book often uses a cabbie metaphor as an illustration. Figure 10.1 shows the UML class diagram representing this class.

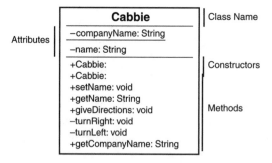

Figure 10.1 A UML diagram of the Cabbie class.

This UML diagram corresponds exactly to the following Java code:

```
/*

    This class defines a cabbie and assigns a cab
```

```java
*/
public class Cabbie {

    // Place the name of the company here
    private static String companyName = "Blue Cab Company";

    // Name of the cabbie
    private String name;

    // Car assigned to cabbie

    // Default constructor for the cabbie
    public Cabbie() {

        name = null;
        myCab = null;

    }

    // Initializing the constructor for the cabbie
    public Cabbie(String iName, String serialNumber) {

        Name = iName;
        myCab = new Cab(serialNumber);

    }

    // Set the name of the cabbie
    public void setName(String iName) {
        name = iName;
    }

    // Get the name of the cabbie
    public String getName() {
        return name;
    }

    // Give the cabbie directions
    public void giveDirections(){
    }

    // Cabbie turns right
    private void turnRight(){
    }
```

```
// Cabbie turns left
private void turnLeft() {
}

// Get the name of the company
public static String getCompanyName() {
    return companyName;
}

}
```

Take a moment to look at the code and compare it to the UML class diagram. Notice how the class name, attributes, and methods in the code relate to the designation in the class diagram. Really, that is all there is to the class diagram as far as the structure goes. However, there is a lot more information to be gleaned from the diagram. This information is discussed in the following sections.

Attributes and Methods

Besides presenting the structure of the class, the class diagram also presents information about the attributes and methods.

Attributes

Normally, attributes are not thought of as having signatures; methods get all the credit. However, an attribute has a type, and this type is represented in the class diagram. Consider the two attributes that are in the Cabbie example:

```
-companyName:String
-name:String
```

Both of these attributes are defined as strings. This is represented by the name of the attribute followed by the type (in these cases, String). There could have been attributes that were defined as int and float as well, as in this example:

```
-companyNumber:float
-companyAge:int
```

By looking at the class diagram, you can tell the type of the parameter.

Methods

The same logic used with attributes works for methods. Rather than express the type, the diagram shows the return type of the method.

If you look at the following snippet from the `Cabbie` example, you can see that the name of the method is presented, along with the return type and the access modifier (for example, `public`, `private`):

```
+Cabbie:
+giveDirections:void
+getCompanyName:String
```

As you can see here, in all three cases the access modifier is public (designated by the plus sign). If a method were private, there would be a minus sign. Each method name is followed by a colon that separates the method name from the return type.

It is possible to include a parameter list, in the following manner:

```
+getCompanyName(parameter-list):String
```

The parameters in the parameter list are separated by commas.

```
+getCompanyName(parameter1, parameter2, parameter3):String
```

Access Designations

As mentioned previously, the plus signs (+) and minus signs (-) to the left of the attributes and methods signify whether the attributes and methods are public or private. The attribute or method is considered private if there is a minus sign. This means that no other class can access the attribute or method; only methods in the class can inspect or change it.

If the attribute or method has a plus sign to the left, the attribute or method is public, and any class can inspect or modify it. For example, consider the following:

```
-companyNumber:float
+companyAge:int
```

In this example, `companyNumber` is private, and only methods of its class can do anything with it. However, `companyAge` is public, and thus it is fair game for any class to access and modify it.

If no access designation is present in the code, the system considers the access to be the default, and no plus or minus is used:

```
companyNumber:float
companyAge:int
```

Protected Access

In Java, the default type of access is protected. Protected access means that only classes in the package can access the attribute or method. A Java package is a collection of related classes that are intentionally grouped together by the developer.

Inheritance

To understand how inheritance is represented, consider the `Dog` example presented in Chapter 7, "Mastering Inheritance and Composition." In this example, the class `GoldenRetriever` inherits from the class `Dog` as shown in Figure 10.2. This relationship is represented in UML by a line with an arrowhead pointing in the direction of the parent or superclass.

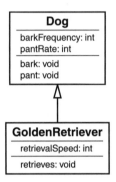

Figure 10.2   UML diagram of the `Dog` hierarchy.

The notation is straightforward, and when the line with the arrowhead is encountered, an inheritance relationship is indicated.

Indicating Interface Inheritance
A dashed line with an arrowhead indicates an interface, which is discussed in the next section.

Because Java is used for the examples in this book, we do not have to worry about multiple inheritance. However, several subclasses can inherit from the same superclass. Again, we can use the `Dog` example from Chapter 7 (see Figure 10.3).

This example illustrates two concepts when modeling an inheritance tree. First, a superclass can have more than one subclass. Second, the inheritance tree can extend for more than one level. The example in Figure 10.3 shows three levels. We could add further levels by adding specific types of retrievers, or even by adding a higher level by creating a `Canine` class (see Figure 10.4).

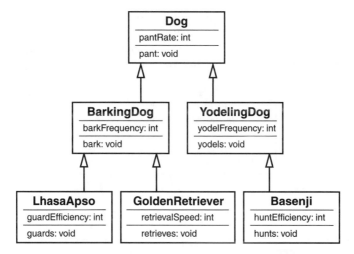

Figure 10.3   UML diagram of the expanded `Dog` hierarchy.

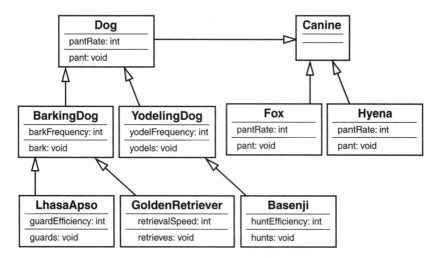

Figure 10.4   UML diagram of the `Canine` hierarchy.

Interfaces

Because interfaces are a special type of inheritance, the notations are similar and can cause some confusion. Earlier we said that inheritance is represented by a line with an arrowhead. An interface is also represented by a line with an arrowhead—but the arrowhead is connected to a dashed line. This notation indicates the relationship between inheritance and interfaces, but also differentiates them. Take a look at Figure 10.5, which is an abbreviated version of an example in Chapter 8, "Frameworks and Reuse: Designing with Interfaces and Abstract Classes." The Dog class inherits from the class Mammal and implements the interface Nameable.

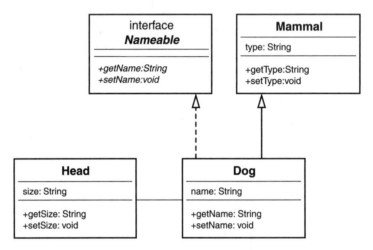

Figure 10.5   UML diagram of an interface relationship.

Composition

Composition indicates that a has-a relationship is being used. When inheritance is not the proper design choice (because the is-a relationship is not appropriate), composition is normally used.

Chapter 9, "Building Objects," discusses two different types of composition: aggregations and associations. Composition is used when classes are built with other classes. This can happen with aggregation, when a class is actually a component of another class (as a tire is to a car). Or, it can happen with association, when a class needs the services of another class (for example, when a client needs the services of a server).

Aggregations

An aggregation is represented by a line with a diamond at the head. In the car example of Chapter 9, to represent that a steering wheel is part of a car, you use the notation shown in Figure 10.6.

As with the inheritance tree, there is no limit (theoretically) to the number of levels of aggregation you can represent. In the example seen in Figure 10.7, there are four levels. Notice that the various levels can represent various aggregations. For example, although a stereo is part of the car, the radio is part of the stereo, and the tuner is part of the radio.

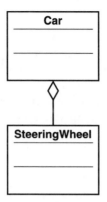

Figure 10.6   UML diagram representing composition.

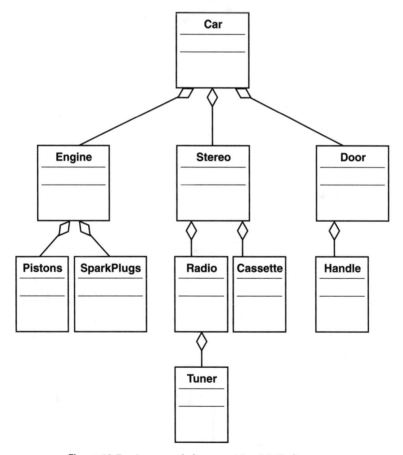

Figure 10.7   An expanded composition UML diagram.

Associations

Although aggregations represent parts of a whole, meaning that one class is logically built with parts of another, associations are simply services provided between classes.

As mentioned earlier, a client/server relationship fits this model. Although it is obvious that a client is not part of a server, and likewise a server is not part of a client, they both depend on each other. In most cases, you can say that a server provides the client a service. In UML notation, a plain line represents this service, with no shape on either end (see Figure 10.8).

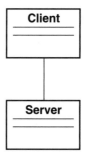

Figure 10.8   UML diagram representing an association.

Note that because there is no shape on either end of the line, there is no indication about which way the service flows. The figure shows only that there is an association between the two classes.

To illustrate, consider the example of the computer system from Chapter 9. In this case, there are multiple components, such as a computer, monitor, scanner, keyboard, and mouse. Each is a totally separate component that interacts, to some degree, with the computer itself (see Figure 10.9).

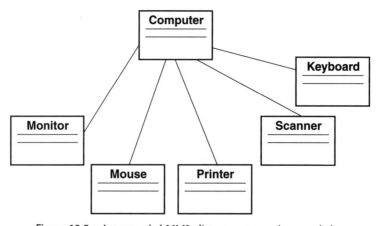

Figure 10.9   An expanded UML diagram representing association.

The important thing to note here is that the monitor is technically part of the computer. If you were to create a class for a computer system, you could model it by using aggregation. However, the computer represents some form of aggregation, as it is made up of a motherboard, RAM, and so on (see Figure 10.10).

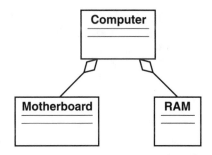

Figure 10.10   UML representation of aggregation.

Cardinality

The last issue to visit in this chapter is cardinality. Basically, cardinality pertains to the range of objects that correspond to the class. Using the earlier computer example, we can say that a computer is made up of one, and only one, motherboard. This cardinality is represented as 1. There is no way that a computer can be without a motherboard and, in PCs today, no computer has more than one. On the other hand, a computer must have at least one RAM chip, but it may have as many chips as the machine can hold. Thus, we can represent the cardinality as 1...n, where n represents an unlimited value.

Limited Cardinality Values
If we know that there are slots for six RAM chips, the upper limit number is not unlimited. Thus, the n would be replaced by a 6, and the cardinality would be 1...6.

Consider the example shown in Figure 9.7, from Chapter 9.

In this example, we have several different representations of cardinality. First, the `Employee` class has an association with the `Spouse` class. Based on conventional rules, an employee can have either no spouses or one spouse (at least in our culture, an employee cannot have more than one spouse). Thus, the cardinality of this association is represented as 0...1.

Making Design Decisions
When designing software, it is important to be sensitive to the fact that there are many different cultures in the world. Thus, making an assumption such as our assumption that an employee can have only one spouse might not be a good thing. If you intend your system to be used internationally, or even nationally within subcultures, you need to think about the design from many angles.

The association between the `Employee` class and the `Child` class is somewhat different in that an employee has no theoretical limits to the number of children that the employee can have. Although it is true that an employee might have no children, if the employee does have children, there are no limits to the number of children that the employee might have. Thus, the cardinality of this association is represented as 0...n, and *n* means that there is no upper limit to the number of children that the system can handle.

The relationship between the `Employee` class and the `Division` class states that each employee can be associated with one, and only one, division. A simple 1 represents this association. The placement of the cardinality indicator is tricky, but it's a very important part of the object model.

More Design Issues

In certain situations, it is possible for an employee to be associated with more than one division. For example, a college might allow an individual to hold concurrent positions in the mathematics department as well as the computer science department. This is another design issue you must consider.

The last cardinality association we will discuss is the association between the `Employee` class and the `JobDescription` class. In this system, it is possible for an employee to have an unlimited number of job descriptions. However, unlike the `Child` class, where there can be zero children, in this system there must be at least one job description per employee. Thus, the cardinality of this association is represented as 1...n. The association involves at least one job description per employee, but possibly more (in this case, an unlimited number).

Keeping History

You must also consider that an employee can have job descriptions for past jobs, as well as for current jobs. In this case, there needs to be a way to differentiate current job descriptions from past ones. This could be implemented using inheritance by creating a collection of job objects with an attribute indicating which job is currently active.

Conclusion

This chapter gives a very brief overview of the UML notation used in this book. As stated in the introduction, UML is a very complex and important topic, and the complete coverage of UML requires a book (or several) unto itself.

UML is used to illustrate OO examples throughout this book. You do not need UML to design OO systems, but UML is a tool that can be used to assist in the development of OO systems.

Learning UML in detail is one of the steps that you should take after you are comfortable with the underlying OO concepts. However, as happens so many times, the chicken-and-the-egg conundrum presents itself. In an effort to illustrate some of the examples in the book, it is very useful to use UML.

It's good to introduce a little of a modeling language (such as UML) and a little of a programming language (such as Java) while explaining OO concepts. Of course, we could have used C++ instead of Java, and another modeling system rather than UML. It is important to keep in mind that whatever examples you use, you should stay focused on the OO concepts themselves.

References

Lee, Richard and Tepfenhart, William. *Practical Object-Oriented Development with UML and Java*. Prentice Hall, 2002.

Ambler, Scott. *The Elements of UML Style*. Cambridge University Press, 2003.

Schmuller, Joseph. *Sams Teach Yourself UML in 24 Hours, Second Edition*. Sams Publishing, 2002.

Fowler, Martin. *UML Distilled*. Addison-Wesley Longman, 1997.

Larman, Craig. "What the UML Is—and Isn't." *Java Report*, 4(5): 20–24, May 1999.

Booch, G., I. Jacobson, and J. Rumbaugh. *The UML User's Guide*. Addison-Wesley, 1998.

11

Persistent Objects: Serialization and Relational Databases

NO MATTER WHAT TYPE OF BUSINESS application you create, a database most likely will be part of the solution. In fact, one of my favorite lines when it comes to software development is "it's all about the data." In short, no matter what hardware, operating system, applications software, and so on is used when creating a software application, the data is usually the reason for creating the system in the first place.

Persistent Object Basics

Recall that when an object is instantiated by an application, it lives only as long as the application itself. Thus, if you instantiate an `Employee` object that contains attributes such as `name`, `ss#`, and so on, that `Employee` object will cease to exist when the application terminates. Figure 11.1 illustrates the traditional object life cycle which is pretty straightforward. When an application creates an object, an object lives within the confines of that object. When the application ends, the object goes out of scope. For the object to live on, it usually must be written to some sort of persistent storage.

When the `Employee` object is instantiated and initialized, it has a specific state. Remember that the state of an object is defined by the value of it attributes. If we want to save the state of the `Employee` object, we must take some sort of action to save the state of this object. The concept of saving the state of an object so that it can be used later is called *persistence*. Thus, we used the term *persistent object* to define an object that can be restored and used independent of the application. Figure 11.2 illustrates the traditional object life cycle with persistence. In this figure, the object is created in application 1, which then writes the object out to a storage device, perhaps a database. Because the object is in persistent storage, other applications can access it. In this figure, application 2 can now instantiate an object and load the contents of the persistent object.

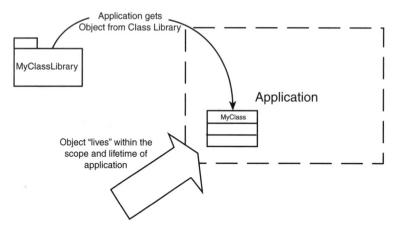

Figure 11.1 Object life cycle.

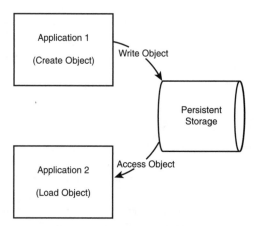

Figure 11.2 Object life cycle with persistence.

There are many ways to save the state of an object. Some of these are as follows:

- Save to a flat file
- Save to a relational database
- Save to an object database

The easiest way to demonstrate how to save an object is to create code that will write the object to a flat file, as most people do not have access to an object database or an industrial strength relational database on their home computer.

Saving the Object to a Flat File

In this section, we will use a flat file to illustrate object persistence. I define a flat file as a simple file managed by the operating system. This is a very simple concept, so don't get too caught up in this description.

Flat Files

Many people do not like to use the term *flat file*. The word *flat* implies that the object is literally flattened, and in a way it is.

One of the things you might have thought about is the fact that an object cannot be saved to a file like a simple variable—and this is true. In fact, the problem of saving the state of an object has lead to a complete software application industry, which we will discuss at length later in this chapter. Normally, when you save a number of variables to a file, you know the order and type of each variable and then you simply write them out to the file. It could be a comma delimited file, or any other protocol that you may determine.

The problem with an object is that it is not simply a collection of primitive variables. An object can be thought of as an indivisible unit that is composed of a number of parts. Thus, the object must be decomposed into a unit that can be written to a flat file. After the object is decomposed and written to a flat file, there is one major issue left to consider—recomposing the object, basically putting it back together.

Another major problem with storing objects relates to the fact that an object can contain other objects. Consider that a `Car` object might contain objects like `Engines` and `Wheels`. When you save the object to a flat file, you need to save the entire object, `Car`, `Engines`, and the like.

Java has a built-in mechanism for object persistence. Like other C-based languages, Java largely uses the concept of a stream to deal with I/O. To save an object to a file, Java writes it to the file via a `Stream`. To write to a `Stream`, objects must implement either the `Serializable` or `Externalizable` interface.

Serializing a File

As an example, consider the following code for a class called `Person`:

```
import java.util.*;
import java.io.*;

class Person implements Serializable{

    private String name;

    public Person(){
    }
```

```
public Person(String n){
    System.out.println("Inside Person's Constructor");
    name = n;
}

String getName() {
    return name;
}

}
```

This class is a simple class that contains only a single attribute representing the name of the person.

The one line of note here is the line that identifies the class as Serializable. If you actually inspect the Java documentation, you will realize that the Serializable interface really does not contain much—in fact, it is meant solely to identify that the object will be serialized.

```
class Person implements Serializable{
```

This class also contains a method called getName that returns the name of the object. Beside the Serializable interface, there is really nothing new about this class that we have not seen before. Here is where the interesting stuff starts. We now want to write an application that will write this object to a flat file. The application is called SavePerson, and is as follows:

```
import java.util.*;
import java.io.*;

public class SavePerson implements Serializable{

    public static void main(String args[]){

        Person person = new Person("Jack Jones");

        try{
            FileOutputStream fos = new FileOutputStream("Name.txt");
            ObjectOutputStream oos = new ObjectOutputStream(fos);
            System.out.print("Person's Name Written: ");
            System.out.println(person.getName());

            oos.writeObject(person);
            oos.flush();
            oos.close();
        } catch(Exception e){
            e.printStackTrace();
```

```
        }

    }

}
```

Although some of this code delves into some more sophisticated Java code, we can get a general idea of what is happening when an object gets serialized and written to a file.

> **Java Code**
>
> Although we have not explicitly covered some of the code in this example, such as file I/O, you can get into the code in much greater detail with a few of the books referenced at the end of this chapter.

By now you should realize that this is an actual application. How can you tell this? The fact that the code has a main method in it is a sure tip that this is an actual application. This application basically does three things:

- Instantiates a `Person` object
- Serializes the object
- Writes the object to the file `Name.txt`

The actual act of serializing and writing the object is accomplished in the following code:

```
oos.writeObject(person);
```

This is obviously a lot simpler than writing each individual attribute out one at a time. It is very convenient to simply write the object directly to the file

Implementation and Interface Revisited

It is interesting to note that the underlying implementation of the serialization of a file is not quite as simple as the interface used. Remember that one of the most important themes of this book is the concept of separating the implementation from the interface. By providing an intuitive and easy-to-use interface that hides the underlying implementation, life for the user is much easier.

Serializing a file is yet another great example of the difference between the interface and the implementation. The programmer's interface is to simply write the object to the file. You don't care about all of the technical issues required to actually accomplish this feat. All you care about is

- That you can write the object as an indivisible unit
- That you can restore the object exactly as you stored it

It's just like using a car. The interface to turn on the car is your key in the ignition, which starts it. Most people do not know or care about the technical issues regarding how things work—all they care about is that the car starts.

The program `SavePerson` writes the object to the file `Name.txt`. The following code restores the object.

```java
import java.io.*;
import java.util.*;
public class RestorePerson{

    public static void main(String args[]){
        try{
            FileInputStream fis = new FileInputStream("Name.txt");
            ObjectInputStream ois = new ObjectInputStream(fis);

            Person person = (Person )ois.readObject();
            System.out.print("Person's Name Restored: ");
            System.out.println(person.getName());
            ois.close();
        } catch(Exception e){
            e.printStackTrace();
        }

    }
}
```

The main line of interest here is the code that retrieves the object from the file `Name.txt`.

```java
            Person person = (Person )ois.readObject();
```

It is important to note that the object is reconstructed from the flat file, and a new instance of a `Person` object is instantiated and initialized. This `Person` object is an exact replica of the `Person` object that we stored in the `SavePerson` application. Figure 11.3 shows the output of both the `SavePerson` and the `RestorePerson` applications.

Figure 11.3   Serializing an object.

Note that in Figure 11.3 the name "Jack Jones," part of the `Person` object, is stored in the file `Name.txt` when the file is executed, and then the object is restored when `RestorePerson` is executed. When the object is restored, we can access the `Person` attribute.

Writing to a Relational Database

The relational database is perhaps one of the most important tools ever devised in the information technology field. Although some people might not buy into this statement completely, and there certainly are many other important candidates, the relational database has had a huge impact on the IT industry. In fact, the relational database remains a powerhouse despite the fact that other technologies may well be technologically better.

The reason for this is that relational databases are the database of choice for most business today. From Oracle to SQLServer in the large applications, to Microsoft Access in small to medium applications, relational databases are everywhere.

Although relational databases are a wonderful technology, they provide a bit of a problem when it comes to interfacing with objects. Just as with the issue of writing to a flat file, taking an object that's composed of other objects and writing it to relational databases, which are not designed in an object-oriented manner, can be problematic.

Relational databases are built on the concept of tables. Figure 11.4 shows a typical Microsoft Access table relationship. This relational model is so widespread that many people intuitively think of all data models in this way. However, the object-oriented model is not table-driven. Figure 11.4 shows the familiar Northwind relational database model that ships with Microsoft Access.

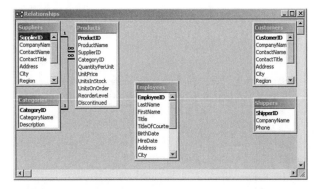

Figure 11.4 A relational model.

Because objects do not map conveniently to tables, object-oriented database systems were developed in the mid-to-late 1990s. An interesting bit of history is that although these databases represented the object-oriented model well, and might even have performed better, there was one major problem: legacy data.

Legacy Data

Legacy data is the decades of data that are stored in various storage devices. In this chapter, we consider legacy data to be the decades of data stored in relational databases.

Because most companies use relational databases, most of today's business data is stored in relational databases. This means that there is a huge investment made in these relational databases. And there is one more issue involved when it comes to these systems—they work. Even though object databases might perform better when writing objects to a database, the cost of converting all the relational data to object data is unacceptable. In short, to use an object database, a company would have to convert all of its data from a relational database to an object database. This has many drawbacks.

First, anyone who has performed the conversion of data from one database to another knows that this is a very painful process. Second, even if the data converts successfully, there is no way to know how the change of database tools will affect the application code. Third, when problems occur (and they almost always do), it's difficult to determine whether the problem is with the database or the application code. It can be a nightmare. Most company decision makers were not willing to take these chances. Thus, object databases were relegated to totally new systems written with object-oriented code.

However, we still have the following problem: We want to write object-oriented applications, but we need to access the legacy data in the relational databases. This is where object-to-relational mapping comes in.

Accessing a Relational Database

All databases applications have the following structure:

- Database client
- Database server
- Database

The database client is the user application that provides the interface to the system. Often it is a GUI application that allows users to query and update the database.

SQL

SQL stands for Structured Query Language. It is a standard way for database clients to communicate with varied vendor database systems that implement this standard.

The database client will communicate with the database server via SQL statements. Figure 11.5 displays a general solution to the database client/server model.

As an example, let's use Java to communicate to a Microsoft Access database, which is a relational database. Java uses JDBC to communicate with database servers.

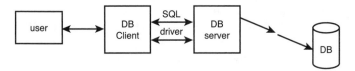

Figure 11.5   Database client server model.

JDBC
Officially, Sun does not maintain JDBC as an acronym. In the industry it is known as Java Database Connectivity.

Part of the problem with database drivers is that they tend to be vendor-specific. This is a common problem with any type of driver. As you probably know, when you purchase a new printer, the printer comes with a driver that's specific to that printer, and you might even have to download specific updates for that driver. Software products have similar issues. Each vendor has a specific protocol for communicating with its product. This solution might work well if you stay tied to a specific vendor. However, if you want to have the option to change vendors, you might be in trouble.

Microsoft has produced a standard called Open Database Connectivity (ODBC). According to Jamie Jaworski in *Java 2 Platform Unleashed*, "ODBC drivers abstract away vendor-specific protocols, providing a common application-programming interface to database clients. By writing your database clients to the ODBC API, you enable your programs to access more database servers." Take a look at Figure 11.6. This figure illustrates how ODBC fits into the picture.

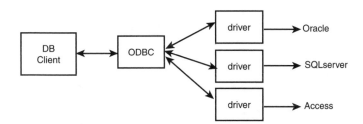

Figure 11.6   Database client server model using ODBC.

Again we see the words *abstract* and *interface* in a definition of a software API. By using ODBC, we can write applications to a specific standard, and we do not need to know the implementation. Theoretically, we can write code to the ODBC standard and not care whether the database implementation is a Microsoft Access database or an Oracle database.

As we see in Figure 11.5, the client uses the driver to send SQL statements to the database servers. Java uses JDBC to communicate with the database servers. JDBC can work in a few different ways. First, some JDBC drivers can connect directly to the database servers. Others actually use ODBC as a connection to the database servers, as in Figure 11.7. Depending on how you decide to write your applications, you might need to download various drivers and servers. This discussion is well beyond the scope of this book, because here we are concerned mainly with the general concepts. For more detailed information on how to actually set up an actual database, and how to connect to it with your applications, please refer to more advanced books such as *Java 2 Platform Unleashed*—it is not a trivial endeavor.

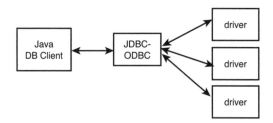

Figure 11.7   Database client server model using ODBC/JDBC.

The JDBC API provides the interface between the application program and the database. These interfaces are found in the Java package called `java.sql`. The API includes the following:

- `DriverManager`
- `Connection`
- `Statement`
- `ResultSet`

Let's explore these topics one at a time in the following sections.

Loading the Driver

Running a database application is not quite as straightforward as running the serialization example in the earlier sections of this chapter. The reason for this is that a client/server connection must be created. Connecting to a local file, as was done in the serialization example, is a fairly basic task. However, remember that when using a separate database application such as Microsoft Access, a connection must be made to the database itself.

This connection actually requires that the database driver be loaded first. To load the driver, we need to use the Driver Manager. In Java, the `DriverManager` class loads the driver into the Java app, and then JDBC is used to make the connection between the app and the database.

To load the Sun driver, you code the following line:

```
Class.forName("sun.jdbc.odbc.JdbcOdbcDriver");
```

Drivers for Other Databases
You can use drivers for database systems other than Access as well. You would then have to replace the string loaded by the forName() command.

Normally the `Class.forName` construct is used for this purpose. You could explicitly assign a reference to the driver like this:

```
java.sql.Driver d = Class.forName("sun.jdbc.odbc.JdbcOdbcDriver");
```

However, the `Driver` class is automatically registered within the application, so this is not necessary.

Making the Connection

After the driver has been loaded, the connection to the database can now be loaded using the `getConnection` method.

```
Connection con = DriverManager.getConnection(url, "id", "pwd");
```

The `url` string format depends on what driver you are using. For example, because we are using the JDBC-ODBC bridge, we can use a `url` like `"jdbc:odbc:myDriver"`.

```
Connection con = DriverManager.getConnection("jdbc:odbc:myDriver", "id", "pwd");
```

You can also connect to the datasource over the Internet with the following form:

```
jdbc:<sub-protocol>:<sub-name>
```

The actual code might look like this:

```
jdbc:odbc//companyserver.com:500/supplierdata
```

Driver Documentation
Remember that you need to consult the documentation for the driver you are using. The syntax may vary depending on the specific driver.

With the driver loaded and a connection made to the database, you are now ready to execute some SQL commands.

The SQL Statements

If you have used Microsoft Access or any other relational database, you have certainly executed SQL statements. This section will provide the basic Java syntax for building and submitting a SQL query to a relational database. It is interesting to note that from now on, everything that we do is not database-specific. Now that the driver has been loaded and the connection made, the rest is basic SQL, which is standard across database platforms.

The first thing to do is create a statement object, which at this point does not yet hold a SQL statement. You can use the `createStatement` method to execute simple SQL statements that do not contain any parameters. In this case, we are simply creating a statement object, which will obtain its SQL information a bit later.

```
Statement statement = connection .createStatement();
```

There are actually two types of SQL statements that we can execute:

- Queries
- Updates

We can use the `executeQuery` method to execute basically any type of SQL query that we are interested in. We can use the `executeUpdate` method to execute something like an update or insert operation, or anything that would actually change the database. The `executeQuery` method only inspects the database, and never physically alters it.

However, before we can actually execute the query, we must build the query. Rather than hard-code it into the `executeQuery` method, let's build a string that we can pass to the `executeQuery` method. This way, we can make the code much more configurable. Here is the code to build a query string.

```
String sqlQuery= "select PRODUCT from SUPPLIERTABLE where PRODUCT = 'Bolts'";
```

What we want to do here is query the SUPPLIERTABLE for any record that contains a PRODUCT of 'Bolts'.

SQL Strings

Note that SQL uses the single quote to delineate strings. Make sure you remember this, because many programming languages use double quotes to delineate strings. This can get confusing and produce incorrect code.

Now that we have the SQL string built, we can execute the `executeQuery` method as follows:

```
ResultSet rs = statement.executeQuery(sqlQuery);
```

You might be wondering what the `ResultSet` is. Well, remember that the SQL query performs a search of the SUPPLIERTABLE for any record that contains a PRODUCT of 'Bolts'. This implies that there might be more than one supplier that supplies bolts. Thus, we have the potential to need storage for more than one supplier. Many object-oriented languages include the concept of a collection. *Collections* not only include traditional data structures such as arrays; they also include data structures like vectors, hash tables, and so on.

Arrays and Collections

Collections are a very useful addition to the Java and .NET toolkits. One of the disadvantages of an array is that you must define its length when the array is declared. Vectors, on the other hand, are basically arrays that can grow, and thus make your programming life much easier.

When a SQL query is executed, we hold the results in a `ResultSet` object, as indicated in the previous line of code. When the `executeQuery` method is invoked, all records in the `SUPPLIERTABLE` that contain the string `'Bolts'` in the `Product` field will be returned in the `ResultSet`. One of the advantages of this is that we can iterate through the `ResultSet`. For example, suppose we want to iterate through the `ResultSet` to simply print all the suppliers that supply bolts that were culled from the database.

```
if (rs.next()){
System.out.println("rs.getString("SUPPLIERID"));
}
```

In this case, when the `ResultSet` is returned, the pointer to the collection is at position 0 (remember that Java and .NET start counting at zero). Each time `rs.next()` is called, the pointer to the collection is incremented by one, basically pointing to the next row. If there are no more rows available, `rs.next()` returns a value of `false`. In this way, you can process the `ResultSet` in a very logical and efficient manner.

If you know the specific row ahead of time, you can actually use the following code:
```
if (rs.next()){
```
```
System.out.println("rs.getString(5));
}
```

This might be very convenient, but it is obviously not that configurable.

Although the statement and the connection will close by default when the application terminates, proper programming conventions dictate that you should close them yourself. This will ensure the integrity of the database. Closing the database is just as important as closing a file. The code for this is quite simple:

```
statement.close();
connection.close();
```

Figure 11.8 illustrates the complete process as detailed in this part of the chapter.

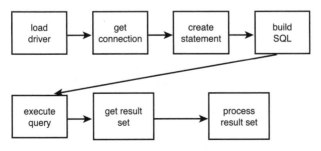

Figure 11.8 The complete process.

The complete code for this example is as follows:

```
public void findVendor(String vendorId) throws SQLException{
    String returnString = null;
    String dbUserid = "userid"; // Your Database user id
    String dbPassword = "password" ; // Your Database password
    Class.forName("sun.jdbc.odbc.JdbcOdbcDriver");
    Connection connection =
    DriverManager.getConnection("jdbc:odbc:myDriver", dbUserid ,dbPassword);
    Statement statement = connection .createStatement();
    String sqlQuery=
        "select PRODUCT from SUPPLIERTABLE where PRODUCT = 'Bolts'";
    ResultSet rs = statement.executeQuery(sqlQuery);
    if (rs.next())
    {
      System.out.println("rs.getString("SUPPLIERID"));
    }
    statement.close();
    connection.close();
}
```

Executing the Code
Remember that you will have to customize this code for whichever driver you are using and the name of your database. Thus, some editing is required before this code will run.

Conclusion

In this chapter, we covered the concept of object persistence. Previously, we had focused mainly on the fundamental object-oriented concepts, and treated the object as an entity that persists only in the life cycle of the application that creates it. We considered the issue of objects that need to persist beyond the life cycle of one or more applications.

For example, an application might need to restore an object that was created by another application or might create an object for later use by itself of other applications. One way to persist an object is to serialize it to a conventional file. Another is to use a relational database.

References

Jaworski, Jamie. *Java 2 Platform Unleashed*. Sams Publishing, 1999.

Flanagan, David, et al. *Java Enterprise in a Nutshell*. O'Reilly, 1999.

Farley, Jim. *Java Distributed Computing*. O'Reilly, 1998.

Sun Microsystems: http://java.sun.com/

12

Objects and XML: Portable Data

OBJECT-ORIENTED LANGUAGES HAVE had a strong showing in recent years. Objects have become a major technology in the programming language space. Objects have also made major headway in the definition and movement of data as well. Much excitement has been generated over the past several years regarding the portability of code. Much of Java's success was due to the fact that it was highly portable across multiple platforms. The bytecodes produced by Java could be executed on various platforms, as long as the system had a Java virtual machine loaded. The .NET framework provides portability across various languages. The assemblies produced by C# .NET can be used within Visual Basic .NET applications, or any other .NET language for that matter. Perhaps in the future there will be a programming language that will be portable across both languages and platforms.

Although portable languages are powerful tools, they are really only half of the equation. The programs that are written using these languages must process data, and this data must be turned into information. It is this information that drives businesses. Information is the other half of the portability equation.

XML is a standard mechanism for defining and transporting data between potentially disparate systems. By using object-oriented languages such as Java and C# in conjunction with an object-oriented data definition language such as XML, moving data between various destinations is much more efficient and secure. XML provides a mechanism for independent applications to share data.

Portable Data

One of the major problems in today's business environment is the diversity of the data storage formats. For example, assume that Alpha Company uses an Oracle database system to operate its sales system. Assume further that Beta Company uses a SQL Server database system to operate its purchasing system. Now consider the problem that occurs when Alpha Company and Beta Company want to do business over the Internet. Although there might be several issues, the one problem we will address here is the fact that the two databases are not directly compatible. Our goal is to create an electronic purchase order for Beta Company using SQL Server, which will interact directly with Alpha Company's sales system, which uses Oracle.

Furthermore, many companies must move the information within their organization, as well as to other companies. Much electronic commerce is transacted over both the Internet and local intranets. The types of business systems that require electronic commerce are obviously quite varied.

XML provides standards to move data in a variety of ways. Often we can think of data as moving vertically and horizontally. The term *vertical* means that data is meant to move through multiple industry groups. Industry groups such as those in accounting and finance (FpML, Financial products Markup Language) have developed their own markup languages that provide standard data definitions. These vertical applications provide the specific business models and terminology to move information across multiple industries. These standards are often called a *vocabulary*. Thus, industry groups are using XML to form a vocabulary.

The other approach to XML standards is that of horizontal applications. *Horizontal* applications are specific to a particular industry, such as retail or transportation. In all electronic commerce applications, the sharing of data is paramount. Figure 12.1 represents how data can move vertically and horizontally through various industries.

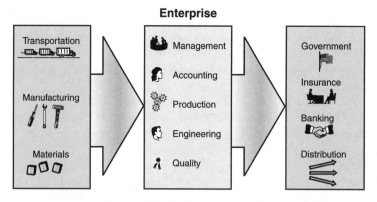

Figure 12.1 XML across industries.

One interesting example of an industry XML application is that of the RecipeML (Recipe Markup Language). RecipeML is an XML vocabulary that defines standards for industries involved with food, such as hotels, restaurants, publishers, and so on. Using RecipeML allows these industries to move data back and forth in a standard and portable manner. Some of the industries with XML-based standards include legal, hospitality, accounting, retail, travel, finance, and education.

Here is where we consider the concept of portable data. Although the low level data (at the bit level) is certainly not portable, we want to create a higher-level portability at the information level. Whereas Java and C# provide certain levels of portability at the programming language, XML provides this information portability that we considered in the previous paragraph.

The Extensible Markup Language (XML)

XML stands for Extensible Markup Language. You probably are already familiar with another markup language called HTML (Hypertext Markup Language). Both XML and HTML are descendants of SGML, the Standard Generalized Markup Language. Surprisingly, SGML appeared as early as the 1970s, and was standardized in the 1980s.

The primary function of HTML is to present data in a browser. It was actually developed to organize data using hyperlinks, and the browser is a perfect vehicle for this purpose. However, HTML is meant to format and present data, not to verify it. HTML is a subset of SGML, and HTML did not include the data verification constructs provided by the SGML specification. The reason for this is that SGML is very complex and sophisticated, and implementing SGML completely can be quite expensive. At least early on, HTML did not concern itself with the data verification issues, among other things.

XML, on the other hand, does concern itself with data verification issues. XML was defined in 1997 as a subset of SGML. XML is much more strict with its format than HTML, and was designed to represent data. XML is controlled by the World Wide Web Consortium (W3C), and is not proprietary.

One of the philosophical problems with Java is that it is proprietary (owned by Sun Microsystems). The .NET framework is also proprietary (owned by Microsoft). The beauty of XML is that it is an open technology. In fact, it is one of the few technologies that has been embraced by most of the IT industry leaders: Sun, Microsoft, IBM, and so on. Thus, XML is not about to go away anytime soon.

XML Versus HTML

Soon after XML emerged, there was speculation that XML would replace HTML. Many believed that because they were both descendants of SGML, XML was an upgrade. In reality, HTML and XML are designed for different purposes. HTML presents data, and XML describes the data. Both HTML and XML are important tools in the development of Web-based systems.

XML actually looks a lot like HTML. This is not surprising, because they come from the same source. However, XML provides two primary advantages that HTML does not—validity and well-formed documents.

HTML tags are all predefined. Tags such as <HTML>, <HEAD>, <BODY>, and so on are all defined in the HTML specification. You cannot add your own tags. Because HTML is intended for formatting purposes, this is not really a problem. XML, however, is meant to define data. To define data, you need to create your own tag names. This is where a document called the *Document Type Definition (DTD)* comes into play. The DTD is where you define the tags that describe your data. When you create an XML document, you can only use tags that are predefined. All XML documents are checked for validity. The XML processor reads the DTD and determines whether the document is valid. If the document is not valid, a syntax error is produced.

Valid Documents

You are not required to use a DTD. However, using a DTD provides a great benefit to validating XML documents. XML only checks to see whether there is a well-formed document. You need to explicitly include a DTD to check for document validity. You define the parameters in the DTD.

For example, if you are creating a purchase order system, you might want to create a tag called `<PurchaseOrder>` in the DTD. If you then misspell the tag like this: `<PurchasOrder>`, the document will not be valid.

A validated document makes XML documents much more robust. For example, HTML has many tags that are part of a pair, such as `<FONT>` and `</FONT>`. If you were to forget to close the pair with the `</FONT>` tag, the browser will still load the document, but the results could be unpredictable. HTML will make a best guess and continue. XML, when used with a DTD, will not attempt a best guess. If the document is not constructed properly, an error will be generated and the document will not be valid.

Enforcing the validity of a document and ensuring that a document is well-formed provides industries with an important mechanism to share information.

XML and Object-Oriented Languages

XML works hand-in-hand with object-oriented languages to provide what I have termed portable information. Often, an application written in a language such as Java or C# is developed to interact with XML. For example, let's revisit the example earlier in the chapter. Alpha Company, a department store, uses an Oracle database, and Beta Company, a vacuum machine manufacturer, uses a SQL Server database. Alpha Company wants to purchase some vacuum cleaners from Beta Company for its inventory. All transactions will be handled electronically over the Internet.

To make a long story short, the problem is that the data is stored in two totally different databases. Even if the databases were the same, the formats of the records in the database would most likely be designed differently. Thus, the goal is to share data between Alpha Co. and Beta Co., which means sharing the data between their databases.

Proprietary Solutions

We could of course create a proprietary application for connectivity between the Alpha and Beta Companies. Although this would work for this one application, it is preferable to have a more general solution (as is the object-oriented way). For example, Alpha Company might be in the market position to require that all suppliers conform to its specification. This is where XML shines. Alpha Company can create an XML specification to which all its suppliers can connect.

To accomplish the goal of connecting the systems of the two companies, Alpha Company can come up with an XML specification describing what information is needed to complete a transaction and store the information in its database. Here is where the object-oriented languages come in. A language such as Java can be used to extract the data from Alpha Company's SQL Server database and create an XML document based on the agreed-upon standards. This XML document can then be sent over the

Internet to Beta Company, which uses the agreed-upon XML standard to extract the information in the XML document and enters it into its Oracle database. Figure 12.2 represents the flow of data from one database to another. In this figure, data is extracted from a SQL database by an applications\parser and then sent over a network to another application\parser. This parser then converts the data into an Oracle format.

Figure 12.2   Application-to-application data transfer.

Parsers

A *parser* is a program that reads a document and extracts specific information. For example, a compiler contains a parser. The parser reads each line of a program and uses specific grammar rules to determine how to produce code. A parser would verify that a print statement was written with the appropriate syntax.

Sharing Data Between Two Companies

At this point, it is helpful to implement, to a certain extent, our example of the collaboration between the Alpha and Beta Companies. The scope of this discussion is to create the XML document that will contain a simple transaction between the two companies. For this example, we will create a simple document that contains the information contained in Table 12.1. This table defines the data that will be transferred from one company to the other.

Table 12.1   **Specification for Data to be Transferred**

Object	Category	Field
supplier		
	name	
		<companyname>
	address	
		<street>
		<city>
		<state>
		<zip>
	product	
		<type>
		<price>
		<count>

Validating the Document with the Document Type Definition (DTD)

In this example, we will be sending an XML document from Beta Company to Alpha Company. The XML document will represent a transaction that contains the name of the company, the address of the company, and certain product information. Note that the information is nested. This is to say that the overall document, which can be described as an object, is that of a supplier. Nested within the supplier identification are the company name, the company address and the product information. Note that there is also information nested within the address and the product identifications. Before going any further, let's define a DTD that will drive all the transactions for this example. The DTD is presented in Listing 12.1.

Listing 12.1   **The Data Definition Document for Validation**

```
<!-- DTD for supplier document -->
<!ELEMENT supplier ( name, address)>
<!ELEMENT name ( companyname)>
<!ELEMENT companyname ( #PCDATA)>
<!ELEMENT address ( street+, city, state, zip)>
<!ELEMENT street ( #PCDATA)>
<!ELEMENT city ( #PCDATA)>
<!ELEMENT state ( #PCDATA)>
<!ELEMENT zip ( #PCDATA)>
```

The DTD defines how the XML document is built. It is composed of tags that look very similar to HTML tags. The first line is an XML comment.

```
<!-- DTD for supplier document -->
```

XML comments provide the same function as any other programming language comments—to document the code. As with any comments, use XML comments to make the document easier to read and understand. Do not put too many comments in it, or the document will be more difficult to read. This document contains only one comment.

The remaining lines actually define the structure of the XML document. Let's look at the first line:

```
<!ELEMENT supplier ( name, address, product)>
```

This tag defines an element called `supplier`. As specified in the DTD above, a `supplier` contains a `name`, an `address`, and a `product`. Thus, when an XML parser actually parses an XML document, the document must be a `supplier`, which contains a `name`, an `address`, and a `product`.

Taking things to the next level, we see that the element name is made up of an element called <companyname>.

```
<!ELEMENT name ( companyname)>
```

The `<companyname>` element is then defined to be a data element designated by #PCDATA.

```
<!ELEMENT companyname ( #PCDATA)>
```

This tag terminates the hierarchy of the element tree. This DTD is named `supplier.dtd`. You can use any text editor to create the DTD. There are also many integrated tools that can be used to create this document as well. Figure 12.3 uses Notepad to show how a DTD for this application might look.

Document Validity

An XML document that specifies a DTD is either valid or invalid based on the DTD. If a document does not specify a DTD, the XML document is not judged either valid or invalid. An XML document can specify a DTD internally or externally. Because external DTDs provide a very powerful mechanism, we will use an external DTD here.

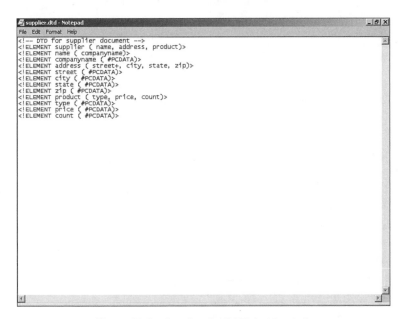

Figure 12.3   Creating the DTD in Notepad.

PCDATA

PCDATA stands for *parse character data*, and is simply standard character information parsed from the text file. Any numbers, such as integers, will need to be converted by the parser.

Integrating the DTD into the XML Document

Now that we have created the DTD, it is time to create an actual XML document. Remember that the XML document must conform to the supplier DTD we have just written.

In Table 12.2, we have identified some of the actual information that will be contained in the XML document. Again, note that the data is only contained in the end elements, not the aggregate elements, such as address and name.

Table 12.2 **Adding the Values to the Table**

Object	Category	Field	Value
supplier			
	name		
		\<companyname\>	The Beta Company
	address		
		\<street\>	12000 Ontario St
		\<city\>	Cleveland
		\<state\>	OH
		\<zip\>	24388
	product		
		\<type\>	Vacuum Cleaner
		\<price\>	50.00
		\<count\>	20

To enter this information into an XML document, we can use a text editor, just as we used for the DTD. However, as we will see later, there are tools that have been created specifically for this purpose. Figure 12.4 shows the XML document written using Notepad. This document is called beta.xml. Note that the second line ties this document to the supplier DTD that we defined earlier.

```
<!DOCTYPE supplier SYSTEM "supplier.dtd">
```

Looking at Figure 12.4, we can see that the tag structure mimics the specification. It is important to realize that the tags are nested, and that only the end tags contain any data. For example, the \<street\> tag does contain information, whereas the address tag does not:

```
<address>

<street>12000 Ontario St</street>
```

Figure 12.4   The Beta Company XML document with the DTD.

There is a better way to inspect the XML document. As stated previously, there are many tools that have been written to assist in the development of XML documents. One of these tools is called XML Notepad, and it has a similar look and feel to Notepad.

XML Notepad

Microsoft does not provide XML Notepad at this time. You can still find XML Notepad by doing a simple Internet search for "XML Notepad." You can download Microsoft's XML Validator at:

`http://msdn.microsoft.com/downloads/samples/internet/xml/xml_validator`

XML Notepad can help us understand the structure of an XML document. After you install XML Notepad, you can open the `beta.xml` file. Figure 12.5 shows what happens when you open the `beta.xml` file with XML Notepad. When the document opens, expand all of the plus signs to look at all the elements. XML Notepad lists each level of the document, starting with the supplier tag. Note that as we have said before, only the end elements contain any information.

The obvious advantage to developing the DTD is that it can be used for more than one document; in this case, for more than one supplier. Let's say we have a company that makes skates called Gamma Company, which wants to supply Alpha Company. What Gamma Company needs to do is create an XML document that conforms to the supplier DTD. Opening up this document with XML Notepad presents the picture seen in Figure 12.6.

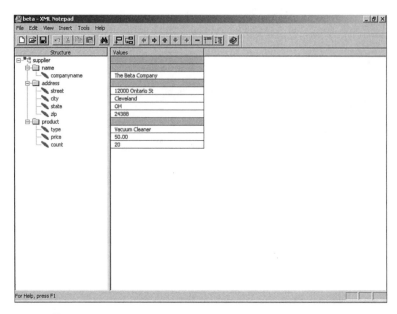

Figure 12.5 Opening the beta.xml file with XML Notepad.

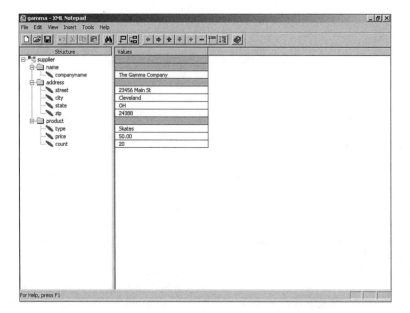

Figure 12.6 Opening the gamma.xml file with XML Notepad.

Note that `beta.xml` and `gamma.xml` conform to the supplier DTD. The question is, what happens when the XML document does not conform to the DTD? It is at this point where we see the power of the DTD. Let's purposely create an error in the `gamma.xml` file by taking out all the information pertaining to the name.

```
<name>
<companyname>The Gamma Company</companyname>
</name>
```

Basically, we are creating an invalid document—invalid per the supplier DTD. The invalid document is found in Figure 12.7. Be aware that Notepad will not indicate that the document is invalid because Notepad does not check for validity. You need to use an XML validator to check for validity.

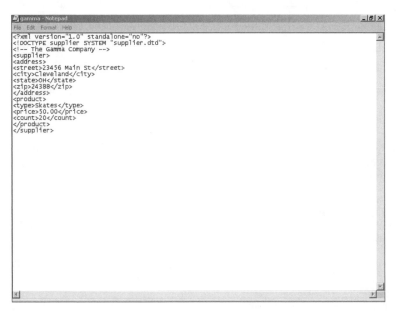

Figure 12.7   An invalid document (no name information).

We now have an invalid document based on the supplier DTD. How do we verify that it is invalid? We can open the invalid `gamma.xml` document with XML Notepad. Notice the result, as indicated in Figure 12.8. Here XML Notepad provides a dialog box that specifies that an invalid document was detected.

Because the supplier DTD was expecting a document to conform to its definition, an error was generated. In fact, the error message is quite specific as to what the problem is. The DTD was expecting the name information. Thus, to create a proper XML document for this system, all the appropriate information must be supplied and supplied in the proper format. The `<address>` tag must be provided for the document to be valid.

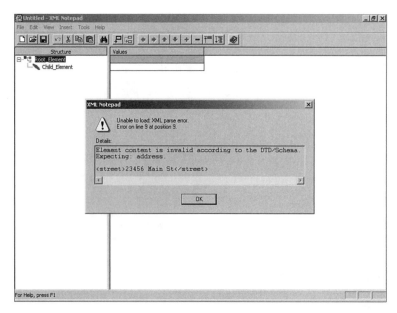

Figure 12.8   The invalid document error in XML Notepad.

One of the primary points to recognize here is that this error checking would not have happened in HTML. In fact, you can open up the XML file with a browser, as seen in Figure 12.9.

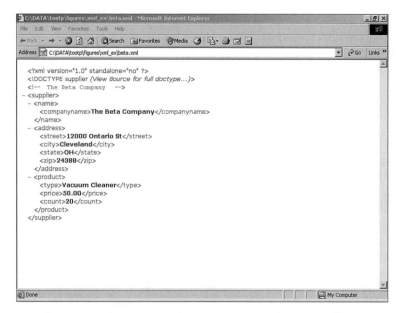

Figure 12.9   The beta.xml document opened in Internet Explorer.

Now let's see what happens when we open up the invalid `gamma.xml` document with a browser. Figure 12.10 shows the `gamma.xml` file when it's opened in Internet Explorer.

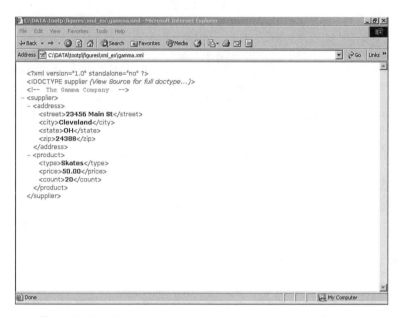

Figure 12.10   The invalid gamma.xml document opened in Internet Explorer.

Note that even though the document is invalid, the browser opens it and even displays it. This is because the browser is not checking to make sure the document conforms to the DTD, whereas XML Notepad does perform this check. In theory, this is one of the major advantages that XML provides when working with data. Although HTML is used to *display* the data, XML is used to *format* the data. This is a very important distinction.

You might ask, what benefit does XML Notepad provide in the overall supplier example, and what is it used for? To answer the first part of the question, XML Notepad, or some editor like it, allows us to verify that the document is valid early on in the process. To answer the second part of the question, XML Notepad or a similar editor can be used to actually construct the document.

Using Cascading Style Sheets

From a technical perspective, the concept of portable data often focuses on the movement of data between two points. However, getting the data from point A to point B provides no real value unless the data is presented in an appropriate way. Thus we must consider how the data used in an XML system is presented to a user.

Remember that although XML is used to define data, HTML is basically a presentation mechanism. However, XML and HTML can be used together to present data in a browser.

Although XML is not generally used for presentation purposes, there are ways to format XML. One of these is to use cascading style sheets (CSS). CSS are used heavily in the HTML world to format content. We can also use CSS to format XML, to a certain degree. Recall that the supplier XML document contains definitions for <companyname>, <street>, <city>, <state>, and <zip>. Now suppose we would like to format each of these definitions as seen in Table 12.3, which provides a specification for how we would like to format the elements of the XML documents.

Table 12.3 **Cascading Style Sheet Specification**

Tag	Font Family	Size	Color	Display
<companyname>	Arial, sans serif	24	Blue	Block
<street>	Times New Roman, serif	12	Red	Block
<city>	Courier New, serif	18	Black	Block
<state>	Tahoma; serif	16	Gray	Block
<zip>	Arial Black, sans serif	6	Green	Block

We can represent this in a CSS with the following style sheet.

```
companyname{font-family:Arial, sans-serif;
    font-size:24;
    color:blue;
    display:block;}
street {font-family:"Times New Roman", serif;
    font-size:12;
    color:red;
    display:block;}
city {font-family:"Courier New", serif;
    font-size:18;
    color:black;
    display:block;}
state {font-family:"Tahoma"; serif;
    font-size:16;
    color:gray;
    display:block;}
zip {font-family:"Arial Black", sans-serif;
    font-size:6;
    color:green;
    display:block;}
```

We can implement this style sheet by adding a line of code in our XML document:

```
<?xml-stylesheet href="supplier.css" type="text/css" ?>
```

For example, in the case of the ZIP Code, the simple text that was displayed earlier will now be formatted with a font of Arial Black, the color green, and a font size of 6. The attribute `display:block` in this case will bring each attribute to a new line.

This code is inserted in the following manner:

```
<?xml version="1.0" standalone="no"?>
<?xml-stylesheet href="supplier.css" type="text/css" ?>
<!DOCTYPE supplier SYSTEM "supplier.dtd">
<!-- The XML data -->
<supplier>
<name>
<companyname>The Beta Company</companyname>
</name>
<address>
<street>12000 Ontario St</street>
<city>Cleveland</city>
<state>OH</state>
<zip>24388</zip>
</address>
</supplier>
```

With the CSS in the XML document, we can now open the document with a browser. Figure 12.11 illustrates how this looks.

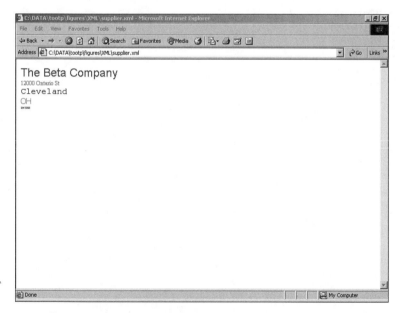

Figure 12.11   The XML document using a cascading style sheet.

Take a look at Figure 12.10 again to see how this document was presented without the CSS.

Conclusion

In this chapter we discussed many aspects of XML and why it is a very important technology within the IT community. It is rare when many major players in the IT market buy into the same standard, but this has happened in the case of XML.

From the object-oriented perspective, you should come away from this chapter with the understanding that object-oriented development goes far beyond OO languages, and encompasses the data as well. Because data is the fundamental part of information systems, it is important to design object-oriented systems that focus on the data. In today's business environment, moving data from one point to another is of paramount importance.

There are many levels of investigation you can visit when it comes to XML. This book is about concepts, and by the end of this chapter you should have a good general idea of what XML is used for, as well as some of the tools that are used. Another level that was mentioned briefly in this chapter was that of the style-sheets. By using cascading style sheets and other technologies you can better format your XML documents.

References

Hughes, Cheryl. *The Web Wizard's Guide to XML*. Addison-Wesley, 2003.

Watt, Andrew H. *Sams Teach Yourself XML in 10 Minutes*. Sams Publishing, 2003.

McKinnon, Al & Linda. *XML: Web Warrior Series*. Course Technology, 2003.

Holzner, Steven. *Real World XML*. Peachpit Press, 2001.

Deitel, et al. *XML How to Program*. Prentice Hall, 2001.

13

Objects and the Internet

P ERHAPS THE MAJOR REASON THAT objects have become so popular in the IT industry has to do with the Internet. Although object-oriented languages have been around basically as long as structured languages, it was only when the Internet emerged that objects gained wide acceptance.

Actually, the object-oriented language Smalltalk became popular during the 1980s and 1990s. And the object-based language C++ gained widespread acceptance in the 1990s. Smalltalk gained widespread support from object-oriented purists, and C++ became the first object language to become a force in the marketplace. Java, which was targeted specifically for networks, is an object-oriented language which has proved commercially successful. Now, with the introduction of .NET, object-oriented languages have become part of the mainstream. This chapter covers some of the object technologies that are used on the Internet.

Object-based Scripting Languages

The primary focus of this book has been on programming languages, specifically Java and the .NET languages. However, these object-oriented languages are not the only domains for programming with objects. We have already mentioned that C++ is not a true object-oriented programming language, but is actually an object-based programming language. Remember that C++ is considered to be object-based. Object-oriented concepts are not enforced. You can write a non–object-oriented C program using a C++ compiler. There is also a class of languages called scripting languages. JavaScript, VBScript and ASP all fall into this category.

Overall Model

Many technologies are used to create Web pages. Programming languages, scripting languages, and markup languages all have a place in the model. Although this book focuses primarily on object-oriented programming languages, it is important to understand that programming languages are just part of the puzzle.

At this point, let's take a brief pause to cover a few of the Internet-related topics that form the basis for our discussion on the Web. First, it is important to review the concepts of a client-server model. Figure 13.1 shows a typical client-server model.

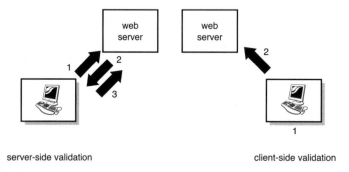

Figure 13.1 The client-server model.

It is important to understand that there really are two sides to the client-server story. As the name implies, the two parts of the model are the client side, which in many cases is the browser, and the server side, which is the physical Web server. A simple e-commerce example serves as a good study for this discussion.

Suppose you are creating a simple Web page that will request the following information from the user:

- Date
- First name
- Last name
- Age

When invoked, the HTML is rendered in the browser, which is considered the client, as shown in Figure 13.2.

This is obviously a very simple HTML document; however, it illustrates the concept of form validation quite well. One of the major issues we must address when developing a client-server system is whether we will do client validation, server validation, or both.

For example, suppose we want to verify that the date entered by the user is valid. We also want the age to be within a valid range—we certainly don't want someone to enter an age of -5. The question is whether to validate on the client side or the server side. Let's explore why this is an important discussion and how it relates to objects.

First, let's address the issue of the Age field. In most business systems, the customer information would be stored in a database that resides with the server. For security reasons, the client is not permitted to access the database directly.

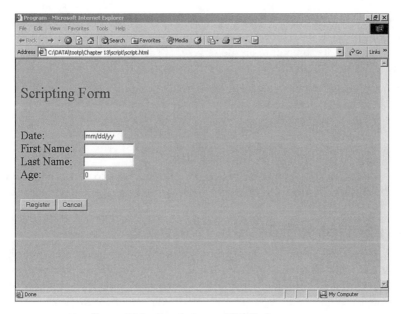

Figure 13.2   Rendering an HTML document.

Client Security
Because anyone can bring up a Web browser, it would be very foolish to let the client (browser) access the database directly. Thus, when the client needs to inspect or update the database, it must request the operation from the server. This is a basic security issue.

The reason why this example is so interesting is because it's a perfect example of the interface/implementation paradigm stressed throughout this book. In this case, the client is requesting a service from the server. The software system provides an interface through which the client can literally send messages and request specific services from the server.

In the example relating to the Age field in the HTML document in Figure 13.2, suppose a user named Mary wants to update her age in the database. After bringing up the Web page, the user enters the appropriate information on the form (including her age in the Age field) and then clicks on the Register button. In the simplest scenario, the information in the form is sent to the server, which then processes the information and updates the database.

How is the information entered in the Date field verified? If no validation is done, the software on the server accesses the Age field in Mary's record and makes the update. If the age that Mary enters is incorrect, the inappropriate age is entered in the database.

If the validation is done on the server, the software on the server checks to make sure that the Age value falls into appropriate ranges. It is also possible that the database itself does some checking to ensure that the age is within proper limits.

However, there is one major limitation to server-side validation—the information must be sent to the server. This might seem counter-intuitive, but you can ask this simple question: Why validate something on the server that can be validated on the client?

There are several points that address this question:

- Sending things to the server takes more time.

- Sending things to the server increases network traffic.

- Sending things to the server takes up server resources.

- Sending things to the server increases the potential for error.

For these reasons, as well as other possible issues, our goal is to do as much of the validation on the client as possible. This is where the scripting languages come into play.

A JavaScript Validation Example

JavaScript, as are most scripting languages, is considered to be object-based. Just like C++, you can write JavaScript applications that do not comply with object-oriented criteria. However, JavaScript does provide object-oriented capabilities. This is what makes scripting languages, like JavaScript and ASP .NET, very important in the object-oriented market. You can use objects in a JavaScript application to enhance the capabilities of your Web page. In some ways, you can think of these scripting languages as bridges between traditional programming paradigms and object-oriented models. I feel it is important to understand you can incorporate objects into your Web applications, even if you aren't using pure object-oriented technologies.

To understand the power of the scripting languages, we must first understand the limitations of HTML. HTML is a markup language that provides functionality, not inherent programming capabilities. For example, there is no way in HTML to program an IF statement or a loop. Thus, in the early days of HTML, there was little if any way to validate data on the client side. Scripting changed all of this.

With the functionality provided by JavaScript and other scripting languages, a Web page developer could actually perform programming logic within the Web page. The capability to perform programming logic allows for client-side validation. Let's look at an example of a very simple validation application using HTML and JavaScript. The code for this simple Web page is presented as follows:

```
<HTML>
<HEAD>
<TITLE>Validation Program</TITLE>
<SCRIPT LANGUAGE = "JavaScript">
function validateNumber(tForm) {
        if (tForm.result.value != 5 ) {
                this.alert ("not 5!");
        } else {
                this.alert ("Correct. Good Job!");
    }
}
```

```
</SCRIPT>
</HEAD>
<BODY>
<HR>
<P>
<H1>Validate</H1>
<FORM NAME="form">
<INPUT TYPE="text" NAME="result" value="0" SIZE="2">
<INPUT TYPE="button" VALUE="Validate" NAME="calcButton"
   onClick="validateNumber(this.form)">
</FORM>
<HR>
</BODY>
</HTML>
```

One of the first things to notice is that the JavaScript is embedded inside the HTML code. This is different from how a programming language is used. Whereas languages like Java and C# exist as independent entities, JavaScript code can only exist within the confines of HTML.

Java Versus JavaScript

Although Java and JavaScript are both based on C syntax, they are not really related.

When presented in the client browser, the Web page is very straightforward, as shown in Figure 13.3.

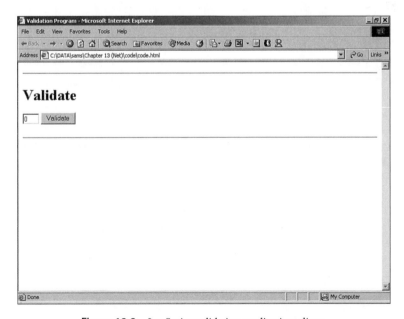

Figure 13.3   JavaScript validation application client.

In this application, a user can enter a number in the textbox and then click the Validate button. The application will then check to see whether the value is 5. If the entered value is not 5, an alert box will appear to indicate that there was a validation error, as seen in Figure 13.4.

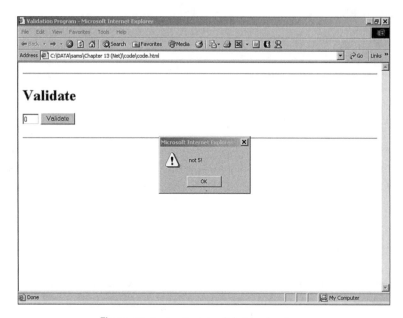

Figure 13.4   JavaScript validation alert box.

If the user enters 5, an alert box indicates that the value was as expected.

The mechanism for performing this validation is based on two separate parts of the JavaScript script:

- The function definitions
- The HTML tags

As with regular programming languages, we can define functions in JavaScript. In this example, we have a single function in the application called `validateNumber()`.

```
<SCRIPT LANGUAGE = "JavaScript">
function validateNumber(tForm) {
        if (tForm.result.value != 5 ) {
                alert ("not 5!");
        } else {
                alert ("Correct. Good Job!");
    }
}
</SCRIPT>
```

JavaScript Syntax

Because we are more concerned with the concepts in this book, please refer to a JavaScript book for the specifics of the JavaScript syntax.

The function is actually called when the Validate button is clicked. This action is captured in the HTML form definition.

```
<INPUT TYPE="button" VALUE="Validate" NAME="calcButton"
   onClick="validateNumber(this.form)">
```

When the Validate button is clicked, an object that represents the actual form is sent via the parameter list to the `validateNumber()` function.

Objects in a Web Page

Object programming is inherent to this process. We can see this by looking at the code within the `validateNumber()` function. Although there are many names, like component, widgets, controls, and so on to describe the parts of a user interface, they all relate to the functionality of an object.

There are several objects used to create this Web page. You can consider the following as objects:

- The text box
- The button
- The form

Each of these has properties and methods. For example, you can change a property of the button, like the color, as well as change the label on the button. The form can be thought of as an object made up of other objects. As you can see in the following line of code, the notation used mimics the notation used in object-oriented languages (using the period to separate the object from the properties and methods). In the line of code, you can see that the `value` property of the text box object (`result`) is part of the form object (`tForm`).

```
if (tForm.result.value != 5 )
```

Additionally, the alert box itself is an object. We can check this by using a `this` pointer in the code.

```
this.alert ("Correct. Good Job!");
```

The `this` Pointer

Remember the `this` pointer refers to the current object, which in this case is the form.

JavaScript supports a specific object hierarchy. Figure 13.5 provides a partial list of this hierarchy.

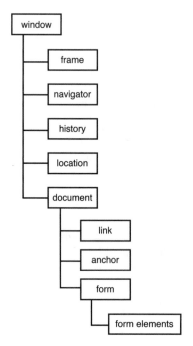

Figure 13.5 JavaScript object tree.

As with other scripting languages, JavaScript provides a number of built-in objects. As an example, we can take a look at the built-in Date class. An instance of this class is an object that contains methods such as getHours() and getMinutes(). You can also create your own customized classes. The following code demonstrates the use of the Date object.

```
<HTML>
<HEAD>
<TITLE>Date Object Example</TITLE>
</HEAD>
<BODY>
<SCRIPT LANGUAGE="JavaScript" TYPE="TEXT/JavaScript">

    days = new Array ( "Sunday", "Monday", "Tuesday",
                       "Wednesday", "Thursday", "Friday",
                       "Saturday", "Sunday");

    today=new Date

    document.write("Today is " + days[today.getDay()]);

</SCRIPT>
```

```
</BODY>
</HEAD>
</HTML>
```

Note that in this example, we actually create an `Array` object that holds the string values representing the days of the week. We also create an object called `today` that holds the information pertaining to the current date. This Web page will display the current day of the week based on the date in your computer's memory.

Java Applets Are Objects

Java Applets provide a great example of what an object actually is because they are totally self-contained and have both attributes and methods. I use this example quite a bit to explain the concept of an object.

Defining an Applet

First, let's define an *applet*. Applets were actually on the leading edge of the Internet boom. My first exposure to Java was a demo that Sun provided with one of the first beta releases of Java. The demo was that of a bouncing head. Applets were introduced to provide dynamic content to Web pages. Prior to the mid-1990s, most Web content was static: basically text and hyperlinks. As the Web became more widespread, people understandably wanted flashier Web sites.

What makes applets really interesting with regard to this book is that they are self-contained objects. Up to this point, all the Java code listings contained in this book are applications. In Java, you can create two kinds of programs: applications and applets. Applications are standalone programs that can be executed independently. Applets, on the other hand, cannot be executed independently—they must be embedded inside an HTML file. In this way, applets are similar to JavaScript. The following code is an example of a very simple applet that displays the words "Hello World Applet" in the browser.

```
// Java Applet

import java.applet.*;

import java.awt.*;


public class HelloWorld extends java.applet.Applet {

        public void paint (java.awt.Graphics g) {

            g.drawString("Hello World Applet", 50, 25);

        }


}
```

Both JavaScript code and applets are literally embedded in HTML code. We have already seen some JavaScript code. Now take a look at the following HTML code, which executes a Java applet.

```
<HTML>
<HEAD>
<TITLE>Java Example</Title>
</HEAD>

<BODY>
This is my page<br>
Below you see an applet<br>
<br>
<APPLET Code="HelloWorld.class" width=200 Height=100>
</APPLET>
</BODY>
</HTML>
```

An applet can only be executed within a browser.

The Object Tag

Although the applet tag <APPLET> was created to work with Java applets, a newer tag called the object tag (<object>), is now used to embed various types of objects in Web pages, including Java applets.

To illustrate the object properties of an applet, consider an applet that provides a banner, which displays several messages that fade in and out one at a time. This applet has all the properties of a valid object—attributes and behaviors. The attributes are things such as color, height, width, and so on. In this case, the behavior is the ability to fade in and out. So, we have met the definition of an object, as the applet has both attributes and behaviors.

Applet Inheritance

A Java applet actually inherits many of its attributes and behaviors from the Java Applet class. This is yet another way that an applet illustrates what an object actually is.

One of the more interesting things about an applet is that it provides a great example of the distributed nature of an object. Consider that an applet is an object that travels across a network. When a Web page is loaded into a browser and an applet tag is encountered, the browser (client) attempts to load the applet by making a request to the server—the same server that contained the original HTML page. This applet is a self-contained object, and is sent across the wire into the browser as attributes and behavior. At this point, a Java virtual machine, which is part of the browser, is launched to execute the applet.

Consider the example of an applet that displays a flashing banner on the Web page. The code that makes the banner flash is actually part of the object. The attributes that represent the color and so on are also part of the object. Even though the color attribute is part of the object, you can actually change the default value by providing a parameter in the HTML code. In this way, each HTML document that uses the applet can be customized. You can actually send parameters to the Java applets by using the following code.

```
<param Name=NameOfParameter Value="ValueOfParameter">
```

Because Java is actually a programming language, it is much better suited to sophisticated programming tasks than JavaScript, or any of the scripting languages. For example, Java can handle the Dynamic Object Model (DOM) object hierarchy described in Chapter 12, "Objects and XML: Portable Data." Java can also create sophisticated user interfaces using its Swing capabilities.

Swing

Swing is the Java package that provides robust user interface capabilities for applets as well as applications. Information on Swing can be found at the Sun Microsystems Web site at http://www.javasoft.com.

JavaBeans Are Objects

Swing is just one of the areas where Java uses packages of classes to assist in the development of software. Because objects are the complete packages we describe, we can extrapolate this concept to that of components. There are many definitions of components; depending on what language or model you're using, you may run into different terms. I teach students that they might encounter one or more of these terms:

- Component
- Control
- Widget
- Bean

Typically, the term *control* is associated with Microsoft products like Visual Basic. The term JavaBean, or simply *bean,* is associated with Java. In his book *Building Web Applications with UML*, Jim Conallen defines the JavaBean component model as consisting of the following:

- Introspection—Enables an external component or tool to analyze how a JavaBean works. It can expose the details of its interface.
- Events—Allow JavaBeans to communicate and connect with one another.
- Properties—Allow developers to customize JavaBeans.
- Persistence—Allows customized JavaBeans to retain their customization.

In essence, a JavaBean is a self-contained, self-aware object. As with applets, beans offer a really good example of what an object should be. Not only are beans self-contained and self-aware, they're objects that are responsible for themselves. Figure 13.6 illustrates the JavaBean component model.

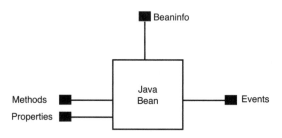

Figure 13.6   The JavaBean model.

A good example of a JavaBean is some sort of user interface component, such as a button. A class is created for the button GUI—a class most probably called `Button`. This `Button` class has many of the typical object characteristics. First, it probably inherits from some other GUI object—perhaps an object called `Component`. Regardless of how the `Button` class is built, it is a totally reusable component. As with all properly built classes, the `Button` class is responsible for itself. Thus, the `Button` class knows how to build itself, respond to appropriate events, and so on.

JavaBeans and GUIs

Quite often, components are thought of as user interface components. Although it is true that components fit naturally into the GUI model, a component can be a non-GUI design as well. You can create a command-line-based component with absolutely no GUI involved. Basically, any type of Java object can be implemented as a JavaBean.

One of the neat things about components such as JavaBeans is that they can be combined to create even more useful and complex components. For example, suppose you want to create a special dialogue box that allows a user to verify that she wants to save a file. You can create a component called `Verify` to perform such a task. Figure 13.7 displays the familiar Microsoft Word implementation of this design. This `Verify` component provides a container that holds three `Button` objects.

Components like this provide a standard look and feel, as well as reusable code. Java can even use components that were written in other languages via special interfaces. Microsoft's Component Object Model (COM) is one example of such a language.

One thing that is important to realize is that JavaBeans are not the same thing as Enterprise JavaBeans. Although they are both components, JavaBeans target the desktop. These components are used for the types of things that we discussed previously, such as client graphical user interfaces. Enterprise JavaBeans, however, are components that target the server. As the name implies, Enterprise JavaBeans are used over a network. Figure 13.8 shows the Enterprise JavaBean model, which we will explore in greater detail in the next chapter.

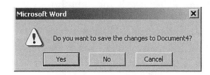

Figure 13.7   Higher–level component.

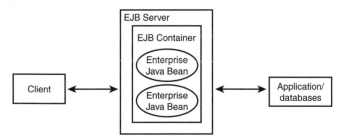

Figure 13.8   The EJB model.

Perhaps the most important aspect of a JavaBean is that applications can inspect the bean to determine what it can do and how to use it. This is often called *introspection*. For example, suppose you are using a graphical user interface. With the toolkit visible, you can inspect all the components available before you even decide to use one. You can also inspect these components to determine what properties and methods are available. Introspection is very important for developing components and objects in general. In this way, you can develop reusable components that can be stored in a collection, such as a package or library. Or, you can place a component on a server and let applications over the network use the component. We will cover this topic further in the next chapter.

Conclusion

In this chapter, we have covered some of the technology available for using objects in conjunction with Web applications. It is important to differentiate between objects embedded in a Web page (such as JavaScript) or objects that are really applications but are used within a Web application (such as Java applets).

In the context of graphical user interfaces, it is common to use components, such as `Buttons`. However, components are not limited to GUIs.

References

Conallen, Jim. *Building Web Applications with UML*. Addison-Wesley, 2000.

Jaworski, Jamie. *Java 2 Platform Unleashed*. Sams Publishing, 1999.

14

Distributed Objects and the Enterprise

IN THE PAST SEVERAL YEARS, THE TERM *enterprise computing* has become a major part of the information technology lexicon. Today, much of the major development in the area of IT technology is that of enterprise computing. But what does *enterprise computing* actually mean?

Perhaps the most basic definition of enterprise computing is that it's essentially distributed computing. *Distributed computing* is just what the name implies, a distributed group of computers working together over a network. In this context, a network can be a proprietary network or the Internet.

The power of distributed computing is that computers can share the work. In a truly distributed environment, you do not even need to know what computer is actually servicing your request—in fact, it might be better that you don't know. For example, when you shop online you connect to a company's Web site. All you know is that you are connecting using a URL. However, the company will connect you to whatever physical machine is available.

Why is this desirable? Suppose that a company has a single machine to service all the requests. Then consider what would happen if the machine crashes. Now let's suppose that the company can distribute the online activities over a dozen machines. If one of the machines goes down, the impact will not be as devastating.

Also consider the situation when you download files from a Web site. You probably have encountered the situation in which the download site provides you with links to a number of sites, and then asks you to choose the site closest to you. This is a means of distributing the load over the network. Computer networks can balance the load themselves. Figure 14.1 provides a diagram of how a distributed system might look.

This book is focused on objects and object-oriented concepts. So in many ways, the entities we are interested in are called distributed objects. The fact that objects are totally self-contained makes them perfect for distributed applications. The thrust of this chapter is this: If your application (client) requires the service of some object, that object can reside anywhere on the network. Let's explore some of the technologies that exist for distributed objects.

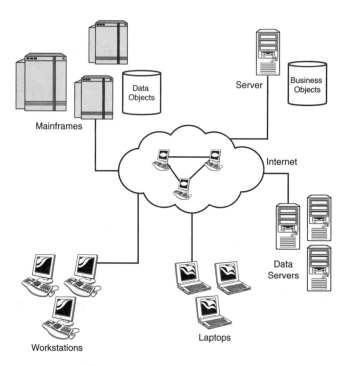

Figure 14.1   Distributed computing.

The Common Object Request Broker Architecture (CORBA)

One of the primary tenets of this book is that objects are totally self-contained units. With this in mind, it doesn't take much imagination to consider sending objects over a network. In fact, we have used objects traveling over a network in many of the examples throughout this book. A Java applet is a good example of an object being downloaded from a server to a client (browser).

The entire premise of the enterprise is built on the concept of distributed objects. There are many advantages to using distributed objects; perhaps the most interesting is the fact that a system can theoretically invoke objects anywhere on the network. This is a powerful capability, and is the backbone for much of today's Internet-based business. Another major advantage is that various pieces of a system can be distributed across multiple machines across a network.

The idea of accessing and invoking objects across a network is a powerful technique. However, there is one obvious fly in the ointment—the reoccurring problem of portability. Although we can, of course, create a proprietary distributed network, the fact that it is proprietary leads to obvious limitations. The other problem is that of programming language. Suppose a system written in Java would like to invoke an object written in C++. In the best of all worlds, we would like to create a non-proprietary, language-independent framework for objects in a distributed environment. This is where CORBA comes in.

OMG

An organization you should become very familiar with is the Object Management Group (OMG). OMG is the keeper of the keys for many standard technologies, including CORBA and UML, among others. Find out more at http://www.omg.org.

The main premise of *CORBA (Common Object Request Broker Architecture)* is this: Using a standard protocol, CORBA allows programs from different vendors to communicate with each other. This interoperability covers hardware and software. Thus, vendors can write applications on various hardware platforms and operating systems using a wide variety of programming languages, operating over different vendor networks.

CORBA can be considered the middleware for a variety of computer software applications. Whereas CORBA represents only one type of middleware (later we will see some other implementations, like Java's RMI), the concepts behind middleware are consistent, regardless of the approach taken. Basically, *middleware* provides services that allow application processes to interact with each other over a network. These systems are often referred to as *multi-tiered systems*. For example, a 3-tiered system is presented in Figure 14.2. In this case, the presentation layer is separated from the data layer by the allocation layer in the middle. These processes can be running on one or more machines. This is where the term *distributed* comes into play. The processes (or as far as this book is concerned, the objects) are distributed across a network. This network can be proprietary, or it might be the Internet.

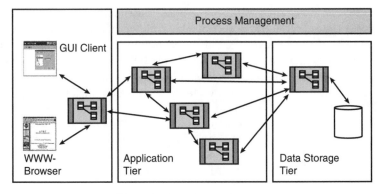

Figure 14.2   A 3-tiered system.

This is where objects fit into the picture. The OMG states that "CORBA applications are composed of *objects*." So, as you can tell, objects are a major part of the world of distributed computing. The OMG goes on to say that these objects "are individual units of running software that combine functionality and data, and that frequently (but not always) represent something in the real world."

One of the most obvious examples of such a system is that of a shopping cart. We can relate this shopping cart example to our earlier discussions on the instantiation of objects. When you visit an e-commerce site to purchase merchandise, you are assigned your own individual shopping cart. Thus, each customer has her own shopping cart. In this case, each customer will have an object, which includes all the attributes and behaviors of a shopping cart object.

Although each customer object has the same attributes and behaviors, each customer will obviously have different attribute assignments, such as name, address, and so on. This shopping cart object can then be sent anywhere across the network. There will also be other objects in the system that represent merchandise, warehouses, and so on.

Wrappers

As we explained earlier in the book, one common use of objects is that of a *wrapper*. Today there are a lot of applications written on legacy systems. In many cases, changing these legacy applications is either impractical or not cost-effective. One elegant way to connect legacy applications to newer distributed systems is to create an object wrapper that interfaces with the legacy system.

One of the benefits of using CORBA to implement a system such as our shopping cart application is that the objects can be accessed by services written in different languages. To accomplish this task, CORBA defines an interface to which all languages must conform. The CORBA concept of an interface fits in well with the discussion we had about creating contracts in Chapter 8, "Frameworks and Reuse: Designing with Interfaces and Abstract Classes." The CORBA interface is called the *Interface Definition Language (IDL)*. For CORBA to work, both sides of the wire, the client and server, must adhere to the contract as stated in the IDL.

Yet another term we covered earlier in the book is used in this discussion—marshaling. Remember that marshaling is the act of taking an object, decomposing it into a format that can be sent over a network, and then reconstituting it at the other end. Thus, by having both the client and the server conform to the IDL, an object can be marshaled across a network regardless of the programming language used.

All the objects that move around in a CORBA system are routed by an application called an Object Request Broker (ORB). You might have already noticed that the acronym ORB is actually part of the acronym CORBA. The ORB is what makes everything go in a CORBA application. The ORB takes care of routing requests from clients to objects, as well as getting the response back to the appropriate destination.

Languages Supported

At this point in time, CORBA supports the following languages: C, C++, Java, COBOL, Smalltalk, Ada, Lisp, Python, and IDLscript.

Again, we can see how CORBA and distributed computing works hand-in-hand with the concepts we have studied throughout this book. The OMG states that

> *This separation of interface from implementation, enabled by OMG IDL, is the essence of CORBA.*

Furthermore,

> *Clients access objects only through their advertised interface, invoking only those operations that the object exposes through its IDL interface, with only those parameters (input and output) that are included in the invocation.*

To get a flavor of what the IDL looks like, consider the e-business example we used in Chapter 8. In this case, let's revisit the UML diagram of Figure 8.7 and create a subset of the Shop class. If we decide to create an interface of Inventory, we could create something like the following:

```
interface Inventory  {
    string[]  getInventory ();
    string[]  buyInventory (in string product);
}
```

In this case, we have an interface that defines how to list and purchase inventory. This interface is then compiled into two entities:

- Stubs that act as the connection between the client and the ORB
- A skeleton that acts as the connection between the ORB and the object

These IDL stubs and skeletons form the contract that all interacting parties must follow. Figure 14.3 shows an illustration of how the various CORBA parts interact.

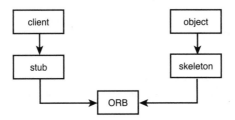

Figure 14.3   CORBA parts.

The really interesting thing about all this is that when a client wants the service of some object, it does not need to know anything about the object it is requesting, including where it resides. The client simply invokes the object (and the service) it wants. To the client, it appears that this invocation is local, as though it's invoking an object that's on the local system. This invocation is passed through the ORB. If the ORB determines that the desired object is actually a remote object, the ORB routes the request. If everything works properly, the client will not know where the actual object servicing it resides. Figure 14.4 shows how the ORB routing works over a network.

Internet Inter-ORB Protocol

Just as HTTP is the protocol for Web page transactions, IIOP (Internet Inter-ORB Protocol) is a protocol for distributed objects that can be written in a variety of programming languages. IIOP is a fundamental piece of standards like CORBA and Java RMI.

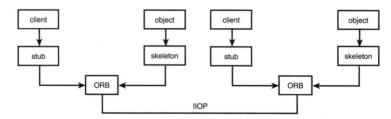

Figure 14.4   ORB routing.

Java's Remote Method Invocation (RMI)

Although CORBA is very powerful, it is also somewhat complicated. CORBA is independent of many constraints, including programming languages. To provide interoperability across hardware platforms, operating systems, networks, and so on, a certain level of complexity is inherent. One obvious way to overcome this complexity is to limit the variables. For example, we could limit the programming language to a single language. Of course, this will impose a major constraint, but it will also make the implementation much more stable.

Java provides such an implementation called Remote Method Invocation (RMI). RMI provides many of the same functions that CORBA provides; however, it is limited to the Java programming language, and thus is not really an open industry standard.

Java 2 Standard Edition

RMI is part of the Java 2 Standard Edition (J2SE). The Java 2 SDK Standard Edition V1.4 provides many enhancements to RMI. RMI is also supported by the Java 2 Micro Edition (J2ME).

In the previous section on CORBA we related many of the concepts associated with distributed computing. RMI implements theses distributed computing concepts in a proprietary way. Although the obvious disadvantage of using a proprietary is the loss of language support, there are certain advantages. The fact that RMI is part of the core Java services means that it integrates seamlessly into any Java application you might develop. This makes the implementation much more stable. You can also take advantage of the various Java services, such as garbage collection.

Using RMI, a Java object can invoke objects on other Java Virtual Machines on networked computers. Again, the concept is very similar to the CORBA model. Figure 14.5 shows a simple illustration of the RMI model.

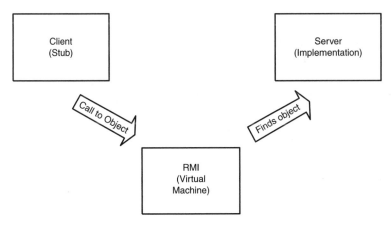

Figure 14.5 The RMI Interface/Implementation model.

One of the primary differences between RMI and CORBA is that there really is no distinct ORB. The client and the server communicate via a transport layer that is basically embedded in the virtual machines of the various applications.

As with CORBA, RMI has the concept of stubs and skeletons. A layer called the *remote reference layer* takes care of referencing the remote objects, using the Transport layer's TCP/IP connection to the server. Again, just as in CORBA, the client calls the object just as though it were a local object. Figure 14.6 shows what the complete RMI model looks like.

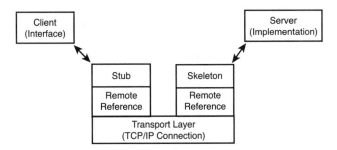

Figure 14.6 The RMI stub/skeleton model.

To illustrate, the server has provided the client with various stubs it can use to invoke objects. The client invokes a specific service provided by the server.

Java's Enterprise JavaBeans

Yet another distributed networking option available to Java programmers is that of Enterprise JavaBeans (EJBs). EJBs provide a standard distributed component model. Do not confuse EJBs with components called JavaBeans. Standard JavaBeans are similar to controls used in the Microsoft model, and are not Enterprise JavaBeans. EJBs are a distributed technology based in part on RMI. Enterprise JavaBeans are considered RMI objects as well as a JavaBean component.

Defining EJBs is somewhat problematic, because the definition includes other terms that themselves need definitions. It is often helpful to get the definition straight from the horse's mouth. Sun defines Enterprise JavaBeans in the following manner.

> *The Enterprise JavaBeans specification defines an architecture for a transactional, distributed object system based on components. The specification mandates a programming model; that is, conventions or protocols and a set of classes and interfaces which make up the EJB API. The EJB programming model provides bean developers and EJB server vendors with a set of contracts that defines a common platform for development. The goal of these contracts is to ensure portability across vendors while supporting a rich set of functionality.*

Enterprise JavaBeans include the following functionality:

- Transaction processing
- Security
- Persistence
- Resource-pooling facilities

Enterprise JavaBeans are actually components that live within an entity called an EJB *container*. The container services the EJB in a similar manner to the way a browser hosts a Java applet. The container manages the aspects mentioned previously, transaction processing, security, persistence, and resource-pooling faculties.

Figure 14.7 illustrates how the EJB container model integrates the preceding bullet items. Enterprise JavaBeans take the concept of distributed computing to a higher level than RMI. Because it encapsulates all the bullet points listed previously, the programmer is free to concentrate on solving business problems, as opposed to figuring out the code necessary to implement the various technologies such as security, transaction processing, and so on. EJBs provide a general-purpose infrastructure so that the developer can concentrate on the business logic.

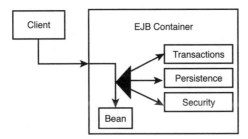

Figure 14.7   The EJB container model.

Transaction Management

One EJB advantage is that of transaction management. EJBs manage transactions so that they can be rolled back at any time before the transaction is committed. A shopping cart example is a good illustration of this concept. If you are in the process of purchasing a product and the connection goes down, you'll want to make sure the system remains in a safe and secure state. The purchase should not be complete until the transaction is actually committed.

The EJB API is an extension to Java. The components of the EJB architecture are illustrated in Figure 14.8.

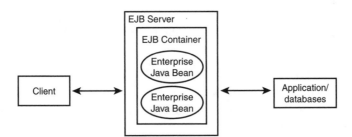

Figure 14.8   The EJB model.

The EJB container is basically the interface between the Enterprise JavaBean and the rest of the world. In many ways, it can be thought of as a proxy. If you have an application that requires the service of a particular EJB, the application must actually interface with the container—not the EJB. A client never interfaces with an EJB directly. Again, this is where the public interface (public methods) comes into play. A client application would invoke public methods provided by the container, which would then manage the access to the EJB itself by invoking the EJB's methods. There are actually two types of containers:

- Session containers
- Entity containers

Session containers hold transient EJBs that are not persistent. Basically, the state of the EJBs is not saved. This is akin to creating a shopping cart EJB that will not survive (persist) if, for instance, you close the browser. There are many uses for session beans; however, there are obvious problems as well. Suppose you have a shopping cart open and then the connection to your machine breaks.

The EJB and Container Contract

Similar to the contracts discussed in Chapter 8, there is a contract between an Enterprise JavaBean and an EJB container. A communication mechanism is created to allow the Enterprise JavaBean and the EJB container to pass information back and forth.

Entity containers hold EJBs that do survive (persist). In short, the state of the EJBs is saved between calls to the container.

EJB servers are very similar to the concept of the CORBA ORB. The EJB server provides services such as the execution environment, transaction services, and so on. The EJB server is also responsible for making the EJB available on the network.

All this talk about EJBs is great, but they are not useful unless you can actually find them. This is a problem that affects many industries and marketing strategies. You can have the greatest product in the world, or in this case the greatest EJB in the world, but if nobody knows about the EJB, it is useless. So, the question is: How does an EJB client find the EJB it's looking for?

This is where the Java Naming and Directory Interface (JNDI) comes into play. By using the JNDI, an EJB client can find the desired services (via the EJB container), and then invoke the desired services provided by the EJB interface methods.

Types of Enterprise JavaBeans

Although the containers provide the actual interface to the client, most people think in terms of the actual JavaBean itself. As with the EJB containers, Enterprise JavaBeans themselves come in two flavors:

- Session beans
- Entity beans

Session Beans

As the name implies, session beans persist for only as long as the actual session. After the session terminates, the session bean terminates. Normally, a session bean is associated with only a single client. Session beans are used when the business model calls for situations when the EJB does not have to survive beyond the session for other applications to user. A session bean can be either one of the following:

- Stateful
- Stateless

Sometimes a session bean needs to continuously communicate with the client. Often, this is called *conversational mode*. In short, the client might need to invoke multiple methods on the EJB, and needs the EJB to maintain its state. Based on our knowledge regarding the state of an object, we can apply this to the EJB.

For example, when the client invokes a method of an EJB and the method terminates, certain state information should still be stored in the EJB's attributes. As we know, the attributes represent the state of an object. The next time the client invokes a method on the EJB, the state of the EJB should still be stored in the attributes. We can say that the client is conversing with the EJB. When this *conversation* is taking place, the EJB is said to be *stateful*.

On the other hand, in the *stateless* mode, an EJB does not converse with the client. For example, a client can invoke a method, which might actually set the attributes of the EJB. However, when the method returns, the state is not tracked. When the next method invocation is made, the pervious state is irrelevant, and the new state is maintained only for the scope of the method's call.

Stateful or Stateless
Regardless of whether a session bean is stateful or stateless, the session bean does not persist.

For example, if an application creates a shopping cart, it would be in the best interest of the store to save the contents of the shopping cart if the system connection goes down. If this is properly done, a user would simply have to reconnect, and the shopping cart would still be available. In this way, the customer does not have to suffer the frustration of having to start over. In this situation, a session bean is not the proper way to design the system because the information will be lost when the session is lost.

Entity Beans

Whereas session beans can be stateful or stateless, entity beans always have a specific state. Entity beans can also serve multiple clients. Thus, in the shopping cart example, using an entity bean will allow for the saving of the state of the shopping cart EJB. You might also want multiple clients to have access to the EJB, but that is probably not the best design for a shopping cart because the user should have a single session. Entity beans can survive both expected and unexpected system terminations. There are also two flavors of entity beans:

- Container-managed persistence
- Bean-managed persistence

In container-managed persistence, the container is responsible for saving the state of the EJB. Because the EJB is in charge, the state of the EJB can be persisted in any type of storage device. In short, persistence is automatically dealt with by the EJB contained. The EJB itself does not contain any SQL code.

In bean-managed persistence, the EJB itself is responsible for the calls to the database and thus contains SQL code. This makes bean-managed persistence much less flexible.

Conclusion

This chapter covered the concepts, and some of the corresponding technologies, for what I call distributed objects. Distributed objects fall into many categories covered by many terms. Some of these categories and terms include the following:

- Enterprise computing
- Distributed computing
- Middleware

Whatever the terminology used, the power of distributed computing is that many computers operating on the same network share the workload. This has several major advantages—not the least of which relates to security and integrity issues. I would encourage you to read further in this area and explore the implementations provided by various vendors, including Microsoft and Sun.

References

Conallen, Jim. *Building Web Applications with UML*. Addison-Wesley, 2000.

Jaworski, Jamie. *Java 2 Platform Unleashed*. Sams Publishing, 1999.

Flanagan, David, et al. *Java Enterprise in a Nutshell*. O'Reilly, 1999.

Farley, Jim. *Java Distributed Computing*. O'Reilly, 1998.

OMG CORBA FAQ:
http://www.omg.org/gettingstarted/corbafaq.htm#TotallyNew

Sun Online Training:
http://developer.java.sun.com/developer/onlineTraining/EJBIntro/EJBIntro.html

15

Design Patterns

ONE OF THE REALLY INTERESTING THINGS about software development is that when you create a software system, you are actually modeling a real-world system. We have seen this concept throughout this book. For example, when we discussed using inheritance to abstract out the behaviors and attributes of mammals, the model was based on the true natural model, and not a contrived model that we created for our own purposes.

Thus, when we create a mammal class, we can use it to build countless other classes, such as dogs and cats and so on, because all mammals share certain behaviors and attributes. This works when we study dogs, cats, squirrels, and other mammals, because we can see patterns. These patterns allow us to inspect an animal and make the determination that it is indeed a mammal, or perhaps a reptile, which would have other patterns of behaviors and attributes.

Throughout history, humans have used patterns in many aspects of life, including engineering. These patterns go hand-in-hand with the holy grail of software development: software reuse. In this chapter, we will consider design patterns, a relatively new area of software development.

Design patterns are perhaps one of the most influential developments that have come out of the object-oriented movement in the past several years. Patterns lend themselves perfectly to the concept of reusable software development. And because object-oriented development is all about reuse, patterns and object-oriented development go hand-in-hand.

The basic concept of design patterns revolves around the principle of best practices. By *best practices*, we mean that when good and efficient solutions are created, these solutions are documented in a way so that others can benefit from previous successes.

One of the most important books on object-oriented software development is *Design Patterns: Elements of Reusable Object-Oriented Software* by Erich Gamma, Richard Helm, Ralph Johnson, and John Vlissides. This book was an important milestone for the software industry, and has become so entrenched in the computer science lexicon that the book's authors have become known simply as the Gang of Four. In writings on object-oriented topics, you will often see the Gang of Four referred to simply as the GoF. The intent of this chapter is to explain what design patterns are. (Explaining each design pattern is far beyond the scope of this book, and would take more than one volume.) To accomplish this, we will explore each of the three categories (creational, structural, and behavioral) of design patterns as defined by the Gang of Four and provide a concrete example of one pattern in each category.

Why Design Patterns?

The concept of design patterns did not necessarily start with the need for reusable software. In fact, the seminal work on design patterns is about constructing buildings and cities. As Christopher Alexander noted in *A Pattern Language: Towns, Buildings, Construction*: "Each pattern describes a problem which occurs over and over again in our environment, and then describes the core of the solution to that problem, in such a way that you can use the solution a million times over, without ever doing it the same way twice."

The Four Elements of a Pattern

The GoF describe a pattern as having four essential elements:

- The *pattern name* is a handle we can use to describe a design problem, its solutions, and conse-quences in a word or two. Naming a pattern immediately increases our design vocabulary. It lets us design at a higher level of abstraction. Having a vocabulary for patterns lets us talk about them with our colleagues, in our documentation, and even to ourselves. It makes it easier to think about designs and to communicate them and their tradeoff to others. Finding good names has been one of the hardest parts of developing our catalog.

- The *problem* describes when to apply the pattern. It explains the problem and its content. It might describe specific design problems, such as how to represent algorithms as objects. It might describe class or object structures that are symptomatic of an inflexible design. Sometimes the problem will include a list of conditions that must be met before it makes sense to apply the pattern.

- The *solution* describes the elements that make up the design, their relationships, responsibilities, and collaborations. The solution doesn't describe a particular concrete design or implementation, because a pattern is like a template that can be applied in many different situations. Instead, the pattern provides an abstract description of a design problem, and how a general arrangement of elements (classes and objects in our case) solves it.

- The *consequences* are the results and tradeoffs of applying the pattern. Although consequences are often unvoiced, when we describe design decisions, they are critical for evaluating design alterna-tives and for understanding the costs and benefits of the applying pattern. The consequences for software often concern space and time tradeoffs. They might address language and implementation issues as well. Because reuse is often a factor in object-oriented design, the consequences of a pat-tern include its impact on a system's flexibility, extensibility, or portability. Listing the consequences explicitly helps you understand and evaluate them.

Smalltalk's Model/View/Controller

The Model/View/Controller (MVC) introduced in Smalltalk (and used in other object-oriented languages) is often used to illustrate the origins of design patterns. The Model/View/Controller paradigm was used to create user interfaces in Smalltalk. Smalltalk was perhaps the first *popular* object-oriented language.

> **Smalltalk**
>
> Smalltalk is the result of several great ideas that emerged from Xerox PARC. These ideas included the mouse and using a windowing environment, among others. Smalltalk is a wonderful language that provided the foundation for all the object-oriented languages that followed. One of the complaints about C++ is that it's not really object-oriented, whereas Smalltalk is. Although C++ had a larger following in the early days of OO, Smalltalk has always had a very dedicated core group of supporters. Java is a mostly OO language that embraced the C++ developer base.

Design Patterns defines the MVC components in the following manner:

> *The Model is the application object, the View is the screen presentation, and the Controller defines the way the user interface reacts to user input.*

The problem with previous paradigms is that the Model, View, and Controller used to be lumped together in a single entity. For example, a single object would have included all three of the components. With the MVC paradigm, these three components have separate and distinct interfaces. So, if you want to change the user interface of an application, you only have to change the View. Figure 15.1 illustrates what the MVC design looks like.

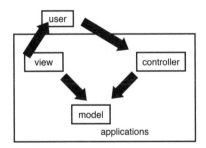

Figure 15.1   Model/View/Controller paradigm.

Remember that much of what we have been learning about object-oriented development has to do with interfaces versus implementation. As much as possible, we want to separate the interface from the implementation. We also want to separate interface from interface as much as possible. For example, we do not want to combine multiple interfaces that do not have anything to do with one another (or the solution to the problem at hand). The MVC was one of the early pioneers in this separation of interfaces. The MVC explicitly defines the interfaces between specific components pertaining to a very common and basic programming problem—the creation of user interfaces and their connection to the business logic and data behind them.

If you follow the MVC concept and separate the user interface, business logic, and data, your system will be much more flexible and robust. For example, assume that the user interface is on a client machine, the business logic is on an application server, and the data is located on a data server. Developing your application in this way would allow you to change the way the GUI looks without having an impact on the business logic or the data. Likewise, if your business logic changes and you calculate a specific field differently, you can change the business logic without having to change the GUI. And finally, if you want to swap databases and store your data differently, you can change the way the data is stored on the data server without affecting either the GUI or the business logic. This assumes, of course, that the interfaces between the three do not change.

MVC Example

As a further example of a list box, consider a GUI that includes a list of phone numbers. The listbox is the view, the phonelist is the model, and the controller is the logic that binds the listbox to the phone list.

MVC Drawbacks

Although the MVC is a great design, it can be somewhat complex, in that there must be a lot of attention paid to the upfront design. This is a problem with object-oriented design in general—there is a fine line between a good design and a cumbersome design. The question remains: How much complexity should you build into the system with regard to a complete design?

Types of Design Patterns

Design Patterns features 23 patterns grouped into the three categories listed below. Most of the examples are written in C++, with some written in Smalltalk. The time of the book's publication is indicative of the use of C++ and Smalltalk. The publication date of 1995 was right at the cusp of the Internet revolution and the corresponding popularity of the Java programming language. After the benefit of design patterns became apparent, many other books rushed in to fill the newly created market. Many of these later books were written in Java.

In any event, the actual language used is irrelevant. *Design Patterns* is inherently a design book, and the patterns can be implemented in any number of languages. The authors of the book divided the patterns into three categories:

- *Creational patterns* create objects for you, rather than having you instantiate objects directly. This gives your program more flexibility in deciding which objects need to be created for a given case.

- *Structural patterns* help you compose groups of objects into larger structures, such as complex user interfaces, or accounting data.

- *Behavioral patterns* help you define the communication between objects in your system and how the flow is controlled in a complex program.

In the following section, we will discuss one example from each of these categories to provide a flavor of what design patterns actually are. For a comprehensive list and description of individual design patterns, please refer to the books listed at the end of this chapter.

Creational Patterns

- Abstract factory
- Builder
- Factory method
- Prototype
- Singleton

As stated earlier, the scope of this chapter is to describe what a design pattern is—not to describe each and every pattern in the GoF book. Thus, we will cover a single pattern in each category. With this in mind, let's consider an example of a creational pattern—let's take a look at the singleton pattern.

The Singleton Design Pattern

The singleton pattern, represented in Figure 15.2, is a creational pattern used to regulate the creation of objects from a class to a single object. For example, if you have a Web site that has a counter object to keep track of the hits on your site, you certainly do not want a new counter to be instantiated each time your Web page is actually hit. You want a counter object instantiated when the first hit is made, but after that, you want to use the existing object to simply increment the count.

Figure 15.2   The singleton model.

Although there might be other ways to regulate the creation of objects, the best way is to let the class itself take care of this issue.

Taking Care of Business

Remember, one of the most important OO rules is that an object should take care of itself. This means that issues regarding the life cycle of a class should be handled in the class, not delegated to language constructs like `static`, and so on.

Figure 15.3 shows the UML model for the singleton taken directly from *Design Patterns*. Note the property `uniqueinstance`, which is a static singleton object, and the method `Instance()`. The other properties and methods are there to indicate that other properties and methods will be required to support the business logic of the class.

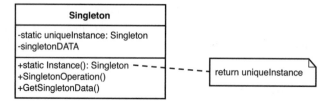

Figure 15.3　Singleton UML diagram.

Any other class that needs to access an instance of a singleton must interface through the Instance() method. The creation of an object should be controlled through the constructor, just like any other OO design. We can require the client to interface through the Instance() method, and then have the Instance() method call the constructor.

The following Java code illustrates what the code looks like for the general singleton.

```java
public class ClassicSingleton {
  private static ClassicSingleton instance = null;

  protected ClassicSingleton() {
  // Exists only to defeat instantiation.
  }
  public static ClassicSingleton getInstance() {
   if(instance == null) {
     instance = new ClassicSingleton();
   }
   return instance;
  }
}
```

We can create a more specific example for the Web page counter example that we used previously.

```java
public class Counter
{
 private int counter;
 private static Counter instance = null;

 protected Counter()
 {
 }

 public static Counter getInstance() {
   if(instance == null) {
     instance = new Counter ();
    System.out.println("New instance created\n");
   }
   return instance;
 }
}
```

```
public void incrementCounter()
{
 counter++;
}

public int getCounter()
{
 return(counter);
 }


}
```

The main point to note about the code is the regulation of the object creation. Only a single counter object can be created. The code for this is as follows:

```
public static Counter getInstance() {
    if(instance == null) {
      instance = new Counter ();
     System.out.println("New instance created\n");
    }
    return instance;
}
```

Note that if the `instance` is `null`, it means that an object has yet to be instantiated. In this event, a new `Counter` object is created. If the `instance` is not `null`, it indicates that a `Counter` object has been instantiated, and no new object is to be created. In this case, the reference to the only object available is returned to the application.

More Than One Reference

There may well be more than one reference to the singleton. If you create references in the application and each reference is referring to the singleton, you will have to manage the multiple references.

Although this code is certainly interesting, it is also valuable to see how the singleton is instantiated and managed by the application. Take a look at the following code:

```
public class Singleton
{
 public static void main(String[] args)
 {
  Counter counter1 = Counter.getInstance();
  System.out.println("Counter : " + counter1.getCounter() );

  Counter counter2 = Counter.getInstance();
  System.out.println("Counter : " + counter2.getCounter() );


 }
}
```

Two References to a Single Counter

Be aware that in this example, there are two separate references pointing to the counter.

This code actually uses the `Counter` singleton. Take a look at how the objects are created:

```
Counter counter1 = Counter.getInstance();
```

The constructor is not used here. The instantiation of the object is controlled by the `getInstance()` method. Figure 15.4 shows what happens when this code is executed. Note that the message `New instance created` is only output a single time. When `counter2` is created, it receives a copy of the original object—the same as `counter1`.

Figure 15.4 Using the `Counter` singleton.

Let's prove that the references for `counter1` and `counter2` are the same. We can update the application code as follows:

```
public class Singleton
{
 public static void main(String[] args)
 {
  Counter counter1 = Counter.getInstance();
  counter1.incrementCounter();
  counter1.incrementCounter();
  System.out.println("Counter : " + counter1.getCounter() );

  Counter counter2 = Counter.getInstance();
  counter2.incrementCounter();
  System.out.println("Counter : " + counter2.getCounter() );

 }
}
```

Figure 15.5 shows the output from the singleton application. Note that in this case, we are incrementing `counter1` twice, so the counter will be 2. When we create the counter2 reference, it references the same object as counter1, so when we increment the counter, it's now 3 (2+1).

Figure 15.5   Using the updated Counter singleton.

Structural Patterns

Structural patterns are used to create larger structures from groups of objects. The following seven design patterns are members of the structural category.

- Adapter
- Bridge
- Composite
- Decorator
- Façade
- Flyweight
- Proxy

As an example from the structural category, let's take a look at the adapter pattern. The adapter pattern is also one of the most important design patterns. This pattern is a good example of how the implementation and interface are separated.

The Adapter Design Pattern

The adapter pattern is a way for you to create a different interface for a class that already exists. The adapter pattern basically provides a class wrapper. In other words, you create a new class that incorporates (wraps) the functionality of an existing class with a new and—ideally—better interface. A simple example of a wrapper is the Java class Integer. The Integer class actually wraps a single Integer value inside it. You might wonder why you would bother to do this. Remember that in an object-oriented system, everything is an object. In Java, primitives, such as ints, floats, and so on are not actually objects. When you need to perform functions on these primitives, such as conversions, you need to treat them as objects. Thus, you create a wrapper object and "wrap" the primitive inside it. Thus, you can take a primitive like the following:

```
int myInt = 10;
```

and then wrap it in an `Integer` object:

```
Integer myIntWrapper = new Integer (myInt);
```

Now you can do a conversion, so we can treat it as a string:

```
String myString = myIntWrapper.toString();
```

This wrapper allows us to treat the original integer as an object, thus providing all the advantages of an object.

As for the adapter pattern itself, consider the example of a mail tool interface. Let's assume you have purchased some code that provides all the functionality you need to implement a mail client. This tool provides everything you want in a mail client, except you would like to change the interface slightly. In fact, all you want to do is change the API to retrieve your mail.

The following class provides a very simple example of a mail client for this example.

```
public class MailTool {
  public MailTool () {
  }
  public int retrieveMail() {

  System.out.println ("You've Got Mail");

    return 0;
  }
}
```

When you invoke the `retrieveMail()` method, your mail is presented with the very original greeting "You've Got Mail." Now let's suppose you want to change the interface in all your company's clients from `retrieveMail()` to `getMail()`. You can create an interface to enforce this:

```
interface MailInterface {
  int getMail();
}
```

You can now create your own mail tool that wraps the original tool, and provide your own interface:

```
class MyMailTool implements MailInterface {
  private MailTool yourMailTool;
  public MyMailTool () {
  yourMailTool= new MailTool();
    setYourMailTool(yourMailTool);
  }
  public int getMail() {
```

```
  return getYourMailTool().retrieveMail();
  }
 public MailTool getYourMailTool() {
  return yourMailTool ;
  }
 public void setYourMailTool(MailTool newYourMailTool) {
  yourMailTool = newYourMailTool;
  }
}
```

Inside this class, you create an instance of the original mail tool that you want to retrofit. This class implements `MailInterface`, which will force you to implement a `getMail()` method. Inside this method, you literally invoke the `retrieveMail()` method of the original mail tool.

To use your new class, you simply instantiate your new mail tool and invoke the `getMail()` method.

```
public class Adapter
{
 public static void main(String[] args)
 {
  MyMailTool myMailTool = new MyMailTool();

  myMailTool.getMail();

 }
}
```

When you do invoke the `getMail()` method, you are using this new interface to actually invoke the `retrieveMail()` method from the original tool. This, of course, is a very simple example; however, by creating this wrapper, you can actually enhance the interface and add your own functionality to the original class.

The concept of an adapter is quite simple, but you can create new and powerful interfaces using this pattern.

Behavioral Patterns

- Chain of response
- Command
- Interpreter
- Iterator
- Mediator
- Memento
- Observer
- State

- Strategy
- Template method
- Visitor

As an example from the behavioral category, let's take a look at the iterator pattern. This is one of the most commonly used patterns and is implemented by several programming languages.

The Iterator Design Pattern

Iterators provide a standard mechanism for traversing a collection, such as a vector. Functionality must be provided so that each item of the collection can be accessed one at a time. The iterator pattern provides information hiding, keeping the internal structure of the collection secure. The iterator pattern also stipulates that more than one iterator can be created without interfering with each other. Java actually provides its own implementation of an iterator. The following code creates a vector and then inserts a number of strings into it.

```java
import java.util.*;
public class Iterator {
  public static void main(String args[]) {

    // Instantiate a Vector.
    Vector vector = new Vector();

    // Add values to the vector.

    vector.addElement(new String("Joe"));
    vector.addElement(new String("Mary"));
    vector.addElement(new String("Bob"));
    vector.addElement(new String("Sue"));

    // Iterate through the vector.
    Enumeration names = vector.elements();
    System.out.println("\n");
    System.out.println("Names:");
    iterate(names );

    }

    private static void iterate(Enumeration enum) {
  while (enum.hasMoreElements()) {
    System.out.println(enum.nextElement());
  }
 }
}
```

Then we create an enumeration so that we can iterate through it. The method `iterate()` is provided to perform the actual iteration functionality. In this method, we use the Java enumeration method `hasMoreElements()`, which traverses the vector and lists all of the names.

Antipatterns

Although a design pattern evolves from experiences in a positive manner, *antipatterns* can be thought of as collections of experiences that have gone awry. It is well documented that most software projects are ultimately deemed unsuccessful. In fact, as indicated in the article "Creating Chaos" by Johnny Johnson, fully one-third of all projects are cancelled outright. It would seem obvious that many of these failures are caused by poor design decisions.

The term *antipattern* derives from the fact that design patterns are created to proactively solve a specific type of problem. An antipattern, on the other hand, is a reaction to a problem, and is gleaned from bad experiences. In short, whereas design patterns are based on solid design practices, antipatterns can be thought of as practices to avoid. In the November 1995 *C++ Report*, Andrew Koenig described two facets of antipatterns:

- Those that describe a bad solution to a problem, which result in a bad situation
- Those that describe how to get out of a bad situation, and how to proceed from there to a good solution

Many people believe that antipatterns are actually more useful than design patterns. This is because antipatterns are designed to solve problems that have already occurred. This boils down to the concept of root-cause analysis. A study can be conducted with actual data that might indicate why the original design, perhaps an actual design pattern, did not succeed. It might be said that antipatterns emerge from the failure of previous solutions. Thus, antipatterns have the benefit of hindsight.

For example, in his article "Reuse Patterns and Antipatterns," Scott Ambler identifies a pattern called a *robust artifact*, and defines it as follows:

> *An item that is well-documented, built to meet general needs instead of project-specific needs, thoroughly tested, and has several examples to show how to work with it. Items with these qualities are much more likely to be reused than items without them. A Robust Artifact is an item that is easy to understand and work with.*

However, there are certainly many situations when a solution is declared reusable and then no one ever reuses it. Thus, to illustrate an antipattern, he writes:

> *Someone other than the original developer must review a Reuseless Artifact to determine whether or not anyone might be interested in it. If so, the artifact must be reworked to become a Robust Artifact.*

Thus, antipatterns lead to the revision of existing designs, and the continuous refactoring of those designs until a workable solution is found.

Conclusion

In this chapter, we explored the concept of design patterns. Patterns are part of everyday life, and this is just the way you should be thinking about object-oriented designs. As with many things pertaining to information technology, the roots for solutions are founded in real-life situations.

Although this chapter covered design patterns only briefly, you should explore this topic in greater detail by picking up one of the books referenced at the end of this chapter.

This book has covered a lot of material. The intent is to provide a high-level overview to the concepts involved in the OO thought process. I hope this book has whet your appetite for this subject and you will seek out other books that go into far more detail. Many of the individual topics covered in this book—such as UML and use cases—have complete books devoted to them. Good hunting!

References

Alexander, Christopher, et al. *A Pattern Language: Towns, Buildings, Construction.* Oxford University Press, 1977.

Ambler, Scott. "Reuse Patterns and Antipatterns." *2000 Software Development Magazine.*

Gamma, Erich, et al. *Design Patterns: Elements of Reusable Object-Oriented Software.* Addison-Wesley, 1995.

Grand, Mark. *Patterns in Java: A Catalog of Reusable Design Patterns Illustrated with UML, Volume 1.* Wiley, 1998.

Jaworski, Jamie. *Java 2 Platform Unleashed.* Sams Publishing, 1999.

Johnson, Johnny. "Creating Chaos." *American Programmer,* July 1995.

Larman, Craig. *Applying UML and Patterns.* Wiley, 1998.

Index

C

E

J

Q-R

How can we make this index more useful? Email us at indexes@samspublishing.com

How can we make this index more useful? Email us at indexes@samspublishing.com

Your Guide
to Computer
Technology

www.informit.com